Best-selling author Michael Murphy is a native of Castlebar, County Mayo. A psychoanalyst with a busy practice in Dublin, he is also an award-winning senior television producer, director and newscaster with RTÉ. He has lectured in psychoanalysis at St Vincent's University Hospital and University College, Dublin. His highly acclaimed literary memoir, *At Five in the Afternoon – My Battle with Male Cancer*, was published in 2009, and was a number one bestseller. His best-selling collection of poetry, *The Republic of Love – Twenty-five Poems*, was published in 2013. The Irish Independent has described him as 'an author of importance'.

Michael lives in Dublin with his partner of twenty-eight years, Terry O'Sullivan.

First published in 2013 by
Liberties Press
140 Terenure Road North | Terenure | Dublin 6W
Tel: +353 (1) 405 5701
www.libertiespress.com | info@libertiespress.com

Trade enquiries to Gill & Macmillan Distribution
Hume Avenue | Park West | Dublin 12
T: +353 (1) 500 9534 | F: +353 (1) 500 9595 | E: sales@gillmacmillan.ie

Distributed in the UK by
Turnaround Publisher Services
Unit 3 | Olympia Trading Estate | Coburg Road | London N22 6TZ
T: +44 (0) 20 8829 3000 | E: orders@turnaround-uk.com

Distributed in the United States by
Dufour Editions | PO Box 7 | Chester Springs | Pennsylvania 19425

ISBN: 978-1-907593-98-7
2 4 6 8 10 9 7 5 3 1

A CIP record for this title is available from the British Library.

Cover design by Fergal Condon
Internal design by Liberties Press
Landscape photograph of Spain by Conor Ó Mearáin

The House *of* Pure Being

Michael Murphy

Foreword by Máire Geoghegan-Quinn

LIB
ERT
IES

Contents

'Aha, so he is the one who is meditating me. He has a dream, and I am it.'

Carl Jung, *Memories, Dreams, Reflections*

'But that kind man, that teacher, lover, friend, who remained indistinct, would be generous with words; she imagined their life together as a long conversation, equally shared.'

Anita Brookner, *Fraud*

'The Jews, Ravelstein and Herbst thought, following the line laid down by their teacher Davarr, were historically witnesses to the absence of redemption.'

Saul Bellow, *Ravelstein*

Foreword
by Máire Geoghegan-Quinn

'*Comhgháirdeachas ó chroí.* I cried. I got very angry. I laughed out loud. What a wonderful story beautifully told with nothing held back. I can't tell you how much I enjoyed reading it.'

That was my letter of congratulations to Michael Murphy after I'd read his memoir, *At Five in the Afternoon.* I meant it. And I suspect I assumed that it would stand alone, since it centred on what prostate cancer did to his life and his perception of his life. Such an experience, dragging a writer face-to-face with death, necessarily gives their work a unique shining harshness.

When he asked me to write a foreword for his sequel, *The House of Pure Being*, one of the reasons he gave for contacting me in Brussels was that when I had been Minister for Justice in Ireland in 1993, I introduced the Bill that decriminalised homosexuality. He told me that this was an act which had set him free.

I agreed without any hesitation to write some introductory words, and then wondered: what could be covered in a second book which would not be overshadowed and rendered trivial by the absence of a life-challenge to match the threat of death? Too many second books are little more than evocative shadows of the first, exemplifying Robert Frost's shrugging comment: 'In three words I can sum up everything I've learned about life: it goes on.'

In a sense, Michael's second volume of reflections and memoir deals with precisely that: the progression of those we met in his first book. Or, in some cases, their failure to progress, most shockingly demonstrated in his account of family members who set an icy silence around the revelations within his first book. That silence invited the kind of surrendered retreat and matching silence often characterised, in the anti-massacred words of our parents, as demonstrating 'common decency'. This book picks apart the concealments, the collusion and the coercion implicit in many of our notions of common decency. That doesn't make it easy reading. But then, anyone who read Michael's first book knows that he is neither an entertainer nor a panderer. To reverse a current cliché: you get much more than what it says on the tin, whether you like it or not, because this is not a man passively examining the shadows on the wall of his life's cage. This is a man engaging with the cruelties of his past with a fury to which he had no access, back then. This is a man baulking, in what he describes as the evening of his life, at events, actions and hurts absorbed in silence at the time. This is a man at one with a writer I know he loves, Federico García Lorca, who held that an artist is always an anarchist, in the best sense of anarchy.

'He must heed only the call that arises within him from three strong voices,' Lorca said. 'The voice of death, with all its foreboding. The voice of love. And the voice of art.'

Those three strong voices unite the varied writings within this new volume. The voice of death speaks, not only to Michael's own experience with cancer, but through the dying of Aengus Fanning, former editor of the *Sunday Independent*, whose conversations with Michael, with their long, companionable silences, establish a side to Aengus that will be new to many who believed they knew him well.

The voice of love sings softly throughout the book. Love of friends, especially when their lives and happiness are unravelling. Love of place and time and the capacity to work. Love, above all, of Terry O'Sullivan, Michael's partner, whom he met when, a quarter of a century ago, making a documentary about the Rutland Centre, where Terry worked.

The portrait of Terry manages to be affectionate and awestruck, culminating in the simple honesty of the poem he wrote as a Civil Partnership gift, the epithalamion: '. . . once upon a time on a Dublin midsummer's day, I always loved you.'

What makes Michael Murphy singular as a writer is his ability to recreate an emotive scene or event, right down to the feel of the wind on his skin or the movement of a curtain against an open window. That ability is based on an almost obsessive acuity of recall, which hammers home a truth none of us needed to understand before Alzheimer's Disease came to live in each of our families: that without memory, we are nothing.

This is a major theme throughout the book, painfully memorable in Michael's account of a meeting with his elderly mother, where she struggles to tell him something she knows to be important, but which will not form words in her mouth.

'My mother is ninety-three years old, and she dwells now in a house of pure being,' Michael writes. 'She has only the present tense, because she forgets what is past, and I'd come to believe she no longer has any idea of the future.'

Terry's mother, too, reaches from beyond death to touch the lives of the two men, and of another who was forced to live a motherless life because of the constricting expectations in the year that he was born.

Michael's poetry appears at different points within the prose of this volume. And, although the extract which follows was not written about himself, it may well reflect the experience of many readers as they finish this startling and beautiful book.

> You will gladden with a smile or with a glance
> When people feel your presence in the wonder
>   of beautiful words
> Lingering in a room like your fragrance
> The blown petals falling to earth like prayers
> Whispering over and over that I have always
>   loved you
> That I have loved you, too

Máire Geoghegan-Quinn,
European Commissioner for Research, Innovation and Science

Part One
My Mother

'Imagine!'

That's what my mother used to say. 'Imagine, just imagine . . .' It was her favourite exclamation of surprise at something suddenly made visible, a version of 'fancy that!' which she'd made her own. She would picture mentally what wasn't present, what she hadn't experienced, and speak about it, clothe it in words, as once she deftly fitted her eldest boy with up-stretched arms into an overcoat. She was filled with wonder and delight at the miracle of creation which happened seemingly without her participation, but which nevertheless had somehow involved her: 'Well, imagine that . . .' she'd say. Today, as I write in my study in Spain, I can see her come out of the kitchen and walk diffidently down the hall, because she's never been in La Mairena. Her ghost calls out to me: 'Imagine!' The invitation is a personal one from a mother to her son to join her in telling a story, and make an emotional connection with her in setting forth in words a fantasy which is unrestricted by reality, and write a fiction that comes flying out of the air from nowhere: 'Imagine!'

The contract requires that I bear her in mind. So here I am on top of a mountain at four o'clock in the morning, with the lights of Fuengirola glittering like the brightest stars down below me in the darkness, my mother's mouthpiece in this dual endeavour, giving voice to a narrative that has known the two of us over the years, and that has also shaped both of our lives, as we strolled around the Mall in Castlebar in Mayo, playing within the protective pathways of its gentle and nudging words, which set safe limits to our known world. Unlike Helen and Anna, those stylishly beautiful women who are my friends in Spain, my mother is an unlikely muse, but I feel safe under the protection of her azure cloak, her *cobija*, which now covers the vast, velvet belly of the sky with softness, pregnant with the possibilities of new life, because I know she has the knowledge that's expressed in memory, best practice, and above all, the miracle of the human voice.

'Imagine . . .' she says.

'. . . that there was once . . .' I whisper back, continuing on her story as she strokes the side of my face with her finger, marvelling at the softness of my beard. And I see the sun begin to shine out strongly from her clear, blue eyes.

'Michael,' she calls, 'I have something to say.'

'What is it, Mum?' as I move even closer to her. She's examining my face intently, and her eyes suddenly fill with tears.

'I don't know what comes next . . .' she says.

I am thunderstruck. 'I know that, Mum.' And I take hold of both of her hands. We remain held that way in the silence, looking at each other, and then the clouds arrive again and darken the sunlight, and my mother leans back into her chair, and I let go of her hands. I realise that I've sunk to my knees beside her.

My mother has gifted to me the awareness that she's lost, that she's without her ability to imagine. I can understand from the outside what a fearful tragedy that is. A fatal flaw in the workings of the brain has led to her downfall, and I grieve with her. But there's also something that has been left unsaid in the dialogue between us, and there are still many possibilities within that gap. I shall continue to visit with her in the nursing home until she's able to say it, or at least until such time as she enters the family home on the Mall in Castlebar for the last time, and closes the hall door in my face forever. Then, from the retrospection granted by that arbitrary end point, everything will have been said from her point of view, and she'll have made her statement.

In the meantime, I shall try to put into words what she hasn't yet said, because in itself it must be of the greatest importance, given my mother's great age, and the wisdom of the personality that she's earned for herself down through the years. It'll be what the French call an *aperçu*, an insight, a summation in a few words, a recapitulation of the main chapters of her life. Perhaps it's one of the reasons why I've written my second book, to give her voice in saying what has become unsayable, what's impossible and unknowable. The disclosure will have the quality of a supernatural revelation, because it will be the truth.

Yesterday, I was reading the publisher's blurb about my first book on his website, and saw that I was described there as 'a soothsayer', a person who tells or speaks the truth. The word also has overtones of being a prophet or prognosticator: one who is robed in foreknowledge of the future. Certainly, that's the direction in which my mother has also pointed me through her being speechless. The words of her first sentence, 'I have something to say', were ordered by the future anticipation of the words to come in her second sentence. She wants me to articulate some imagined future state of conclusion. It's a completion which I doubt can ever be achieved. Steve, my publisher, had brought forward his conclusion from my writing. Now I too was in the position of a reader looking over his shoulder. I saw myself through his eyes, and to my surprise, the effect on me was alienating. It split me in two. I was looking at myself in a looking-glass, except that the judgment Steve had delivered caused me to switch places, so that I was the insubstantial reflection confined within the singular word he had chosen, from whence I was looking back at myself, helplessly in thrall to what he had in mind.

I can remember coming around the back way from where I lived with my grandmother, and peering in the kitchen window at my brother and my mother and father, who were laughing and joking around the dining table. At that moment, I felt I was the stranger looking on, extraneous to the family's enjoyment. And when they all turned their heads to look at me, I reddened under the sting of their gaze, ashamed of what they saw. The terror rising was for me to be held outside, and I wrongly believed that the glass barrier didn't permit the transmission of my feelings of deprivation. But my younger brother had scrambled off his chair and pressed his face grotesquely against the window pane, mocking my isolation. He'd read the singular truth that I was set apart, egregious, and he was reacting to it. I read in his gaze that it was I who was the *stróinséir*, an odd stranger who wasn't part of the household, the one left over as a remainder. I also experienced for the first time that people could travel from my outside in as if my skin were permeable. Or perhaps it's because I was born inside-out; it certainly feels that way.

I hope I do my mother justice. I seem destined to fail in the attempt to express what's been left unsaid between us. My words will be inadequate and partial, merely an approach, an approximation, which may do violence to her. 'Imagine,' she has instructed, furnishing me with all the information that's required. She's invoking my powers of imagination to supplement her deficiency, but inevitably I'll fall short. Maybe somewhere she understands that too: that I've failed her, inasmuch as she has herself been failed by words, which have run away over the ridges of sand, leaving her lost in the desert. Somehow I'm complicit in that abandonment, and by exploring the something my mother has to say, I shall uncover the truth of my role in her life, and ultimately my transgression.

When I finished writing my memoir *At Five in the Afternoon*, I understood that what I'd written no longer belonged to me, but to the reader. He brought his own being to the words, and breathed into them a life which was different to what had inspired me. Even though it was recognisably my life story, it brought forth a different book which gave off a smell I didn't recognise. A reader from Kinsale sent me an email containing a

Jehovah-like denunciation: 'You have shamed yourself, your family, your friends and colleagues in the manner you portrayed them.' That was taking my text and stretching it out, leaning forward with it, an effort that I hadn't made. The wording of what I'd written was an obstacle to the flow of his being that obviously lent itself to such an interweaving, but I felt that the resulting garment didn't fit out my soul, while it thoroughly went along with someone else's. I'd been displaced from my mooring, which made it doubly difficult to feel certain of the truth.

If my mother gets to make her statement in my hearing, I wonder will I be able to accept it willingly, without straining to make it fit into my reality? I was genuinely at a loss as to how to reply to that reader's words, because he spoke in a different language, and sought to discredit my experience of abuse: 'In fairness, the only character who comes out well is your partner Terry, who has a real – not imagined – situation to take from his early life.' What I have learned from living with Terry, and from many years studying psychoanalysis, the obligation to hand back abuse to the perpetrator no matter from whence it came, eventually dictated my response, although it left an after-taste of intolerance. And did the scolding over shaming reveal a truth I couldn't accept, that his characterisation was a darker mirror-image of myself, an alien that I didn't want to know lest I be forced to make room inside for an awkward, unmanageable stranger, and have to welcome him back home as my brother?

Paradoxically, the publisher's word 'sooth' aligns me with the previous generations back through my mother and father. In the time of my ancestors, what is true derived from being. So were I to bypass the disjunction and describe myself as a soothsayer, the particular truth I'd tell would necessarily draw from that universal and ancient wellspring. I admire the wisdom in the way that the word has been constructed and handed on down to me in an eternal relay, but still I feel dislocated. When I read my own book myself, which details my slow recovery from prostate cancer, I'm unable to resume possession of the land, because the enclave of my being inscribed in the book belongs to a different time with a different set of circumstances, and I have moved on. My mother suffers from dementia, which is a chronic deterioration caused by organic brain disease, so that when eventually she speaks her truth, it will have to articulate in distinct syllables a being that we share now in the present, without referencing the past. And consolingly, either of us can attempt to say what we hold in common.

As a writer, I see what is true flicker about in the words and the phrases as I set them down. It surprised me to discover that truth is like a *fóidín mearaí*, a sod of confusion, on which you can easily lose your step and be led astray. Truth surfaces briefly in the gulf between what has happened for me in the past, and what has not happened to me yet. And the continuous flow of my words onto the page as I type in this no-man's land names for me a coming-to-be in language that approximates to the truth. I wouldn't say that the full truth is in the brutal reality of my existence which has been scored onto paper by the printer. Rather, it's the rising into the air of my spirit, which is momentarily visible in the words on my computer screen, always open to change at the flick of a flying finger, where it produces the music of poetry, as in mythical times the wind would pass lightly over the strings of an Aeolian harp to produce a deep musical chord, rising and falling with the breath of air.

And just like truth, my spirit seems to escape capture, no matter how carefully I try to control the various arbitrary syllables being taken together in phrases. I feel like a composer jotting notes of music onto a stave. When they're read horizontally, they sound vertically down the page, down through the memory of the years which are immediately present to me: they make my being sing. I catch myself, hearing myself say 'I be's, employing Hiberno-English usage. It permits my voice to inhabit the patrimony of the verb, and be more emphatic. 'I be's' gives body to the tenuous pointillism of those dots of living colour, truths that briefly break cover as I watch them. They coalesce into a luminous 'present continuous' stream that can sweep me along in its wake for the length of a breath: my singular contribution to the symphony of life. The choir has been singing for millennia in a fusion of instrumental and vocal forces, but without the addition of my individual voice or that of my mother, until recently.

My mother is ninety-three years old, and she dwells now in a house of pure being. She has only the present tense, because she forgets what is past, and I'd come to believe she no longer had any idea of the future. Certainly, the logical structures of time and of space don't define the world that she's living in, which is that of the dreamtime. People who aren't fixed in her memory appear randomly in the three or four seconds of the now that draw her attention. They're without a context, and speak to her in puzzling fragments: '. . . well today . . .' '. . . milk in . . .' words detached from meaning that are sent skimming over the waves like fragments of slate until they sink into the deep, phrases that pat lightly over the top of her head with the same childlike tones, before evaporating into the ether above. The imaginative thoughts that participate in my mother's overflowing reality are like that medium, which was once believed to fill all space hypothetically.

When last I saw her, I hadn't recognised her at first. I retreated from the large lounge where she usually sat, and asked the nurse at the nurse's station, 'Where's Sue Murphy, please?' She brought me back almost to the door of the room, and indicated towards a huddled figure lost in a corner. My mother was sitting alone, slumped on a settee in the nursing home lounge, and her shoe was off. Framed by the doorway, I was removed from the static scene within, a dispassionate observer of inanimate objects, a still life by Cézanne, dull and without colour. My expectations were of an encounter with a neatly dressed, alert woman, a person of note who would continue to carry the weight of her ten decades with elegance. I walked across the room until I appeared in front of her, and she recognised me: 'Well I never think about the boy visiting me . . .' she announced smiling shyly with delight, rising to the occasion as I bent down to kiss her puckered lips. It was the only coherent sentence she was to form that day, but to me it was like opening up the score of a Bach cantata, a revelation inscribed in the master's handwriting with '*soli Deo gloria*', for the glory of God alone. I savoured in my mind the concerted collection of utterances she brought forth: 'Well I never . . . I never think . . . I never think about the boy . . . the boy visiting me . . . visiting me . . .' The additional voices with their different emphases chased each other putting the previous one to flight and resonated around the room, interweaving a counterpoint with the main subject in their various combinations, and adding layers of harmonic complexity which continued to build for the duration of my visit. They also formed an airy counterpoint around the rapid assortment of syllables, the neologisms that she began to create in my presence and continued to say. Nothing was dwelt upon: the notes were left as soon as they were sounded.

Her speech is now reduced to a substrate of language that she urged on me, cupping it together in her hands: 'Tissue Paris laboringly *taoiseach taoiseach* . . .' she said, English words and Irish words that appeared to be spilling out from between her bony fingers. It was a sieve I made from the rushes up in Flannery's field as a boy that she placed trustingly into both my hands so that I could buttress it, and catch the runoff of what she was saying. 'You, you, you . . .' she said, re-affirming in votive speech the umbilical cord that tied a mother to her son in a rainbow of love. My mother was performing a religious act for me, a sacrament, because in that gesture she was gifting to me a ciborium, and entrusting me with her being, whose fragments she was holding tenuously between her thumb and index finger. From now on I was to be the golden container who was her salvation; it was up to me to make sense out of the babble she'd placed before me. I was to separate out the extraneous particles that cluttered up her speech, and give birth to the truth of what she had to say, because in that ritual she was demonstrating to me that she was no longer able, that it was beyond her. She needed the containment that a mind ordered by time and space could provide. I felt the responsibility of her heartfelt cry as she desperately gripped onto my hands above the abyss. It overruled the pressure that deadlines can enforce on me, and the exertion I can feel from trying to attain to some other place. The ambiguous bestowal of these gifts has been cruelly confiscated from my mother.

I'd sat companionably beside her on the couch, so that she could lean back into the hammock of my warmth. I'd brought with me some regenerating cream, whose cold drops I began to massage into her dry and misshapen hands. This was an anointing, which even today in a mirror image still tried to facilitate my living by gifting to me all that she had to offer in return: rubble from the building blocks of words that formerly had upheld the architecture of her life. Once upon a time these hands used to play the piano so expertly, hands that bestrode the keys generating music of the highest rank from deep within, soul-feeling which still poured out fluently even as her grasp on words had become hesitant and faltered like her skin, which to my horror began to disintegrate and peel away into slivered rolls of worked clay beneath the vigour of my kneading. I looked up, anxious lest I hurt her, and her blue eyes were scanning my face. 'Are your hands sore, Mum?' I asked.

'No,' she replied. Then, 'Tissue, tissue, tissue . . .' she instructed, as I modulated my touch so that it became gentle, warming the coldness of her confounding world, supplying for a few moments a familiar, external reference with which she felt secure. I hoped my presence could give back to her once more the consistency of sameness, without me having to immediately move away from her as the busy carers in the nursing home have to do. Held now in my gaze, and embraced by the loving tones of my voice, the flesh of her flesh, I hoped that I could keep her from disintegrating, from being drawn in different directions: someone sitting talking to her, a plate with biscuits, then coming into her line of sight, sitting up close and saying to her, a hand being rubbed of skin: fragments of being from the outside imbued with the nonsensical logic of dreams.

Like an author writing down the words about one of his characters and plotting out their lives, I was unsure whether it was I or my mother who was in control of the dictation. At least I could continually be there for my mother to keep her in mind. My thinking about her wouldn't be as alienating as that 'soothsayer' phrase which was chosen for me by my publisher, who knows me professionally, but who doesn't know me at all. I could be her voice, in a method which is familiar to me from my psychoanalytic work, where the stream of a person's being is gathered together under the constraints of the couch so that as much as possible is channelled into speech, in a message sent to the analyst, and back to themselves by way of my interpretation, which punctuates the discourse suddenly belonging to both of us.

There've been many occasions, a falling down in wonder, that have witnessed the daily miracle of my mother issue forth from my behaviours. I move food around my plate with a fork, before isolating an irregular object, 'What's that?' tapping at it like her. I also do her reproving glare, a fierce look which I see in the photograph of her McGauran grandmother, and which unmistakably says, 'Never make noise!' I register her bodily delight at rag-time, stride piano, and dance an impromptu Charleston with my hands as she plays the piano. I can also sit rapt, carried away with spiritual awe at the complexity of Bach's music, which is an advance on what would've held her interest. But the grounding we have in common is a similar, reverent attitude towards all forms of music, sounds in time that always belonged to the Muses. These are the inheritances which have anointed me my mother's heir. But to incarnate a voice that is so characteristically hers is of a different order of magnitude. And now that she's fading, the task of travelling that road takes on increasing urgency. I always remember the colour of her voice speaking Hans Christian Andersen's words aloud to me slowly, so that I could understand and live within the dream world of his fairytales. But what I remember most is the quality of her silence, clasping me to her, underpinning with bated breath and delight my excitement at telling her my own stories, the fantastical adventures which happened for me with her in mind.

Recently, when she'd had a short stay in hospital to regulate her Warfarin, I was talking away at her bedside, filling up her silence with how well she was looking, that I hoped she was trying to eat what they gave her because it was good for her – maybe she would try some of the jelly? – and I caught sight of her peering at my leather jacket. She reached forward with her hand and fingered the soft brown leather appreciatively. I broke off from what I was saying to ask, 'D'you like that, Mum?'

She looked up and into my eyes: 'It's wonderful to be loved,' she whispered to me.

The misalignment in our conversation, the shock of the truth had the effect of repositioning me within a flow of words that I realised had never ceased for my mother, despite her confusion. I saw that it would continue on for as long as she drew breath. It was immaterial whether she was referring to me, and to my partner Terry's birthday gift of the leather jacket, or whether she was the person who felt loved by the presence of her son: the import of her narrative embraced us both. After all, love is love. And love matters.

The hi-fi in the nursing home began playing a CD from the wartime era, when my mother was in her early twenties. Vera Lynn sang slowly in her clear, determined voice, 'There'll be bluebirds over the white cliffs of Dover, tomorrow, just you wait and see . . .'

I started singing it for her too, and quickly faltered to a mumble, choked with emotion, overwhelmed by the sudden grief. It pained me that we didn't have any more tomorrows, and that we'd come to the end of the idyll. The poem that was our lives together had been simple and charming, and short. The promise of tomorrow which the song held forth wasn't the truth. My mother would never again take her place at the head of the dining table in the big kitchen of the family home on the Mall, empty now, cold and succumbing to dampness.

'There'll be love and laughter and peace ever after, tomorrow . . .'

The love and laughter which had once echoed off those plastered walls blistering with rusting, brown patches of damp belonged with the cobwebs, and with the dust settling silently like Dickensian fog onto the old-fashioned furniture that nobody wanted. There were going to be no more tomorrows for the Murphys of the Mall. The song mustered courage to help people face the burdens of the day, but as I held onto my mother's hand, I heard an ironical lament for an era of family which had begun at that time, but which was now, some seven decades later, definitively over.

I looked around the day-room at the helpless, elderly patients, some of them dozing, slack-jawed in their chairs, others moving restlessly, muttering out loud for nobody to hear them, or to pay them attention. I could clearly see our irrelevance, numbering myself among those in the frontline facing 'peace ever after'. That was to be our tomorrow, and the implication of the relegation brought me up short. It shocked me to observe that today's generation bustling about, helping patients out to the toilet, wheeling some of the chairs with their protesting cargo in to the dining-room for lunch, had within the unthinking possession of their youth the many tomorrows that had been taken from the two of us in a re-distribution of realities. My mother and I were suddenly left alone in the empty lounge. The valley would indeed bloom again, but we wouldn't be there to see it. And I was surprised to feel pangs of jealousy at being displaced.

Before I left, Aileen took me aside and said that they'd increased the number of times they changed my mother's pad during the day, because her incontinence was getting worse. I know it wasn't Aileen's intention, but I felt berated by the effort of care that the Polish assistants were giving to my mother. Not one of them had passed us by as we took tea and I fed my mother the buttered scones topped with strawberry jam from the generous tray they'd provided for us, without saying a loudly cheerful 'Hello, Sue!' And yet, they were the ones who were ministering to her in private several times a day. As I drove back to Dublin after my brief visit, I was tormented by the thought that I'd profaned my mother. After she'd twice attempted to boil the electric kettle on the range, compromising her safety, I was the one who'd been instrumental in turning her out of her home, so that she was abandoned to this life of exile among strangers. The shock to her system had so affected her that she'd progressively withdrawn her interest from the surroundings of the nursing home, and lived amidst her memories turning deep inside her being. Suddenly my voice seemed to take on an added importance, if only to undo what couldn't be remedied.

When I sat beside Mary, a bookshop owner, for dinner in an Italian restaurant after the intimate signing of my book she'd organised in Village Books of Malahide, and she asked my partner, Terry, about his work with abuser priests, and whether those who'd been abused went on to abuse, my mind went directly to my mother, and how she was folded into my earliest decision to go live with my Granny in the house next door, and apart from my immediate family. As the conversation continued on around the table, I wondered whether I was avenging that hurt by visiting the same exclusion on her. The son on whom she believed she could depend had robbed her of what she'd made known to me about her being. I'd taken with me the supplement of continuity, the joining together of moments of being that enabled her to connect with a son whom she continued to love, and driven it back to Dublin, forgetting my mother to the care of strangers for another fortnight, leaving her bereft of meaning, because she has no context.

During those first few months of settling in, when we'd arrive back at the nursing home following an afternoon drive, my mother would protest as soon as she caught sight of the building. 'No, no, no . . .' she'd cry out, distressed. My mother is lost, and I've deprived her of the future hope that she could re-find herself again in my continuous presence. Even in the etymology of the verb 'to be' in Old English, while it didn't have a past tense, I could see that it was always open towards the future. My mother had clearly demonstrated to me on more than one occasion in the nursing home the possibility that she was about to be in language, and I'd pillaged that from her by walking away. I'd turned my back on her again, a rejecting action that is replaying on a loop in my life, and that's beginning to infiltrate my text like a virus. By continuing to involve her in what was my own fractured response, I'd committed a sacrilege. '*Tu es ma mère: tuer ma mère*': according to the French homophone, in affirming my mother, I kill her. I'm guilty of murder.

Occasionally I suffer visitations at about a quarter past three in the morning. There's no aura, no warning of any kind to prepare me as I make the ritual preparations for bed. At three-fifteen on the dial, I blunder into instant wakefulness, panicked from a nightmare, when the default setting of not being able to pay my way, the ghost of money, is rattling his chains around my bedroom. A catastrophe which is beyond rectification – exceeding the overdraft limit at the bank, the important receipt I sent without a record, the unexpected invoice – will have wormed its way into consciousness as I slept, and poisoned my mind with certainty. In the dream I'm swimming and swimming in an ocean too far away from a glimpse of land on the horizon, when the unreasoning terror begins to weigh my body down, and I can't shake off his unwanted attentions. The ghost of despair ducks my head over and over under the water, but still I swim, slower and slower and with greater effort, until I start to sink into the measureless depths from exhaustion. I wake with a start to find I've wet the bed, an occasional side effect of the prostate surgery that has saved my life from the clutches of cancer. I get up, and out of my pyjamas, wipe myself down and the bed, spread out a clean towel on the sheet. I lie down again on the dampness. In that twilight hour before the dawn, I can see with enhanced vision the truth of myself that I'm able to suppress during the day: as a person without the distraction of my clothes and the roles that they imply, I'm beyond forgiveness. I lash myself with condemnation for having abdicated my responsibilities on so many levels, particularly with regard to my mother, and for having failed in my task, that ultimate concern around which I built my life. Loving and the grief surrounding it, latterly bitterness, even disappointment, hurt my heart so much that I hesitate to give it voice. The ghost of death insinuates that I've come to the end and have ceased to exist, and that this suffering I feel is the pain of non-being, that instant at the point of death which flashes into an eternity. I'm no longer able to preserve my being against the all-engulfing threat of danger, and my anxiety is naked now. For sixty years it had been eating away at the centre of my existence like the hidden, slow-growing tumours of prostate cancer, which have recently erupted in my flesh, to be laid bare in all of its ugly messiness upon the bed. Other ghosts lose their form, and I sink back into a spasmodic, dreamless sleep until the radio alarm comes on with news of the latest atrocity, followed by the collapsing economy. It's a daily lightning rod for the projection of unmanageable feelings of paranoia, to which I know my mind is vulnerable as I take my shower. I've learned from experience not to entertain these thoughts before noon, when the day takes on a different temper, and the effort of upholding my being buries the terrifying potential of non-being into an open hole in the ground, and covers it over with a comforting cushion.

When I was three and a quarter years old, my younger brother Kieran was born, and I was displaced from the unquestioning position I'd held as the only son. I can reconstruct from the nightmares I suffer at 3.15 AM, that they're an echo of this childhood trauma. A fatal doubt was brought home from the hospital along with the baby with the big head, who took pride of place in my mother's bedroom, in what had been my cot. My parent's action undermined the innocent certainties of the world I inhabited, and robbed me of bliss. There's a painting which captures the moment of alienation perfectly, which is on display in Berlin's Picture Gallery. It's of a mother and child by Pieter de Hooch, and shows a mother lacing up her bodice seated on a chair smiling down into a covered cradle. Behind her back in the next room, a young girl stands irresolute in the shadows, pensively looking out through an open doorway at the sunlight. I walked out through that door, and went to live with my Granny; I'd no other means of redress. Mum and Dad laughed heartily at my proposal to them sitting around the big dining table in the kitchen that they send the baby back to where he came from, that we'd no need of him.

'That's not possible, Michael . . .'

Their amusement about such a grave matter to me, and the realisation that inexorably they were closed to any discussion, that there was no reaching out to help me with my difficulties, meant that I could never bring to them again questions that I pondered over, or that were forced upon me. Anxious tentacles began to imprison me at that tender age, a cage that was destined to remain forever in place, and to be reinforced over time. It was plain from their mirth that I'd misspoken, and that I was suffering because of it. As I played alone at their feet, my wounds hidden beneath the long white folds of the linen tablecloth, I saw that I'd been replaced by a younger version of myself, and with terror I understood that it was I who was superfluous.

From the many children's storybooks of fairytales and myths that were read to me, and from the pictures that I'd studied, and dreamed over, I knew that the three bears had threatened Goldilocks and that the house of the Three Little Pigs was blown down. Before I was chosen to be slain by one of the Valkyries, who were depicted in colourful paintings flying through the air on their horses, drawn swords at the ready, I determined to withdraw to my Granny's. I realised that she too was under threat from Red Riding Hood's wolf, that neither of us was safe, but I believed that since she was older than me, Granny was in a better position to handle it. Psychologically, I needed to put in place a barrier against an overflowing, all-encompassing familial sea which threatened to drown my survival as an individual. Displacement was a happening and a conclusion which I arrived at fully formed. They were part of a piece, a beaten path to be followed through the forest, rather than a logical thinking through of the options. Granny lived alone in the house next door until I arrived there with my pyjamas. I knew that I could retake my rightful, solitary place under her tutelary care, and that I'd live longer there, hidden away in my cottage in the woods.

The simple time of innocence had passed, leaving a fracture at the heart of how I perceived the world, which has festered over the years. The mask of being a sunny child covered over my dejection. I heard a lens make a sharp, splitting sound, and when I looked through the steel-rimmed spectacles that I wore, I saw a puzzle. The dissected piece of glass bent the light from a straight course, and the strangeness of the world that I inhabited, twisted as it was in different ways, underlined for me the foolishness of relying on an external reality which could change irrevocably in an instant, switch 180 degrees, and on people who professed to love me, but who were capable of betraying me without warning. As I grew more and more the introvert, and tried to negotiate my own ambivalence with greater skill, I saw that I was no longer guiltless, harmless, without blame. When I stood before an altar glittering with candles and decked with boughs of dark-green holly, I sang joyous Christmas carols with my classmates in the choir, but felt no nostalgia for an Eden from which I'd been expelled: '*Natum videte regem angelorum . . .*' With sinking heart I'd already seen the bicycle helmet, the board games, and the knitted pullover stacked in my parents' wardrobe that Santy would bring later on that night. Suddenly, I was too old to be a believer, no longer an innocent.

'*Venite, adoremus Dominum . . .*' After the goodwill of the Midnight Mass, I'd no interest in visiting the church crib to see the baby Jesus in the manger, because '. . . there was no room at the Inn.' That phrase tortured me because it led in two directions: when baby Kieran arrived in my life unexpectedly, I concluded there was no room for me in my parents' house; and yet, I too was displaced from my home like the baby Jesus. Which of the two rivals did the story of Jesus represent? And which of the two emphases best represented the truth? Whatever way the sentence was pronounced, I believed there was no room for me; and no further words were available to resolve the conundrum, just the silence of God from without.

It was the first of many absences. I had to live within that soundless sentence, and make the best of it: but all the while I was learning, and coming up with my own responses from within. I felt as I did walking home down Chapel Street that Saturday morning in springtime after my first confession in the Church of the Holy Rosary, when I remembered that I'd eaten a sweet during lent and that I'd forgotten to tell that sin to the priest. Others' violent certainties must have informed me of God's known will, since I was aware of transgression, and at the time I applied it to myself. The earth underneath the pathway trembled so much that I felt dizzy, and then it roared open. A blast of heat from hell's furnace scorched the surface of my skin. I oscillated in silhouette over the raging orange chasm which had opened up from underneath the path, and I could see devils that were bigger than me coming towards me, taunting me, and I went cold with fear. They surrounded me with mocking jeers and began to push and to pull at me, kicking my legs with their boots trying to trip me up, mussing up my hair, until a shove to my back sent me sprawling out into the abyss, and they continued on their way, laughing at my shock and humiliation, and the embarrassment which suddenly squeezed tears down my cheeks. The ground became solid again, and I pulled myself up out of the grate into a seated position, and tied my shoelaces which had become undone in the scuffle. I spat into my hanky, and then tried to wash out the grit from my grazed knees, staunching the dripping rivulets of dark blood that were staining the tops of my knitted stockings. There was a sudden painful clatter across my ear from a devil passing back up the path. God was letting me know that I'd failed to let the priest hear the truth. I'd spoken against the Holy Ghost by not telling the full truth in confession, and I'd committed the unforgivable sin. '. . . it shall not be forgiven him, neither in this world, neither in the world to come.' From the start, trying to make sense of my primitive experiences led me to conclude that I was destined to be unforgiven.

That unforgiven status was a registration which was to have many effects, both good and bad. It served to strengthen my sense of uniqueness: I had no like or equal, I was unrivalled. Because of the recording of that condition onto a list in my soul that I stumbled across in my own psycho-analysis, and which was carried back to me in various interpretations later on, relentlessly repeating in my life, I led a solitary life, moving through the silence of the empty house next door like a monk around a monastery. I tolled the bell announcing the Divine Office, and members of a ghostly community would sweep down polished corridors in their gleaming white habits like great, gliding birds to sing the canonical hours, Lauds and Matins on shadowy winter mornings, and Compline in the yellow warmth of summer evenings. Each of them was a word which had materialised out of the air. They jostled close together in serried rows to express themselves in lays, short sung poems that foretold of the divine.

Terrorised by the memory of my damnation, which continued to dictate behaviour even as it sank into forgetfulness, I was impelled into confessing the whole truth of experience to myself, naming it aloud in language as if my salvation depended upon it. 'In the beginning was the word . . .' I whispered to myself the widest range of words which formed incantations on the tongue, magic formulas, a layering of language which I employed to keep me company. They were playmates who defended me, and helped to control the *anima mundi* of my environment. Up the fields on my own, I was conscious of clambering out among the yellow primroses in hedgerows from which I would materialize as a fox, of being ravished by the bluebells blanketing sun-dappled glades as they took up residence inside me, or getting myself trapped by the sucking sedges which grasped at my wellingtons like the dentist, Billy Bourke, extracting a wisdom tooth with superhuman effort. I was being scratched at by attacking whitethorns, whacked about by the blasts of winter wind in a galleon's sail, and drenched by sudden summer showers from the cloud static over me and nowhere else, which melted onto the heat of my skin as I sheltered under the warmth of hedges, watching worms burrow holes in the bodies of

Spanish mariners, buried where they were felled under a double ditch. Out among the hills I became a sorcerer of language in which the marvellous partook of the real, and the strange adorned the mundane. I painted my world like Caravaggio and Zurbarán and Rubens, adorning the walls of baroque churches and palaces with robustly dramatic and colourful canvases, this time constructed out of words. And that's the truth.

In fellowship with the sharp reflections in my Granny's sitting room mirror above the fireplace, which caught the cold image from the mirror on the opposite wall and multiplied it, I chanted aloud Shakespeare's seven ages of man over and over, and gave voice to each of those imitations until I had them off by heart. It was part of my homework from secondary school, but unknowingly I was fathering myself into the various roles that over time would beckon to me successively with crooked finger from outside in the street, broadcaster, psychoanalyst and author, like shapes requiring to be filled: reflecting copper moulds on the kitchen table that my Granny filled with a gelatine mixture over the flesh of chopped fruits on every Saturday evening of my childhood. As I stepped out from the wings of adolescence, I knew that this was going to be the performance of my life. It would be a continual coming-out into the purest truth of words, which eventually would become more and more refined, truer, as I grew to inhabit them; a movement away from the coarse and serviceable sackcloth clothes made from jute into the fine and lustrous silks. It would be a progressive revelation of otherness, the communication of divine knowledge so that more and more I could be imbued with God's spirit, a breath which I understood could never belong to the unforgiven, but at least it could pass through me to another, filtering the words which were hidden in the air, as Granny would pass the gelatine through a muslin strainer to extract any films of skin that might have formed. I could give them voice, 'This is my body . . . This is my blood . . .' as one after another the words which I conjured out of nothingness were hurled forward into a future eternity, taking with them as a gift the imperceptible fragments of my being which had made those words my own.

Back then, even at the beginning, I was aware that the mind full of words could fail. It was borne in on me that there was always the possibility of silence. Inexplicably, I could lose colour until I too would be shining white, suspended, noiseless, and candid, like the whitest dove, from whose vantage point high up on the classroom ceiling I'd see a spinning De La Salle dervish down below dexterously wield a heavy window pole. Brother Flavian was a cogwheel in the life of Castlebar children, clicking around to iambic pentameter: 'The infant, schoolboy, lover, soldier, justice . . .' beating out a lesson, beating it into First Year upper arms and shoulders, beating, beating as he went through the lines of desks, pausing only to beat the terror out of those youngsters who shook with fear in the classroom because they were aware that they'd forgotten the words, words in whose talons the boys were held dangling for an instant within sight of the dawning horizon, and then inexplicably let go of, so that they were helpless, all control gone, plunging, streaking down like stars from the heavens to their lonely fate, at one with the unloving nothingness, derided, worthless as if they never had been, simply because their reach for a future possibility had flown away and left without them, and left them without. There was silence, suddenly: oblivion.

Part Two

Live Big Young Man

I re-formulated versions of the sentence in my mind, relieved that the anguish of my uncle's insult no longer undid me. The phrase I eventually settled on, 'I reject out of hand your controlling silence,' seemed to hold me somehow from caving in. All morning I'd felt scalded by feelings of worthlessness and failure at allowing myself to be given across to him on the generous platter of my openness. I'd rung my uncle and aunt on New Year's Eve to wish them all the best for the coming year. I said, 'It's going to be a great year for me, Robbie: you know I've got a publisher for my book . . .' and my uncle had changed the subject. He ignored the statement as if it had never been made, and I found myself continuing on a cheerful conversation, at odds with the cutting silence which had just deleted my wonderful news. Initially I was puzzled, thinking that this younger brother of my father, who's now in his late seventies, had misheard. But as we continued to talk, with a deepening sense of shock I realised that not only had he ignored what I'd said, but that he'd so seamlessly elided it from our conversation, that it had become delusional. We breezily wished each other a happy new year, and I put down the phone, very aware that there was something wrong. 'I shouldn't have spoken about the book!'

'What d'you mean,' Terry interrogated, 'you shouldn't have spoken about the book?'

'I just didn't think . . .'

We looked at each other in disbelief. The revelation for me was that my uncle didn't wish me well, despite his cheery protestation. And the revelation for Terry was that I'd acquiesced in having my voice silenced. He pointed out that I hadn't said anything about it during the conversation, or given any indication that something was amiss. He was exasperated that I'd behaved like a shivering pup with its tail between its legs. Breathing strength into my discomfort, he suggested rightly that something would have to be done about my behaviour.

That briefest altercation over the phone was the first brushstroke of an impressive tenebrist painting, where the large areas of dark colours are relieved with an inspirational shaft of light. The picture would continue to be worked on over the next couple of years in conjunction with Terry's recommendation. It was way too early for me to have a considered opinion about that first daub of colour on a very large canvas: there wasn't yet a second one with which to compare it. However, I realise with hindsight, that Michelangelo already knew where he was going with a baroque masterpiece, even though the initial swipe of shadow hit hard and with a sweeping blow. The final portrait, when it emerged, would be balanced in every degree. Despite the blanketing silence from my uncle, I was left even more determined that my words would see the light of day.

I'd been outmanoeuvred in the field of conversation, and been turned about. I'd registered immediately that this was happening by the imperceptible ripple of disquiet that had passed across the blank canvas sheet of my credulousness. Because nothing was said, because I was presented with silence, it took time to register the event, and to transcribe it into meaning; only then could I evaluate the level of the danger. I remember in particular the silence of the wind that surrounded my sexual abuse as a small child by a young man from the garage next door, when he'd crushed me to him, the strangeness of our situation up against a wall, hidden in the crackling, overgrown thicket of small trees and shrubs at the end of our back garden, the man bending over me supporting me in his arm, his urgency against me in the shadows, the hoarseness of his breathing against my ear fogging up my glasses, and I could see the sunlight way, way off shafting through a gap in the fluttering leaves of ash and their swaying branches, and I imagined that I was a little baby bird, a *scaltán*, high up at the top of a tree in a nest of twigs, swaying back and forth, back and forth in the breeze. Nothing was ever said then either, nothing was referred to afterwards as he released me slowly, exhausted now, his other hand supporting himself against the wall, and I gently escaped from under his awkward embrace, out of the shadows and into the silence of that wind washing all about disturbing the peace, walking straight ahead with tentative steps on ground that had suddenly collapsed beneath me, head held high without a backward glance leaving him behind, blinking self-consciously in the sudden sunlight, until the next time that I'd be waylaid. I see now that the emphasis I place on naming, on putting everything into words, is to counter-act the silence of that sexual abuse by telling the truth.

When complex waves of feelings – strangeness, and intimacy, and sexual curiosity and conflict and shame – were aroused by an older sexual predator in the early years of my childhood, I didn't have the words with which to paint them, so that the feelings floated away over the ripples of time and out of reach. Only the disturbed traces remained in their wake, lapping gently now at the edges of my mind, so that the memories I conjure up are perilous reconstructions in which the present partakes of the past. And on occasion, feelings of anxiety and anguish have had to be unwillingly walled up alive in a secret panic room inside me. Like a ravening pack of dogs, they went bad, or mad, and took every opportunity to join in the barking proper to other angers.

Further strips of material attached to the written evidence holding an abuser's appended seal are more difficult to erase once they've been jeeringly stamped, branding-ironed into the flesh of childhood memories that recorded every new moment of the burning horror exactly as it was happening. A heroic effort forced out against the odds is required to close the eyes of the mind, afraid to sleep lest an elaborate spectacle of dreams on a wheeled platform trailing excited children arrives like a thunderbolt in Market Square. It gives to the actor a tragic stature on this stage, and gives a semblance of truth to his performance, which he raises from many sources. His voice has a resonance, which comes not just from reverberating off sinuses, but up, up from the echoing depths of his being. It is sonorous and produces a deep song, a *cante jondo*, which expresses the purest feeling of his soul, thrilling those children to their core. His face wears a mask: the skin is pulled back tight against the pain. The character in this play mirrors in the shining key light of his eyes that a person's purchase on the life of the mind is sorely won in a battle against fate, which never will have armistice.

There are times when I'm occupied with putting up some book shelves in the apartment, changing a plug, or re-potting plants out on the garden balcony, and the actor on stage faces me with an image of my father. He looks wounded from what I've said about him in my first book, and I hear his reproach, 'How could you have done this, Michael?' And the painful feeling lingers. His face comes near to mine, and I see that the picture I painted is a mirror: it leaves me vulnerable to attack. At the same time I tell myself that courage demands I speak the truth, because I'm defying a faithfulness to the past. I look at myself, and reiterate like a mantra, 'Self-affirmation, in spite of . . .' And the obstacles within take into themselves the gentle, insistent anxiety of doubt, a wavering which I find is not easily entreated.

I know the codes that regulate behaviour within the family that influence me. It's a *vade mecum* I carry around with me in my satchel, a book of rules to which I never have to refer, because I felt that I knew all of them off by heart. If I think to disregard them, I feel anxious, and if I violate them, I know I shall be punished. I've a heightened awareness of them in Terry's company, because when he transgresses familial rules to which he's indifferent, I feel apprehensive. In all cases, the default setting is fear. My response to these is up at the level of terror, completely out of proportion to what's happening. It's a very young one in age, that of the tiny child who's thunderstruck with fear when faced with a giant who turns into a monster. From the bodily evidence, I can piece together that I must have been terrorised by the potential retributive punishment from my parents and teachers. I remember vividly the many beatings I received from my father. That triangular situation involved my father, my mother, and me. Although I was barely three years old, my father was definitively taking me out of my mother's sphere of influence, while at the same time he was depriving his wife of enjoying unfettered access to her child. By exercising his power so brutally and beating me to within an inch of my life, he was showing to the both of us that as a rival for her affections, there could be no competition: my father always won. The tensions within that psychological drama are mundane, but the trauma involved seems to have been out of the ordinary.

Possibly because I grew up elsewhere, still desperate to withdraw from fraught familial situations, those regulations which were inscribed upon my psyche early on weren't subject to the natural process of change and wearing away, so that I live life within the archetype of a primitive triangulated family, under a feudal system of government. It's the anxious fee granted to this vassal for maintenance, which I'm fearful is always subject to being withdrawn without warning. Many times Terry has looked into my eyes with a rueful sympathy and said, 'God, they certainly did a job on you at the Mall in Castlebar!' I've constantly to remind myself that family conversations are historical battlegrounds, dangerous because ownership of the family, certainly where a stranger is concerned, is perpetually in dispute. And yet I feel bound by my surname, and proud of my father's name.

Terry is right: a courageous sedition, a going apart is needed of me, to breach the stultifying laws of what's considered to be acceptable deep down in my psyche. However, the penalty for any infringement of fealty is immediate banishment, at least, that's how I register it. Once upon a time, an explorer who was three and a quarter years old undertook a bravely impossible journey through the frightening shadows of the forest. He collected his pyjamas from under his pillow, leaving behind all that he had come to know, and went to live with his grandmother in the house next door. He was making his escape from the terrifying, giant woodsman, whose evil axe was following the child and attempting to hack his being in two. When this explorer was older, and before it was too late, the imperative of his soul seems to be that he has to cover the same ground again, this time as an adult with more knowing eyes. It's an exploration that can only be carried out in the field of words, because the once-upon-a-time of the fairytale is over, and nowhere else exists,

Terry was reversing into a parking space, when he said, 'You know that Robbie and your Aunt Mary will never speak to you again if you publish the book. Are you prepared for that?'

'Don't be ridiculous!'

He persisted. 'Are you prepared for that?' Blue eyes looking straight into mine, momentarily, in the rear-view mirror, locking hard.

'The book has to be punished; there's no question about that.'

Terry put his foot on the brake and withdrew the keys. 'The book has to be punished, or published?'

I was taken aback. Then we both laughed uproariously by the assent signalled in my Freudian slip: my unconscious thought had told the truth.

I've tended to revere the book that I've written as the manifestation in words of a benevolent, wiser personality, who has my best interests at heart. He is pre-eminent above all others, and naturally takes first place. To my mind, he commands unquestioning obedience and devotion. He has certain requirements regarding artistic truth, because words are clearly apprehensible, and I'm able to seize them fearlessly in my hands like bricks, to build a dwelling there for my soul. This person is an emotional taskmaster of late maturity, who makes demands on me to attain the highest possible standards of literary creation. When I've achieved those, he requires me to go beyond myself, and to comb through the opening chapters of the text again to take account of the latest chapters I've written, and bring all of them into alignment. From the viewpoint of this divine perspective, I can look forward and back in time at my life as it has revealed itself to me through my writing. The text has registered a new amalgam, which opens up further possibilities and also requires a rewriting of what I'd laid down before. As the words slip easily onto the page, they reorganise the memories I have of the past. This sets me up differently inside with regard to my future, which has been altered at a stroke of the keyboard. This is the person who is speaking me, and giving me audible expression.

That's the broad street of the imagination in which I can be inaugurated as a domesticated Archangel. The Spanish poet, Ferderico García Lorca, described the scene:

> *San Miguel se estabo quieto*
> *en la alcoba de su torre,*
> *con las enaguas cuajadas*
> *de espejitos y entredoses*

> St Michael was resting calmly
> in the alcove of his tower,
> his petticoats frozen
> in spangles and lace.

Bemused members of the town council in their robes of office, the awestruck parish priest on hand to bless the occasion, bourgeois dignitaries and burghers accompanied by the town's brass band, assembled on the Mall by the steps of the Castlebar Courthouse. They all took favourable omens from the completely unexpected shock of my soaring flight. The Taoiseach, our Prime Minister Enda Kenny, said, 'This is a book about the stream of being of its author, a meandering down and across the thought-processes of Michael Murphy . . . Most of all, this is a book about humanity: your humanity . . . To write as you do is an act of courage in which you open your soul to the reader and to the world.' But to cause hurt to anyone has never been asked of me. I was conscious when writing the book of handing back to their rightful owners some of the abuses that had been projected onto me; however, in telling the truth as I saw it, I was never consciously malign. What I apprehended as a child could have been inadequately understood. The truth I made of it at the time, and the inferences I drew, account for the childish blind spots that can still cripple me today. But in matters of feeling, the inner child is intuitively accurate. I still scan the environment instinctively for a place of safety. That childish wonder also feeds into the artistic vision of the literary sage, who's the only person I take into account when writing. His cloak slides comfortably around the shoulders of my father, fitting him out with ease, because it was he who initially held out the coordinates of literary idealism to his eldest son, through his encouragement. I'm grateful for his patronymic gift of humming wings.

My pioneering Dad walked with me up to the Mayo County Library one sunny Thursday afternoon, which was a closed half-day in Castlebar when I was about twelve, so that he could sign out for me in front of the librarian a copy of James Joyce's *Ulysses*. The Saturday morning before, which was the allocated time for youngsters, she'd refused to let me have the book, and I'd to go and place it back on the shelf. Me and my Dad carried the tome home to the Mall as a spoil of war, replete with its strong and definitive Irish words, which had never been banned by the Irish censor because the book had been published abroad. On the way we paid a visit to Brady's shop by the post office, where Dad bought two slim bars of Cadbury's chocolate as a celebration, because, as my father told me, 'the milk in it is good for you!' As a health professional, my pharmacist father had foresight. He supported the nourishment of my literary education, and the potential for its unknown and subversive effects. James Joyce, the exile, was the first saint who was righteous in my Dad's eyes. Later on we were to read together Samuel Beckett's *En Attendant Godot*, about which we argued, and which didn't appeal to him. Mum told me he was disappointed with my eventual decision to live my life in the big city, as opposed to small-town Castlebar. But he passionately understood what the stoic Greek philosopher, Epictetus, pointed out. He quoted him for me, that '. . . the well-educated alone are free.' I was given an education for which my father had made provision and to which he gave his blessing over the ongoing years.

I've paid for this wreath of words with my life's experience. It's a garland, a festoon of summer flowers twisted around my neck which others can see, even if they don't wish to advert to it, smothering the sight with silence. Terry's mother, Sarah, was having a row with her twin sister, who withheld mention of the beautiful new outfit that Sarah was wearing especially for the visit. Sitting around the fire in the old family homestead in Laois, and sharing afternoon tea, Sarah could stand the silence no longer, and she asked, 'Well, Nan, what do you think of my rig-out?'

Nan looked at it, thought for a few seconds while balancing the best china cup and saucer in one hand, and wiping an invisible crumb off her skirt with the other, said even-handedly, 'Nice, mind you . . .'

On the sharpest of learning curves about writing a book, I've come to realise that there are countless steps on the path that I've chosen. Every one of them has captured me with surprising changes of perspective, and some of those advances have taken me unawares. As I look back, I seem to have lived life before as a blind and deaf mute, whereas now after the consolidation of writing, all of my senses have come alive to the giving of colour and the making of music: *Soli Deo gloria*, as J. S. Bach wrote on his manuscripts. What I've always prized the most are the vibrant colours which shine with light, the Titian blues I saw in the Prado in Madrid, the brightest vermilion reds of Matisse, and his leaping, dancing figures full of joy which now adorn the walls of the Hermitage in St Petersburg, and the sun-disc yellows of Van Gogh cornfields: these are the vivid, translucent tones with which I paint my life. Strolling through the fields of golden sunflowers that surround Castello di Gabbiano outside Florence, where I was attending my friend Ruth's fiftieth birthday party, I asked Aaron, a ramrod-straight American Navy SEAL in his early thirties to have an experienced word with her fifteen-year-old cousin, Richard.

'Yes, sir!'

The teenager had landed a summer job in a diving shop in Marbella, and his payment was to be the free dives, about which he was passionate. Aaron stood tall in front of the younger man, and told him that when he was growing up in the States, he always considered life to be a fairground, and that he was determined to take every ride: 'Live big, young man, live big,' was what he counselled.

This second chance at life after being inoculated by Death means that I'm obliged to make my life count for something. Ten days after the prosta-tectomy, I asked for my laptop to be brought into the hospital. Writing my first book has been the beacon of hope in the desert that served as an inspi-ration to lead me on: it goes before me, flaming with the divine light of truth. The fire has aroused my creativity. It has enabled me to continue liv-ing life in a new way, so that nothing is wasted, not the pain, nor the suf-fering, nor the hopelessness, not even the silence that I admit I subscribed to for over half a century, and that now I see coming at me again across the desert like a suffocating wall of sand, which tells me I'm outside it, that I've breached through. I've cleared my throat to speak out, a step forward into the spotlight that serves to leave others behind in the shadows. The shin-ing light can gather together in clarity all the facets of my life, and then reflect outwards the events that have shaped me in order to advance and create something brilliantly new.

On an earlier visit to my uncle and aunt, I told them, 'I'm determined to live as healthily as I can, free from the many forms of cancer that beset all of us, each and every one of us. My stance has to be the positive one of gratefulness for the further gift of life that's been granted to me. My book will be a celebration of that survival, and be more than any of us can envisage at this moment: I'm certain of that.' After sifting through the words that made up my preliminary manuscript, I was sure, resolved in my mind that it was good, and that my time is now.

The Daffodil

For all those who have been touched by cancer.

I desire to be free as the daffodil
For daffodils dance in the wind and the rain
Like children at play laughing and waving
Celebrating in the green spring

Those brilliant yellow Lent lilies
Are risen from the dead after suffering underground
And offer the promise of a resurrection
Nodding their assent to the dream of the impossible

Their glance is more tenuous from having survived the past
Fearless of tomorrow they live only for today
And give prodigally blooming in profusion
Delighting the soul with yellow brightness
Inviting me courageously onwards towards the summer
Illuminating little steps with lighted lanterns

So changed from having lost
Aware of limits lacking that much more
I embrace the cost of a new life
A second time around

Another chance to flame with love
The last dance better than before
I have endured like the daffodil
I too am above ground
And mostly I am childishly grateful

Shortly after the book was published, Robbie was being brutally definitive, stretched out in his living-room armchair, when he turned his head towards me and declared out of the blue, 'If anybody asks me what I thought of your book, I'll tell them I haven't read it.'

His words were completely unexpected, but my face remained impassive.

'And that will be the truth!' he added proudly.

Mary asked, 'Can I get anybody more tea?'

The floor gave way beneath me like the trapdoors of a scaffold under a man who was to be hanged. The shock when Robbie's words hit home rammed underneath the diaphragm as if my uncle physically collided with me. My throat was constricted, and I found it difficult to breathe. The unspoken text was that his version of the truth would supersede mine, because he'd decided not to grant the acknowledgement of reading what I'd written about my life, about the abuses I'd suffered, and the joy of recovery from cancer. And when asked, he was determined to stand over that rejection publicly. My truth was to be ignored, I presume, so that the status quo ante, the state of affairs that existed both within and without the family before the book was written, could prevail. I'd attempted to write myself into that family history from the exile of the house next door, but the present head of the family was going to expunge that contribution through his foreclosure.

The unyielding front that Robbie had adopted manifested the tight battle formation with shields joined I faced from both my uncle and my aunt. They balanced five metre lances on the shoulder to keep me out

THE HOUSE OF PURE BEING

there, hanging, twisting in the wind at the end of a rope, untouchable. Their solidity of union, the phalanx that confronted, meant that once again I no longer belonged. There was no place to go with this: no reply was expected, no rebuttal was possible, there was no way forward out of this situation. In any case, how to express an opinion about something, which simply didn't exist? Once again there was silence. I and my book counted for nothing, and Robbie was letting me know that brusquely, sweeping us out of the way with a butcher's broom like offal. I'd been convicted in criminal proceedings by the hanging cohort sitting in judgement, and Robbie had now formally pronounced the sentence. My unforgivable crime was to have published a book.

As they cheerfully waved me away from their house in Terenure towards the road for home, the impression remaining was that I was a slave bound hand and foot by the oppressive chains of language, taking part in a triumphal procession honouring a victorious general. I felt deeply aggrieved by Robbie's contempt. Although at the time the thoroughgoing depths of his denunciation hadn't fully penetrated, when my powers of speech returned somewhere beyond Rathgar village, in the heat of battle I vowed resolutely never to enter their house again. 'You're always welcome here,' they intone regularly, but it's a conditional welcome. I'm welcome in their home as long as there's no reference to the book, or to the exciting events that have followed on its publication, about which they've never made enquiry. It's as if there's no freedom to begin a sentence with the personal pronoun 'I' because Robbie has killed that in me.

Some days after that encounter, I signed for the ten author's hardback copies of my newly published book which arrived at the hall door from the distributors. It felt as if the well of words was overflowing, because the first-edition copies that I'd mentally ear-marked for Mary and Robbie as a valuable gift on into the future, were now redundant. They were never to receive them, a symbolic absence which had suddenly roared open into an eternal void.

It feels as though I've deliberately turned my back on the people who understood my language in a way that approximated my own, in a considered betrayal of a part of myself, and that I'm the lesser for it. Isn't that telling, the way I express the sensation as though it were my fault? Terry pointed out the pertinent question: 'Who has turned their back on whom?' It hardly matters now, because the devastation which has been wrought is the same. I shared a common field with my family, and I've had to cede my portion of that, and to withdraw, set out in a different direction on a journey all by myself, because they've chosen to take their stand with the abuser. It's a sundering, a severance, without, apart from, separately, far away, different.

The happening has also revived the anguished memories of my brother Kieran's death from cancer fifteen years ago, which was the death of future possibilities. His death left me orphaned, and I'm experiencing that same loss again, or perhaps anew, given the protective safety of distance. Now is the time for the frozen emotions around that catastrophe to be reclaimed and honoured, which were buried in a hole in the ground with that final decade of the rosary, the last time we stood in a line as a family together and shared in sorrow. And we were left all alone in the cemetery.

Part Three

The Silence . . .

'How are you?' has always struck me as an absurd question, out of tune with what's really being asked, until I discovered that 'how' is a derivation of the Old English 'who?' And yet, after the early morning pleasantries – 'You're welcome! May I get you something to drink – coffee, tea, water?' – it's the question with which habitually I begin each psychoanalytic session at my consulting rooms in Dublin, after the client has settled comfortably onto the couch: 'Well, how are you?'

For me, that unasked question, 'Who are you?', which is hidden deep in the expectant silence of the room, is the invitation to say something intimate about the self, the fruit of ongoing thought and knowledge which has been ripening unbeknownst in the shadow of other trees, way out on the edge of the orchard, over time. It implies that I'm open to hearing what the client has to say, and committed to the work of developing being, and being there, for the length of time it may take to arrive at the truth.

'How are you?' seems to be another question entirely to do with bearing, the manner in which you uphold your being in the world. Such a body language only serves to emphasize the full speech that's required of that register to express the gesture articulately, and without inference, so that the hidden *who* question can be encouraged like a delicate plant deep in the unconscious, and brought forward to flower in the person's conscious speech as well. And yet, there's also something comforting and soothing in the simplicity of a tender 'How are you?' It's a full-faced question that heals the soul, and makes the loneliness of being recede, if only for a moment. I'd never realised that my denigration of that *how* question has had the profoundest implications for the manner in which I've conducted my life to date, because it's not a question that I usually ask of myself, being more concerned with constructing who I am through the various scenarios of the drama of the day.

My brother's knowing question, 'And how are you now?' meaning how are you given the present circumstances, the question with which I began and ended my first book, certainly has within it the sense of bracing your-self against the vicissitude of life, a two-handed protective shield against variation and mutability. He was giving the nod to a person hiding out of sight around the corner of language, and respectfully inviting them to break cover and speak, if that was their wish. By employing my brother's quote open-handedly in my book, I believed that I too was giving such an entrance to all comers, more than willing to accept what they have to say. 'And how are you now?' invokes the ceremony of a blessing, the bestowal of a divine gift which has the effect of consecrating both parties. That val-ued communication is a spiritual safe house where the fragile gossamer of life's mystery can be shaken out in speech, like St Martin's summer in November, when cobwebs draping garden foliage reach out to brush your face with gentle filminess, nature's softest fingertips, renewing the spirit with precious moments of golden autumnal tenderness, before this time in a side-by-side gesture of solidarity we can face again into the icy blast of winter's north-easterly chill, arm in arm together; unless, of course, a silent blanket of snow starts to smother everything.

From my years of psychoanalytic work, I'm very mindful of people who proffer the most valuable gift possible, that of telling me about themselves, or as we say with greater accuracy in Irish *mé féin a labhairt*, to speak myself. There are some exceptional individuals who have the courage to speak themselves out into the eternal stream of language. Like a cuckoo in a nest, they make a space for themselves there by deliberately elbowing others out of the way as they grow, constructing who they are out of the building blocks of words, a patrimony that belongs to all of us, but which they strive mightily to ingest and make their own. They've to struggle to do that, because others won't yield them a place without a fight: every word of the language has to be gained, and then held. As Samuel Johnson, with huge insight, put it: 'Every man has a right to utter what he thinks truth, and every other man has a right to knock him down for it. Martyrdom is the test.'

Some people begin their analysis by speaking to me about themselves almost in the third person, which only serves to shine a spotlight on the fearful pain of their alienation that has condemned them to live elsewhere, in the wrong person, or even in a different grammatical tense. It's a punishment they suffer for not being able to interrupt the silence, and speak the truth about themselves. In all likelihood, the reasons for this have been outside of their control, trammels to which they may never even have adverted, and which had been imposed on them by someone else, essentially to control them. In the very few words of hope that I'd offer (my place is to hear, after all) I hold out a flaming torch that by the end of their analysis, after labouring for possibly many years, gradually they shall have inhabited all the memories of who they are in a language of their own choosing, and begin to live life in the present. They'll have reclaimed old ground, and have brought those recollections up to date through a software update, and a rebooting. Their speech will have been pruned of other's prescriptive voices, unoriginal reproductions that took to themselves the right to inscribe rules upon another's body, to inhibit them with corrupting cursive chains that dug painfully into the flesh, behaving rather like computer viruses. Then for the first time, they'll be able to speak to me in their own voice, and after time, in the most assured manner. As a final step, they'll have taken home that torch blazing with the light of truth, for it will have belonged to them always and in the first place, but without their recognition or realisation.

'Yes, I've got something to say.' And isn't that in itself something to be grateful for, because it enables me to continue on from day to day. I can expand upon that opening line, give a gloss as if the *something* were an unusual word requiring an explanatory note. And one word borrows another, hanging together and making further connections. Silence would bring that continuity to a shuddering halt. My story doesn't yet have an ending, and it would be wrong of me to insert a final full stop before my allotted time ran out.

Just imagine murdering the artist! Not only closing over the wing panels of a triptych and blocking out the blazingly beautiful central section, but actually removing it from view. Somebody deciding to deliberately disappear the artist, a mirror-image of what happened in Spain during the civil war. People weren't allowed to wear mourning after a loved one had been disappeared: they had to carry on as if nothing had happened. From the retrospection given by that premature conclusion, I was sixty-five when I died unexpectedly, the much-loved partner of Terry, sadly missed by my mother, and deeply regretted by my uncle and aunt, although they too wore no black, so that their neighbours would never suspect somebody else had blood on their hands.

It's the same way that I behaved after the surgeon removed my cancerous prostate. Every day I mourned in silence the absence of a penis that once ejaculated semen, but I didn't burden anybody with my complaints; there's so much more to be grateful for. Yet, from that narrow perspective, focussed in on the symbol of creativity that shoots blanks, I've continued on a different track. My spirit is invited by each new dawn to try again in a beyond of death. It's a bodily resurrection which has fitted seamlessly with my life before, making unrecognised appearances on a lonely road. At the very least, I can always say something which has the power to change matters.

The something I've got to say, and it's a subversive imperative now burgeoning up as it does from underneath, is about my sexual identity. I'm homosexual; now there's an admission that has the potential to change matters. I don't announce it normally, because I used to wonder what people would make of the label, about which they'd feel obliged to have an opinion, for or against. I'm sure people with a high level of awareness register the fact subliminally when they meet me, but it's not a topic that would come up in general conversation. I'd be wary of discrimination, when a particular person is singled out for subtle disfavour. I'd be disappointed to experience an acknowledged lack of interest from people, because of my perceived sexual difference.

Homosexuality has been innate in me from the first gleaming rays of the rising sun, although I didn't open up anything about that orientation until I began to experiment sexually in my late twenties with members of my own sex in whom I was mirrored. The loud cry of joy I set up on that first night of seduction was my delighted reaction to having freely explored the texture, the curves and folds of another man's body, a man who'd held me reverently in his arms. It was the inevitable next step into adulthood, from having lived cheek by jowl with my brother, who shared with me his humour, love and loyalty, and in the varying expressions of his being, who was the first to ground my masculinity, after my father. The dramatic uncovering of the phallus was a sacrament to which I came late in my personal development, a benediction by a priest of Dionysus, who raised the monstrance of which I shall always speak well. I was in my thirties when I knelt before him smelling of incense, and worshipped there: received the white host melting onto my tongue. The phallus became a whetstone of humanity which has sharpened my understanding of what it means to be a man. Over the years, it has kept me sane within the symbolic presence of its parameters, my life regulated according to the rise and fall of its tides. Now, since the operation for cancer, it incarnates nothingness for me as well.

Early one morning in the broadcasting studios, there was a retirement gathering for a technician when he'd completed his final shift. As we cut the cake, and toasted him with glasses of cava and orange juice, a young man was standing across from me, with his legs apart and arms raised, holding the camera of his mobile phone to his eyes with both his hands, taking photographs of the occasion. A large, circumcised penis was clearly outlined in the bulge of his grimy jeans, and a sudden surge of desire took away my breath and confounded me. I looked at this young technician with renewed interest, admiring the generally easy appearance of the thirty-year-old with the curling brown hair, the bigness of his body, its shape and muscular development. He lowered the camera and held my gaze with bemused blue eyes for a moment, and then he raised the camera again, this time turning his torso to the side to take another photograph from a different angle, which had the effect of emphasizing the curving thickness of his member sloping over heavy testicles, trapped against his right leg by the zip. The size of this young man's penis astonished me, and it looked to be lazily semi-erect.

Under the pressure of my gaze, the young man lowered the mobile phone, made a point of checking it briefly, and then he turned around until we were directly facing each other. He raised the camera again and focussed up on me through the lens: guiltily, I averted my eyes from his crotch, like a man caught looking enviously at the massive bonnet of a BMW 5 Series Touring. He grinned, so he was aware that I was disturbed by him. He bent his knees a little and thrust his appendage forward shamelessly. I was sure that he was being deliberately displayful towards me now, confidently proud of his vigorous endowment, and I was overwhelmed at such a sight: we seemed to be alone together in the room. He gently lowered the camera and gave me a broad smile. He'd have known that I was gay, and I presumed that he was straight, but there was no malice in that smile. I felt it as a gentle gesture of solidarity man to man, a sympathy which I was too emotionally retentive to acknowledge with the even slightest nod of my head: I knew not to go there. I had to walk away, out of the room and down the corridor, and for the first time I was stung with the anguish of being an old man, old enough to be that young man's grandfather. My sexual life was over. After the prostatectomy, I'd been left with the stump of a non-functioning penis that over the past three years seemed to have withered away into nothingness, something I could never let another see. I considered the dart of my sudden desire to have been an obscene anachronism, out of place and time, depraved, unworthy because it no longer seemed to arise naturally from within myself, but had to be generated by an outside stimulus.

I was plagued by the pathetic, romantic fantasy that he was going to follow, catch up with me and invite me back to his untidy bachelor flat for a mug of coffee, both of us trembling with excitement at the improbable adventure. As soon as we'd cross the threshold, we'd embrace. I'd sink to my knees and worship this character I seem to have idealised, as he rolled back his head and groaned. I heard those deep, inarticulate sounds expressive of sexual desire in my head, and they wouldn't leave me alone. They tormented me, and continually broke my concentration. The sensible facts of my age and of his youth, that I was gay and he was straight, didn't intrude to save me. I became angry that I was being subjected to such heart-scalding imaginings, a ludicrous drama in which I hadn't taken a role since I myself was in my early thirties, when I was coming out. 'What's the point of this suffering,' I muttered aloud, 'now that I'm incapable of doing anything about it?' I drew amused glances from my colleagues passing by, talking to myself. It felt as if I'd overdosed on caffeine. 'You're insane,' I concluded, alive with the madness.

It was late evening before I thought to analyse what it was in the chance encounter that invited such a strong reaction. The particular young man didn't concern me: I'd never paid any attention to him before; indeed, I knew nothing at all about him. The essence of what shocked me, what had provoked me, was catching sight of the shape moulded by the cloth, and the breathtaking bigness of the shape. It was a talisman that resonated with me, for whatever reason: the visible representation of something abstract, undefined, a phantom out of a dream, intangible.

Two days later, a memory came back of being sexually abused in the thicket at the end of our back garden at home by the young mechanic from the garage next door. I was seven years old, and it was the first time that I'd felt a burgeoning penis become fully erect against my body. In all of the encounters with that young man, I remembered he'd never opened the zip of his blue overalls. I'd never seen something then either, or so I'd thought. But I must have registered the imprint of his penis beating against his clothes, even though I didn't have the words at the time to fill out the shape, or even to understand what was really happening to me out of sight of the others, and how I'd felt about it. Those episodes, and they were repeated many times, had sunk into the depths of unconsciousness, to surface now with all the frightening excitement of secret trysts, just the two of us, me and the youth whom I took to be my older friend, that I'd experienced out among the bushes and the trees at the end of our back-garden.

When I was absorbed playing games by myself, the young mechanic used to creep up on me from behind, tap me on the shoulder, and when I turned he'd ask, 'Would you like to come with me, and I'll give you more lessons in how to wind an opponent?'

I was appalled that I should be so captivated by an image, tangible to me now in that historical context of my extreme youth. What I remembered above all was the urgency of his voice, the hoarse whispering against my ear in a rough embrace, almost a rising chant repeated over and over, gently and with increasing desperation: 'Are you winded yet, oh tell me, aren't you winded yet, be sure to tell me when you're winded, do let me know when you feel that you're winded . . .'

'Yes,' I'd say: 'Yes . . .'

I was filled with sadness that the passion of sexual activity was consigned to the past, now that I'd been emasculated by prostate cancer. Because of the radical prostatectomy, the fantasy of the mutilation of the penis has become a reality for me. Sometimes the poor, withered thing can hiccup up gobs of urine, never semen anymore because the surgeon has removed my prostate gland. As a man, I've been rendered voiceless in that department, uttering nothing: I have no thing. The echo of what I was missing, of what I'd been deprived of, pained me grievously. At least I was able to take delight in the healthy exuberance of that relaxed young man from a different generation, who'd so unselfconsciously inhabited his body that he was able to share it with all comers. Or perhaps towards the end of his display, he'd performed that erotic dance especially for me, whom he'd recognised as being thunderstruck, although he could never have surmised the reason why. I'd like to think that a connection was made, if only with my past, because it somehow redeemed the frank openness of what had happened between us. I'd witnessed his enjoyment, and he had recognised my desire. There was no trace of judgement involved, although I was full of self-reproach that I'd committed an offence through being seen to be desirous. And yet in his manifest enjoyment of his body, the young man represented for me a generous future. He held out to me the promise of further development, and the freedom to live life in ways that I never before would have deemed possible, nor even permissible. That young man's erection enabled me to flesh out with words the nothingness of an image that breathlessly I'd experienced once upon a time as something tactile. Through his intervention, I found out that the power which had shaped and moulded my sexuality for the past fifty years or so was a memory. It has been alive in me for all of that time unbeknownst, sending me off like a medieval knight of old on a never-ending quest to find again the Holy Grail, which I'd lost. It's the bowl that has dictated my responses, a rounded, hollow container used for serving food and holding liquid. And yes, this desire which has motivated me, this particular truth which has moulded me, has been my life. Only now it's no longer consigned to the underworld of my past, but resurrected into life-giving words that are free-floating, and that also have the sovereign power to consciously collaborate with my future.

Terry and I were invited to have dinner in the Hodson Bay Hotel with Chris Forde and Eileen Donohoe (who has since become the Principal of

Athlone Community College) before their awards night, at which I was to be the keynote speaker. Eileen shocked me with how she began her speech in front of the 750-strong gathering of pupils and their parents. 'First I want to welcome Michael Murphy and his partner, Terry O'Sullivan.' While her remark was a polite expression of good manners, her recognition that the two of us shared a reality, overtook a reticence, a silence, that I'd imagined appropriate for the secondary-school atmosphere of a town in the centre of Ireland, although I hadn't been inside a secondary school for upwards of forty years. The principal's founding statement outed the narrowness of my own homophobic prejudice. With hindsight, she was also speaking to those children in her school whose sexual identity was homosexual, recognising their inalienable equality in her eyes, and that of Athlone's Community College.

Unconsciously I'd painted in advance a portrait of a gay man, which I'd always known was hanging neglected on the wall of a corridor in my house, but which her greeting had forced me to pause and to confront, really examine for the first time, noting the slap-dash nature of the work, the thin, inadequate texture of the paint, the deployment of garish colour, and the unsubtle modelling of the figure which seemed to be lost in the deepest shadow. As I glanced around the ballroom trying to read a momentary reaction on the blank faces in the close ranks of seats, it was borne in upon me that my depiction was of a gay man set against the context of the powerful massed ranks of heterosexual society, a painting which had been coloured in by memories of my shameful secret growing up in Castlebar, which I'd always pretended to ignore, but which had left me solitary. There's an Old French word which expressed my attitude perfectly: *desdeignier*, which means to do the opposite of treat as worthy, to take from worthiness. Eileen's gentle perspicacity enabled me to see that as a person I was de-centred, that I'd painted a self-portrait from the outside using someone else's perspective. I'd so hated the loneliness of that likeness, that I'd smothered it with silence. She gently showed me that I was the only one who turned up at the party wearing a mask and a fancy-dress costume, which was the real reason that I was feeling out of place.

It was the second part of her sentence, '. . . and his partner Terry O'Sullivan,' that hit home. Backstage, when I met the elegantly suited Spanish singer, Diana Navarro, after her concert in the football stadium in Marbella in August, Terry reminded me on the way home, that in company, I often neglect to introduce him as my partner, and I treat him as though he's invisible. He had to say to her, *'Yo soy su compañero,'* that he was my companion. The push of Terry's interpellation interrupted the business of giving her a copy of my book in which she's mentioned twice, whereas the dowry of his daily life interest in my estate is absolute, and reiterated daily. I'm full of gratitude for his recurring forbearance on so many levels. It was salutary to realise that unconsciously I've afflicted him with my own disdain, which hurts him, because the brushstrokes which have blackened his ebullient personality paint him with my Shadow. This is a character I've rejected and consider inferior, made up of traits which I've attempted to cleanse from my conscious persona, in a vain attempt to fit in with what I took to be the prevailing public mood. The perspective of exile seems to have nurtured this ambition, like a pointless yearning for the illusory innocence of the past. I also diminish myself by holding back from speech a vital part of who I am, an energy bursting with the rude and playful, priapic vigour of the primitive, but whom I've been unwilling to let loose through fear of censure and humiliation.

I took a further step forward into the light when I appeared on *Spirit Level*, a religious television programme hosted by Joe Duffy, in which I talked about Cardinal Ratzinger's document of 1986. In it, he describes homosexuals as 'intrinsically disordered . . . with a tendency towards evil.' I pointed out to Joe on air, 'If I were to say to you that I think all Jews are intrinsically disordered, and that Jews as a race have a tendency towards evil, you'd be horrified!' I had to consciously take that step, and not falter: I am never to detract from another's humanity. And yet, I've been guilty of disparaging my partner, and treating him as if he were of lower rank, an *untermensch*. It's not the truth, and as I can see from the lessons of history, my contemptuous attitude is dangerous.

Ironically, the theme of my speech to the students in Athlone that evening was 'Inhabit who you are . . .' Following on the principal's introductory words, the mantra became for me an avant-garde dwelling place of open spaces and light. The moment of epiphany was reminiscent of the time when the floor in Benalmadena's Torrequebrada Casino began to turn around in a circular movement at the end of the Flamenco *Tablao*, and the principal dancers stepped forward to the edge of the stage. In the end, it was they who warmly applauded us as we went sailing past them and out into the balmy smoothness of the Spanish night. As my gift to the students, I offered them a defiant poem called 'The Poppy', and promised that in whatever collection or book it would appear, the poem would carry the dedication, for the Athlone Community College Student Award Winners 2010.

The Poppy

Because there is no point to anything anyway
It is necessary to be defiant and protesting
Like a single red poppy in a field of yellowing corn

And because I care so desperately that there is no point
I keenly feel the deadly sadness underlying it all

I know there is no voice that is like unto mine
There never was nor will there ever be again
For my time under the warmth of the sun which will set

And so there is no reason never to be
Outrageous or resplendent as a poppy

Bright-red

    erect

        and generously

Giving difference to the sameness of that field of corn

Shouting out that I was born for better or for worse

Waving my flag and making my colourful noise

And frightening away the darkness for as long as possible

To become the best poppy that ever there was

Is no mean ambition because it means

To take on the responsibility of caring for myself

And not to lean on or to take from other's kindnesses

And for today's eternity how glorious a thing it is

To be alive and laughing in the wind

Extravagantly scattering my seeds of happiness and hope

And being wild

        and flagrant

            and dancing

Like a single red poppy in a whole field of yellowing corn

Experiencing events like the Athlone awards night have helped me to build a more authentic personality, by joining words together in a way which would have seemed unthinkable before. I see now that my reality is a linguistic one, discursively constructed. I swim each night and each day in a river of words, which has the effect of pitching me into the truth. When I was growing up in Ireland, being gay was something I had to hold back from passing into speech, because I feared the violent release of energy from the word would have upended me onto the left-hand side of God. The life-changing revelation triggered by that Athlone awards night is that I can act out of who I am through finding that all of language is allowed. Words don't have to be silenced, and certain words that give a person life should never have to be incarcerated. This disclosure has permitted me to use an open-hearted speech that has strength, forcefulness and vigour, which represents all of me fully in performance. Such liveliness has released me and my partner, Terry, from the shadows, and a self-imposed repression that attacked at the basis of who we are, through wearing a respectable outer cloak and the mask of invisibility, essentially through my silence. It frightens me that I could so easily have ended up living an anonymous life. I have cancer to thank for changing the poverty of that outlook.

Having to cope with the fear and pain surrounding cancer, and handle the reality of the ultimate physical assault from Death resolutely knocking on the hall door of my heart, has already developed in me the courage to face danger head-on. The imperative of survival has led me to battle and to overcome all of these obstacles like a man. What I need for the future is the courage of confidence, to act in accordance with my own truth, without undue care for the baggage that others will bring to the idea of who I am. I've already entrusted into Terry's keeping the disclosure of my secret self, so I've a positive experience of what it means to be known intimately by another. His love is shown in the Charles Eames chair he bought in secret, and had installed for me when I arrived home from hospital after the prostatectomy. This was the chair that was made for the film director, Billy Wilder, when he was directing *Some Like It Hot*: 'I thought it would be appropriate for an RTÉ Producer/Director,' he'd said, delightedly. He fills the coffee machine for me the night before I go to the radio station to read the early morning news, and leaves my flask ready, to involve himself in the effort I make getting up at four in the morning to work. It's out of such big and little acts of continual thoughtfulness that love has taken hold. Terry upholds my being through the commonplace interactions surrounding cooking and cleaning and plans and duties. I love his smile, and the way that his blue eyes light up with enthusiasm. This daily engagement has led me on to accept my inalienable freedom, which is growing stronger under the care of his love, and simple well-wishing.

Benedicite

Benedicite means a blessing – literally, to say well.

'Yes' is a courageous commitment
As delicate as the air that it displaces
To be received with reverence
And venerated for its holiness

'Yes' is an assent to life
An annunciation heard
Nine months before the nativity
A foundation stone with which
To build a home within
'Yes' is a sacred word

She shyly proffered us the ring
A glittering diamond crystal
That seemed to be floating on air
'We got engaged this Christmas Eve' she said

They both were beaming happily
Inviting praise and recognition
Commending themselves to each other
And to us for their achievement

'I had a dream that I was choosing children's names' he said
'Middle-class names of saints like Paul and Mark
She was sure of the ring in the window
So I asked her marry me'

She said 'Not like this not now outside a jeweller's shop'
And then she said 'Why not ... ?'

Such is the logic of how lives intertwine
The pattern of how decisions are arrived at
Commitments are that are timed to coincide irregularly
Cut like the facets of a diamond ring
Facing away from each other

They were walking back arm in arm
To their car in the Phoenix Park
When a stranger had called after them
'You look well together'
Setting them up to suit each other
For a whole lifetime of continuous hope

'Yes' a feather-light kiss to the forehead
'Yes' a whispered grace
'Yes' the tenderest of looks
And a determined proclamation
'Yes' is the bravest undertaking
Of all the continuous covenants

For unto us is born from heaven above
On every Christmas morning of our lives
Love the divine redeemer
Benedicite
Say 'yes'

The great prize of living above ground after cancer, that resurrection, has been to write my first book. This accomplishment was one of the effects of having been shocked back into life. I watched myself slowly emerge, like a colossus breaking free from the chains of others' speech that had bound me tightly for so long. My body was newly clothed in diaphanous words which glittered free as the thousands of stars in the night sky when I rose up, up into the blue yonder from out of the dripping ocean of language: a being swollen with a primitive energy constructed out of the powerful words that I've made my own. When I saw Goya's painting *The Colossus*, one of his black paintings in the Prado, I recognised it. The head and torso of a powerful man with his back to the viewer hangs over a fleeing procession of people and carts and wagons. This blinding vision, which I had painted with the words in my book, was my definitive reply hurled out like a thunderbolt at an unheeding universe, the living out of my truthful answer to the question that life poses as to who I am in my heart. And I've cancer to thank for bringing that analysis towards a completion.

As my book was opened up, I imperceptibly began to shine before a group of like-minded individuals. Soon they sank to their knees in prayer before the supernatural vision that was occurring for them in their imaginations. The feelings that were evoked by my words reverberated off incidents from their own experience, to register a new amalgam which never had existed in the world before. It gave birth to angels with wings, spiritual beings attendant upon God who took unto themselves the likenesses of men, messengers and guardian spirits who brought to mind divine words and phrases, and conjured up patterns of light which focussed onto the retina representations that weren't immediately present to their senses. And after this mystical ecstasy, those visionaries went forth, and spread the word abroad. They wrote an account of their rapture, and sent emails to me afterwards, saying that they were moved to tears, that they found my book to be beautiful. I registered their comments on my website, and gave there the authorisation of their Christian names as well, where they formed an online community of souls. These individuals had the ability to hear the poetry in my voice, because it had also resonated deep within them. The stream of images I continue to create draws strength from the magnanimity of their collective sustenance. We form a gathering of souls that emits much light into the universe. It shines ever brighter with intense and vivid colours.

I found a genuine prophet in Steve MacDonogh. He was the herald who assented to make me appear by publishing my first book. The apparition when it happened was fulgent, radiating light. Jen Kelly, the couturier, and Garrett Fitzgerald immediately offered their beautiful Georgian mansion on North Great George's Street in Dublin's city centre as a backdrop for the book launch.

'Where are you going to get the candles?' asked Jen, in his soft Derry accent. And when he saw my incredulity, brought forward with a northern directness his insistence on the truth, 'Of course you have to have candles; if you're doing it, it has to be right.'

This elegant house was decorated with enormous displays of sweet-smelling summer flowers and trailing ivy. Delicate Chiavari chairs in gold were placed in the two enormous reception rooms up on the first floor, where the caterers circulated amongst the crowd with several types of finger-food, offering glasses of *rioja* and a choice of juices. An *a cappella* quartet of former St Patrick's Cathedral choristers in solemn suits sang baroque music on the return of the stairs. And everywhere, the large beeswax candles I'd sourced gently flickered on the ledges of the tall windows, and above the marble fireplaces, so that a magical atmosphere of shadows and light was created.

Steve had arrived earlier with a portable stand which carried large posters of the book's cover. On a table in front of this, he laid out copies of the paperback and hardback editions of the new book, which people could buy as they arrived. They came in their droves, despite the first major crash of the newly opened Luas light rail system, just off O'Connell Street, when the train ploughed into a bus and injured twenty-one people, three of them seriously. This major emergency had blocked off direct access to people arriving by the main road artery from the south side of the city. I spent the evening signing copies of my work, so engrossed in greeting people, that I didn't have time to eat or drink. Those snatched conversations, the embraces, were exhilarating and full of warmth. As a thank you to all of the supportive friends who took the trouble to turn out that evening, and to the Minister of State for Health and Children, John Moloney, representatives of the Irish Cancer Society, especially to Tom Lynch, the surgeon who'd operated on me in St James's Hospital to correct the incontinence problem, I sang my heart out in a Spanish thanks to life, 'Gracias A La Vida', which was written by the Chilean songwriter Violetta Parra. Regrettably, she was unable to sustain what she'd written, and she committed suicide in 1967. The sadness of her death gave an added poignancy to her words, a stinging of which I was aware on the night:

Gracias a la vida que me ha dado tanto.
Me ha dado el sonido y el abecedario,
Con él las palabras que pienso y declaro:
Madre, amigo, hermano, y luz alumbrando
La ruta del alma del que estoy amando.

Thank you, life, for giving me so much.
You've given me sound and the alphabet,
With them the words in which I think and declare:
Mother, friend, brother, and shining light
Illuminating the way of the soul of my beloved.

Part Four
Hanging from the
Balcony by One Hand

The three women at the next table in the Marbella Club Café had determined not to pay for their meal, and they laid about the waitress with words: '. . . spilled our champagne . . . cold, inedible . . . were truly sorry, you wouldn't charge . . .' Their sharp and sweeping strokes cut the surface of Mira's skin. The poisonous emotions propelling the torrent lodged themselves into the slits and gashes multiplying on her body. The women stood up, gathering up their bags, Anna noted a changthangi pashmina draped over the back of a chair, and they loudly walked away, talking and laughing about their intended visit to a nightclub, dismissing Mira from further consideration. The waitress bent to tidy up the remains on their table, shamed under the weight of words that the women had left behind. It was an ignominy read by everyone in the café: she knew that they could hear the words echoing about her body like the crackling flames in a funeral pyre, whose fierce blaze was uninterrupted by the sudden silence.

Anna and James had noticed the women immediately, blonde forty-somethings wearing miniskirts. They'd been made aware of the demanding, English voices: women who were used to being indulged by wealthy men. But they'd also seen that the waiter service had been impeccable. Before they left, they made a point of speaking to the manager on Mira's behalf, to set him straight on the misrepresentation. A week later, when they visited the MC Café again, they were shocked to discover that Mira was dead. The manager told them that on her way home that early morning, Mira had toppled off her scooter just down the road outside the Puente Romano Hotel, and she died later in hospital from multiple fractures. He said it was an incomprehensible accident which had deeply upset the staff, and that the hotel had paid for Mira's mother to come from Greece.

'Not an accident,' mumbled Anna, her cheeks scalded by the sudden tears.

The cars were whizzing by the small, sad shrine at the side of the road. On the tufts of yellowing grass, her colleagues had placed four red plastic holders that had contained candles, and they'd laced to a post with black, Marbella Club ribbon, three flowers of coloured paper, and an A4-sized photograph which was protected by a plastic covering, under the heading 'Our Mira'. It showed a smiling girl with an open face, but whose gaze didn't penetrate the lens, so that the image remained locked in on itself, on the far side of the camera. Maybe that snapshot caught the genuine aspect of her vulnerability, the aloneness of her lack of connection in southern Spain, which Anna had recognised many weeks before: she'd given Mira some left-over garden pots for the balcony of her new apartment in the centre of Marbella. She understood that the young woman's stability had been overturned by a verbal assault, that words had assailed her. She'd witnessed the violent blows that words had landed on her body earlier that evening. She recalled how the words had punished the politeness of Mira's spirit, flogging repeatedly at her courteous deference to the judgements of those vulgar women. Anna felt guilty that she hadn't intervened directly to shield her from the barrage, and she was confident in the truth that Mira had been battered to death by the deadly substance, words.

Day after day, the sun shines down on the Costa del Sol, baking the clusters of white-walled villages, driving the dust with the wind through uneven alleyways. And, for a few days' holiday each year, the Mediterranean sunlight warms northern European bones. For those of us who live under the intense gaze of its unseeing eyes, the Spanish sun is an unappeasable

God, primitive and ageless, without empathy. Two thousand years ago, the Roman legions stationed in Hispania Baetica worshipped it as *Sol Invictus*, the unconquered: in any struggle for victory, the sun always wins. That's an immutable law, a secure foundation stone which can uphold a person's sanity, or break it, under dogged pursuit from the frightful sun of Spain. But the otherness of its nature, unmediated to humankind, evokes the silent horror of a snake. The sadness of Mira's accident, the sorrow of those colleagues who raised an altar at the side of the road to remember their friend, are clandestine emotions, hidden from a God who has no conscious awareness. In the face of this daily personification of death, the survivors who assemble on the shores of southern Iberia clasp each other easily in the arms of language. They weave a mellow fabric with the pale blue flowers of words, five-petalled words which are immediately thoughtful and kind, tender and considerate, loving. It's the cool, linen awning clacking in the breeze that hides the fragile, living weave of their connections from incineration by a baleful gaze. It's the enclosed patio garden shaded by fragrant orange trees, protection from fused eyelids and a fatal strike for the interconnecting pathways which are led hither and thither by their words. And sometimes, unthinking security can be inverted: the linen sheet can fold, the snake can penetrate the garden. Devastation happens quietly from within.

I stood up in Ojén's Town Hall at the annual general meeting of the Comunidad de La Mairena, and told everybody about our tenant, who lives in the far extension to our apartment; my indignation at the unfairness of the situation swept me along. 'Stefan Schmidt hasn't paid his rent for the past nine months, since last summer. And we've also been paying his electricity bills for the year and three months that he's been living there. He owes us nearly seven thousand euro.' I was interrupted by gales of laughter which echoed around the large assembly room. I thought they were laughing at our predicament, but Terry whispered not at all, they were laughing at the insolent boldness of the 'renter', as a glamorous German woman subsequently called him. Somebody then suggested that we shouldn't speak to those who owe the community money. And afterwards, when I was having a word with the secretary from the administration, she told me, 'My heart sank when I heard you mention Stefan Schmidt. I have had experience of him over the past few years. And when I heard you say that he is now in La Mairena . . .' She looked stricken. 'Tell your solicitor to go very powerful against him.'

There was a note attached to the hall door: 'Hello Michael, hello Terry. When you have time for a meeting? With or without lawyers. I think we should find a good solution for the apartment! Then you will have your rent and I can stay. Stefan.' He came across to our apartment on the Saturday morning at ten o'clock, unshaven, and wearing a dark tracksuit. Stefan is a tall, lean man with black, oiled hair swept back from his forehead. He looked like an ungainly insect, a locust, as he folded himself into the armchair opposite; he was very much in charge of himself. 'I cannot see you because of the flowers,' he said in his dry, accented voice, almost a rasp, as our friend Anna leaned forward from the couch to put the vase of lilies onto the lower table. She and her boyfriend, James, had arrived beforehand, and they sat in on the meeting: 'But you have to pay your rent . . .' they kept repeating periodically in an incredulous tone, because of Stefan's effrontery.

He was calmly explaining that his lawyer had advised him to try for a solution. He'd come to tell us about his bill for damages to his furniture, and I told him to examine the contract for where it says that he's responsible for insuring his own belongings, and that we weren't liable. Terry pointed out, 'Six weeks ago, you showed us a bill for six thousand euro for repairs to the apartment, and now you're saying that the damages bill has gone up to nine thousand euro – in little over a month? What happened, Stefan?'

'Yes,' he said happily. 'I have a Persian carpet which was destroyed.'

'I notice that the rug we left in the apartment, you put it out on the balcony in all that wind and rain,' I said.

'Oh, that's only two hundred euro,' he replied.

'Yes, but it's our two hundred euro!' reminded Terry.

I explained that as good landlords we were concerned for him and his children, but he seemed taken aback at my suggestion that the best solution would be for him to move out of the apartment now (his three children attend the Colegio Alemán across the road) before the difficulties were compounded. Anna pointed out that we need his rent in order to pay the mortgage, the community fees and the electricity.

Stefan was unmoving. 'My solicitor has advised me to withhold the rent, yes, and we are going to take the two issues of the rent and the damages together.'

'Stefan, you have to pay your rent. And if you don't, then we shall pursue you for the back rent that you owe us, you will be removed from our property, and we're also going to sue you to reclaim the costs of the legal fees involved.' He remained impassive. 'The *burofax*, which is the certified copy of a letter to be used in court, has already been issued, Stefan, and I'm aware that you haven't picked it up, but it's still legal. You have a few more days before we leave for Ireland to stop this matter from escalating.'

The discussion with him went around and around for about three quarters of an hour, but got nowhere until James, in exasperation, stuck it to him: 'Are you going to pay your rent?' he asked.

'No,' said Stefan, emphatically. It was out before he could help it.

I got up from the couch as Terry began to speak, and went to open the hall door. 'You're an angry man, Stefan,' said Terry.

He demurred.

'This is what I work at, Stefan: I'm a psychoanalyst, and I'm saying that you're an angry man; I'm reading your body language.' They were standing, and Terry moved up close to him and into his space. 'I don't know who it was who hurt you – your father, your mother – but take it to them and not to us.'

Stefan suddenly reddened under Terry's gaze.

'We're good people. We did nothing to you, and yet you're hurting us by not paying your bills. I know when I'm being rolled over.' Stefan said nothing, and later, Terry explained that he'd had the feeling he was looking at a shamed little boy. He asked him, 'What sort of a father are you? We're paying for the light and the heat for your children, and they're not even ours.'

Stefan leaned away from him to shake hands with Anna and Jimmy on the couch before walking out. I called after him, 'We're here until Wednesday, Stefan . . .' but he didn't look back, nor slacken his stride. Nor did he communicate with us directly again.

His wounding action, and our vulnerability to his assault, was shocking. In the short term, we were powerless. The attack he'd launched was two-pronged: on the one hand, withhold the rent from us, and with the other, press home his advantage by billing us for damages at a price more than what he owed us in rent: a lose, lose situation. It undermined our belief in the Spanish dream to such an extent that when we opened the door into our beautiful apartment that Saturday evening, it had lost its lustre. We moved around it clumsily, as if the comforting shelter that had been our home in Spain had been sold from under us.

Four days later, on St Patrick's Day, when I sat on a bench at Barajas airport in Madrid waiting for the connecting flight to Dublin, I looked at the river of men who passed me by, a river in flood. I observed the colour of their skin, I listened to the myriad languages they were speaking, I noted their age, their physical condition, but most of all I examined the expressions on their faces to see if I could detect whether they were ineffective men: frightened eyes, a defeated, tremulous mouth? What was the missing piece in our education that rendered us incapable? Or were we so overeducated that we were effete? Did Stefan think he could harry us because, as Terry alluded to, we're not fathers, that we're gay? Had he been assessing the situation that evening he sat beside us signing the contract, taking in the Christmas flourishes in our apartment, the brightly coloured cushions scattered like flowers across the couch, the fun of the multi-coloured chandelier, and did he say to himself then that these men are like children playing house? At what stage in our dealings with him did Stefan feel so masterful, so certain of winning that he cut off from feelings of altruism and decided to set his malicious game in motion? It had to be because he felt that he could revile us.

Terry came up to my seat at the airport. 'I've forgotten my walking stick in the *minusvalido* toilet . . .'

'I'll get it,' I offered, but when I searched there, it was gone; just the smell of cigar smoke in the air.

'Isn't that a shitty thing to do to someone who obviously needs a walking stick,' Terry complained. 'And I really liked that one – blue, with the flowers on it.'

The next time we travelled abroad was some months later, and we were at Rome's Fiumicino Airport. We'd parked in the underground car park at the Centro-Commerciale Leonardo. Terry went up into the shopping mall to buy a pair of plastic spectacle frames in blue, a striking colour one can find in Italy: they brought out his lively blue eyes, which blaze with intelligence. We were gone no more than forty minutes. As we got back to the car, Terry called out to me, 'We've been robbed!' At first I thought he was joking, but there was a showering down of glass when Terry slid open the door. With a panicked feeling in the pit of my stomach, I saw that our two suitcases, the brown leather Bally bag, and the new Toshiba laptop containing the first three chapters of my second book had been taken. The shock was explosive. My book was gone, and I didn't have a backup. I was finding it difficult to breathe: my lungs seemed to be drowning in the humidity, and my heart was in flitters, *stracaithe*. Terry's walking aid was upended between the back seats. We'd been left with only the clothes we were standing in, which were sticky with sweat. 'It's my fault,' he said, desolately. I turned and ran to the escalator to get help.

The two sets of keys to the apartment in Dublin, with the keys to both cars on the same key ring, were in the pocket of the Bally bag. The red shoes we bought for Anna as a present were in one of the suitcases, and my reading glasses were in the pocket of the laptop bag. Terry's wonderful, candy-striped Signum shirts that he bought in Germany, all of them were gone. I felt burdened with the sorrow as each new memory of what had been in the luggage arrived for us like leaden weights, and my head hung lower. It was similar to a death. Terry was to say later, 'They've taken our emotions as well . . .' I think his perception was about us being numbed with shock, and that we'd been plunged into mourning suddenly.

Since the violent assault from cancer, I've found living, the response to that 'How are you?' question about upholding your being in the world, very hard to sustain at times. The tendency to expect the best and see the best in all things has been undermined to such an extent that I can experience survival as a futile exercise, as if the easy outpouring of my being has been too rapid, and I'm left depleted, and go into spasm. The weariness I feel reminds me of the fatigue associated with recovery from cancer. At such times, my head falls down onto my chest with the total loss of hope, and in the moment I can visualize throwing myself off the terrace of our apartment in Spain, six stories above the ground, to end the overwhelming pain of an effort without end: *quietus est*. When I told Terry what I was feeling about having been so comprehensively robbed in Italy, and what I wanted to do, he said calmly, 'Please don't do that to yourself, or to me.'

The Italian police didn't want to know about the robbery, passed the buck to the police at the airport, where we met a woman cop named Claudia who'd grown up in Long Island on a diet of *Cagney and Lacey*, and who even looked like Tyne Daley. Claudia finally took charge of our report for the insurance company. She told us the robbery was most likely carried out by Roma, and she alarmed us by saying that they had a network throughout Europe, so we should change all of the locks in Dublin without delay. We rang our friend Barbara, who organised a locksmith for the apartment, and had the cars clamped in the garage, but still I'm hanging from that balcony with one hand.

The robbery was an unforeseen event without an apparent cause. On the surface it seemed to be chance, but I concluded it had happened to us because we'd been careless. We'd acted without giving sufficient attention to our surroundings, and had put our belongings at risk, so that now our attention was being seized in a brutal and violent fashion. Fate had given us a harsh wake-up call that had left us bereft. The inevitable fortune had befallen us predetermined by our own actions, so it wasn't strictly speaking like the trauma of cancer, which is extrinsic to meaning and truly arbitrary. The temptation for us was not to move beyond a 'This is Italy' type of explanation, having witnessed the total breakdown of whatever chaotic system they'd put in place for the breakfast in our hotel the morning before, and blame a people whose ancestors had once ruled the known world with efficiency and order, a people who had brought to fruition the civilisation that we enjoy to this day. The last time Terry had been in Italy thirty years ago his car had also been robbed, and it was found burnt out as well. We both had known this, and yet we'd walked away from a car full of luggage. We'd been foolhardy.

Is that the weakness that Stefan had intuited: a gay carelessness or frivolity which lies concealed behind our eagerness to please and to be useful? I'd told him, 'Of course you can pay the rent every two months, if that suits you better, Stefan.' And Stefan had stopped paying any rent at all, because from the outset he knew that I hadn't taken a stand on the contract which both parties had signed up to, nor had I strongly insisted on an upright position based on the law: *pacta sunt servanda*. I'd surrendered our state of being manly, of being law-givers. As Terry facetiously puts it, 'Beat me up if you want to!' And my version of that saying is, 'Why don't you hit me and get it over with!' Beneath the sharp humour, both of us are recognising a fault in our characters. From the phrases we employ, what's enfolded within the words is a reference to another repeatedly striking a blow with a fist, a distinguishing symbol which has left its mark on the body or an imprint on the soul. This battery was engraved or scratched onto our distinctive natures, so that the furrows which are cut there direct us to the pages of a book where the information may be found: on our memories.

Being pleasant towards another is expressed in the form of an invitation to hurt, in both cases: 'I give you permission to hurt me, yes.' As a child, Terry was repeatedly beaten up by his older brother, Joe. In my case, the frightening figure was my father. He seems to have so undermined my being at a critical point in my childhood that I never really recovered from the shock, and live life at a regressed and lower level than is appropriate. I can understand the taking control of an intolerable situation by making the choice to allow the inevitable, but seeing clearly that I make an equation between being agreeable and inviting an assault is more difficult to grasp, unless it's viewed through the psychoanalytic lens of castration, the normalising psychic function of accepting castration in order to take up a symbolic sexual position not defined by anatomy. 'Why don't you hit me and get it over with?' is essentially, in its positive form, a passive 'Fuck me!' In its negative form, it seems to rein in the verb *to be* through enforcing limits, obscuring my attempt to shine throughout the universe with an omnipotent burst of spreading, divine light, painfully aware of my lacking and the losses that I suffer, appropriate restrictions which go with being successfully human.

We were in the Habitat store in Marbella's La Canada shopping centre yesterday, and I could see out of the corner of my eye a burly man begin to cut ahead of me in the queue for the checkout, so I moved ahead of him decisively. I'm beginning to learn from this debacle with Schmidt that an assertion of my rights matters for my sense of wellbeing as a man, and that my stance has to be the masculine one of challenge, as opposed to the yielding feminine one of response. I'm astounded to discover that the latter has been my unthinking, natural position up to now. The cause I'd plead and the accusation that I'd make, my motive which rightly reproaches me, has been to tell myself that the battle encounter, the joust in particular from those I'm next to so that I can see their expropriating soul flicker in their eyes, robs me of speech. I stand dumbstruck, unmoving, passive. I should realise that they can read the beaten imprint on our bodies, and have no compunction in profiting from that.

I can see Terry take the battle to people who park in spaces marked disabled without displaying a disabled person's parking permit. Years of painful suffering from polio have taught him the importance of this small concession from the Government and the Irish Wheelchair Association. His argument is that his pain can be that less if he isn't forced to walk excessively, which is why we now use a wheelchair where necessary. Terry is a vociferous warrior, waving his cripple-fabulous walking-stick in the air, loud and noisy, defending a right which the able-bodied could usurp with impunity, without reckoning on his belligerence. In the Lidl supermarket, as Terry approached the checkout with his trolley, he saw a tall and stately, elegantly dressed woman, who was wearing a wig, drop a packet of waffles onto the roller belt and walk away. Terry unloaded his items onto the belt, and just as he arrived at the top of the queue, the woman returned with a large box of groceries, and pushed past him, jostling him out of the way. He immediately confronted her. When the woman explained that she'd been there first, that the packet of waffles reserved her place, he pointed out that that he'd seen her leave the waffles on the belt and walk away, but that was several minutes ago. 'People join a queue – that's what we do.' And gesturing to the line, 'Look at all of these people waiting.'

She loudly berated him, looking him up and down. She'd raised her voice for others to hear. 'You are very rude for an elderly man,' she called out imperiously.

Terry held her gaze, 'I'm in my fifties – not much older than you are.'

And she caused a scene, began to shout at him and gesticulate, waving him away with her arms.

Terry pointed out, 'You're not accepting your responsibility in this.'

But he was shaking with shock at the eruption of her sudden hysteria. So he continued to speak determinedly over her cries, responding to her charges: 'You've obviously done this before and gotten away with it because nobody has dared to challenge your behaviour up to now. I'm telling you, you won't bully me!' And he was unyielding against her rant, until eventually she carried the box of groceries like a battering ram back away down into one of the aisles, still roaring at him. The line of people looked stunned at the commotion, and a few at the end moved their trolleys to join another queue. The manager arrived, and Terry was feeling shaken and angry. He told him it was shameful that customers had to put up with such bad behaviour. He was very upset by what had happened, which overshadowed how well he'd dealt with it.

My defence in the future will also involve the active approach of not yielding, whereas in the past I'd have suffered from quietism. Again, I infer from those words that what I term active, i.e. not yielding, is very much a static approach, which omits the confrontational aspect of the behaviour undertaken by Terry. My words barely draw near to the ideal. So the paradigm inside which defines how I interact with those around me is more deeply ingrained than I'd imagined at first. Perhaps it truly is structural, because it's an apparently fixed position that I've always held with respect to others, rather as the various words – nouns, adjectives, verbs – take up their accustomed places in a sentence. I seem to have an internal representation of these interpersonal relations, which is in control of my behaviour. It's a compass I've relied on automatically to find direction, and pace out steps that increasingly have become pointless, even dangerous. Like Terry, I need to pursue those who would encroach upon me, take the battle to them and push them away. The effort involved in paying minute attention to how I interact with my surroundings should pay off. It demonstrates my consequent commitment to the importance of how I want to live my life in the now. I hadn't realised that I've to be oh so careful of my being in the world, so that it can truly become a house of pure being in the present, clean, clear and unmixed. It will be a gentle and serene dwelling where my soul can remain, appropriate to the vibrant colours therein. I have to expand the dream, and live it big, so that I can always affirm that 'The sun lives in my house!'

The eviction, when it happened, was an anticlimax. The judge in the Marbella court had found in our favour on all counts. Stefan had to vacate the apartment, or he would be evicted in three months' time on Wednesday, 27 September, and he also had to pay all of the back-monies he owed us in rent and for his electricity bills; however, to retrieve the money would necessitate another court case, which we decided to set in train. Our lawyer, Roberto, assured us that it wasn't necessary to be present for the eviction, because the court would organise all of the personnel: the process-server, the barrister, the locksmith. But in a stepping-up to the plate, Terry and I decided we should go down to Spain to be present, because the matter pertained to Stefan the tenant, who held our property legally through a lease which we'd signed.

The idea of an eviction, to recover property by judicial means, at best is an ambiguous concept for any Irishman. More particularly, eviction has been blackened by the folk memory of the terrible fate that befell the people of Mayo, and those who made their living around my hometown, Castlebar, during the Great Famine of the late 1840s. When their crops had failed, and they were unable to pay their rent, Lord Lucan, a military despot, had the starving families evicted from his estates in County Mayo, and he employed what was known as the Crowbar Brigade to level the homes on their smallholdings so that the wretched people couldn't return there to find shelter. Newspaper reports of the time document these living skeletons stalking the countryside in a desperate search for food, and dying in their thousands, famished, by the wayside. Death and emigration accounted for the loss of 114,057 souls in Mayo, almost a third of the county's population, during those hungry years, and their tragedy has seared itself into the memory, so that the word eviction still evokes horror.

It comes from the Latin *ex vincere*, meaning to conquer. The Irish were a conquered people, evicted by force from their ancestral lands through centuries of domination and plantation by the British, and the five years of pitiless evictions clearing Lord Lucan's 60,570 acres in Mayo were the culmination of this penal system. Michael Davitt, who went on to found the Land League, a mass movement which campaigned for reform of the land legislation, wrote in his autobiography, 'Straide [in Mayo] was my birthplace, and almost my first remembered experience of my own life and of the existence of landlordism was our eviction in 1852, when I was about five years of age.' For me, eviction lacks the force of will which the law invokes: rather it results in a real uncertainty about the ethical nature of its pursuit, particularly where there are defenceless children involved. There's a going around the concept involved before it can be taken in and assented to, however falteringly.

Because Stefan's behaviour had been so bizarre to our way of thinking, we didn't want to meet him by chance. Also, we didn't know if he'd been informed of the eviction, and we didn't want to give any indication that the process was underway. Stefan hadn't attended the court case, and our lawyer, Roberto, intended not to contact Stefan's solicitor until the Monday beforehand, so that there could be no time for objections. We skulked in the apartment over that weekend, conjecturing from the footsteps overhead about the various comings and goings of Stefan and his children. It was Tuesday before we heard the commotion, heavy weights being dragged across the floor, furniture being moved about, and loud hammering, as though beds were being dismantled. 'He knows now,' said Terry, relieved, standing listening in the centre of the living-room. Stefan and a friend of his were packing up a van, climbing up and down the steps outside with furniture and cases. During the day, judging from the brief, sudden silences, he made several short trips away to another location somewhere in the vicinity, and then back again. Suddenly, by evening, all was quiet overhead. I went out to reconnoitre. His section of the apartment was in darkness, and the car tyre that had been dumped outside the hall door from the day that Stefan had moved in, was gone; just the black tread marks that had dirtied the tiles remained.

The following morning, as I turned my landlord's key in the door lock for what was the last time, under the eyes of the officials from the Marbella town hall, I felt relieved when I saw that Stefan had left the place clean. The sun was slanting in through the sliding French doors and glittered off the polished marble floors.

Terry's mobile buzzed. 'Look!' he said, handing me his mobile. The text message consisted of just two words: 'Stefan Schmidt'.

I promised, 'The day will come when you'll hand him back a similar message, just as odd and pointed, like the tip of a weapon!'

The officially appointed locksmith set to changing the lock, and then he handed me a new set of keys. It signalled a new beginning for Terry and for me. To start to say or to speak, and to use words that draw from a source that's been restructured in such a way that it yields a stressed syllable at the end of a line of verse in a masculine ending, is what was symbolically put in place when I received into the warm palm of my hand a ring of shiny, new keys. The apartment was empty, because Stefan had wanted to rent it unfurnished, and we'd unthinkingly acquiesced in that. We'd sold all of the furniture for a derisory amount to Daniela, the smart German agent who'd recruited him for us. She'd assured us that she knew Stefan personally, that he was a friend of hers. To our relief, we had vacant possession of the little apartment. And the view from the balcony of the sun shafting through clouds, and striking the Mediterranean Sea in a glittering pathway of light which seemed to lead directly towards the balcony, was a welcome home that invited our participation in the open-hearted Spanish dream once more.

It was many months before the court in Marbella finally concluded that Stefan had no bank account in Spain, so we couldn't pursue him for the 20,000 euro he eventually was to owe us in back rent. However, Stefan used an antique Mercedes E Class van in Spain that was his pride and joy. Whenever we saw it, the van looked immaculate on the outside, and everything inside was kept ordered and clean and tidy. We determined to sequester it, and to sell it on by way of payment. This would be a taking of the fight to the enemy, that final stage in the bullfight, when the matador, killing sword in hand, walks slowly out to the centre of the bullring, to face the bull before a fight to the death. And despite the temptation to have packed his belongings into black bin bags, and to change the locks on the door, even to have him visited by James's friend from Birmingham, 'Mick the Brick', we'll have done it legally. It was to be a further year before the Spanish court sanctioned the embargo of Schmidt's cars, all three of them.

Part Five

On Writing . . .

I'm always in the process of constructing a narrative, weaving words to tell my story. I make up my reality, and my desire stages the *mise-en-scène*. Like Aristotle in the summer heat of Greece, who strolled within the shady walkways of the Lyceum grove teaching and debating with his fellow Athenians, I too walk about in the south of Spain, disputing in my mind. Shopping in El Corte Inglés in Fuengirola, working calmly with expatriate clients at my Spanish consulting rooms, cleaning the apartment in La Mairena after the dusty mess of having had new bathrooms installed, I leave traces of my being strewn across the landscape, which in turn engraves itself upon my life in a mutual intaglio, making cuts in the surface. Unlike the wrinkles which can be read upon my face, these incisions etched onto me and my environment are invisible. I know that if both were to be smeared with ink and the surfaces wiped clean, the ink in the recesses would print off our collaborative story onto the fabric of existence, as naturally as the words that I write are scored onto a page.

I was here, I made a difference, and I said it. While those three actions can be grasped by my mind, they only have real substance and become tangible for me when I can experience them in words, and can reflect upon them. These three statements make permanent in definitions modelled from the finest silver and gold what otherwise would be fleeting, escape capture, or be deemed never to have happened because they're not consciously remembered. I also understand at the same time that every detail is inscribed on the unconscious as on a computer, so that nothing is ever lost irretrievably.

It was another Greek philosopher, Socrates, who said, 'The unexamined life is not worth living.' That's one of the reasons why I work as a psychoanalyst, helping people to put their lives into words, asking them to explain and to clarify, particularly when a word they use seems to have a more personal meaning so that it drags a familial lexicon in its wake, made up of ancient proscriptions. My clients have the ability to put something out into words, to examine it, take it back, change it around, and even return to it the next day we meet. It's as if their narrative is always dependant on there being a future, a next time, which I can hear is forever re-working their past. Through writing, I'm able to examine my own life, which also becomes a life lived in words. Following the assault from cancer, Death hovering at my shoulder seems to be much more present to me. Unlike my clients, I write as if there's no tomorrow, as if Death greedily swallows words that envisage a future, leaving me with no opportunity for further change. There's a fixed quality to the ordering of the words, as if I'm writing out my last testament. When I write, there's an onus on me to get it right the first and last time, because the finished book means that my life is over. It's as if the potential death sentence in cancer has been pronounced, Death's cloak extending outwards silently like a spreading pool of black oil until it covers everything

The narrative also has its own logic, and requires an ordering, with which the editor looking over my shoulder was able to assist. I confess that at times I could see no reason for moving certain chunks of text around. I'm not so sure that editing should be undertaken in the cause of meaning: there are certain aspects in life which are opaque, unintelligible: they don't transmit light, just don't have to be understood. Editing also highlights certain episodes over others, while Freud said, an analyst should listen with an evenly suspended attention, giving everything equal weight. I find the world of the book is a closed world, where everything has an equal and self-referencing importance. And maybe a person's life is like that as well.

In relating, recounting or explaining, a listener is implicated in what I have to say. That dialogue is initially with myself, a conversation of such celerity that speaking and listening alternately results in a seamless text that seems to write itself, coming from elsewhere, the words bobbing about in the air like *putti*, cherubs peeping out from underneath the cupola of a baroque cathedral ready to be engaged, awaiting the reader's contribution. I have the power to change, refine, and weigh each word, to judge how it impacts on the ear as it reverberates off the exuberantly ornamented concave and convex surfaces, so that the full range of sound can deck out my story beautifully in the most gorgeous of vestments. That audience is with my soul, ushered in with trumpet blasts on the organ, and the throwing open of ornately carved double doors at the west end of the cathedral by liveried pages, when I advance into the nave in solemn procession, regularly moving forward past the serried rows towards the chancel, and after the deepest, camp genuflection, take my place at the high altar in the sanctuary. I turn and begin to speak into the tremulous hush, so that the projection of my words suddenly infuses the air with clouds of incense, and a thousand beeswax candles burst into flame at the sound. That's what the formal invitation to read what I write is for.

In the forgotten language of the church, the Old Latin *gnarus* means knowing or skilled, so that this masterly conversation is always completed on the most verbally literal level, which can alter the complexion of what I want to express. I'm led on through unexpected pathways to say what I wouldn't have said otherwise, through paying attention to the formal characteristics of the words that materialise. The offering of such interpretations has the effect of subverting the conscious meaning of what I want to say, hearing through different emphases what pushes forward from the unconscious to be heard at the same time in a reverberating choral polyphony. Confirmation that the dislocation is correct is more music, a further efflorescence of narrative, the sudden blossoming of living words which continue to adorn the fine and lustrous silks of my soul like wild flowers enchanting my wayside, inviting me to pursue a path that's opening up before me through the living thicket of language.

For the speech of a writer comes from elsewhere, the other place: radically other, like the apparition of the Holy Spirit in Piero della Francesca's *The Baptism of Christ*, a white dove hovering with widespread wings invisible to all but the viewer, like a white afterthought compressed between the Father and the Son, or a sudden slice of gleaming white light on the surface of the sea at the horizon uniting the sky with the ocean, an inspiring sight with which I'm familiar from the terrace in La Mairena. It staggers my steps with shock and upsets the direction of my compass. After having been dazzled by such a divine revelation of the word that has escaped incorporation up to now, it's no longer possible to approach the everyday routine with equanimity. The feeling is that of an Irish monk in exile on the continent, inscribing beautiful letters of relative application onto a fine parchment prepared from the skin of a calf. I paint decorations, naturally coloured by ochres and iron oxides, with hog's bristle, sometimes with a sable brush, so that the flapping of ghostly wing beats can be heard to swoosh through my text eternally.

The light is a constant in the south of Spain. It never loses its surprising intensity, painting the clear blue skies with a highly glossed enamel finish around the green leaves of gnarled Mediterranean oaks, their terracotta trunks denuded of cork bark. The heat lies heavy during those somnolent afternoons in midsummer, when the breath of the wind has been sucked out of the dry air, and the white marble tiles on the terrace, baking under the unrelenting sun, scald the soles of the feet. At such times, I shelter on top of a rumpled bed sheet and doze, with the door to the balcony flung open to encourage the gentlest breeze, which sometimes flaps open the curtains in a blinding flash of light to sidle sideways into the bedroom like a bashful ghost. The Spanish *siesta* is one of life's sybaritic pleasures to be savoured with gratitude, especially since I rise at four o'clock in the cool of the early morning to write at my desk. Then the *levante*, the fresh easterly wind, blows through the open windows of the apartment, dispersing the stagnant warmth with the smell of the sunburnt grasses and caressing my skin with coolness, before a lightening at the horizon throws the black silhouette of a tree outside the balcony into relief, heralding the majestic arrival of the sun, to the sudden hissing accompaniment of the water sprinklers in the gardens.

At home on my mountaintop in Spain, golden light spilling out from the computer screen at four in the morning to form an illuminated cocoon in the velvet darkness, I accept the opening 'How are you?' question symbolically as a deceptive verbal feint, an initial flash of yellow and magenta with the matador's *capote* as the powerful black bull charges into the arena. I toss off the gesture without paying undue attention to the impaling power of words. For I also hear that question as the opening ritual of writing, which has to do with the music, with feeling, and the strong incandescent flame of pure being. Always, I'm wary of the power of words. Without adverting consciously to the collective heritage of scratching runes into bark, when the characters were once believed to have a magical significance that possessed supernatural powers to influence events, today I know from my psychoanalytic experience that the ancestors had divined the truth. In an age of unbelief, I can profess those letters up there on my computer screen to be meaningless. But from personal experience of dealing with people who deliberately set out to undermine, I know that when letters are written onto flesh by cruel aggressors, often repeated over time, words can wound and cripple.

I abstain from speech when somebody shocks me with the power of an unexpected verbal attack, because momentarily I'm blown off my feet by the rotating winds which propel their assault. When I remember, I've been able to begin a sentence with an 'I feel . . .', which names the situation I find myself in, even though it leaves me completely exposed to the other's judgement. 'I feel . . .' seems to place the devastation in a category beyond argument, which can momentarily discomfit the attacker. It gives me time to gather my resources, and face the attacker head-on. But like the sudden thundering forward of the bull, a terrible storm of aggression can erupt at any moment and engulf the finest thread of being, which I know to be tenuous. I tread lightly and live life warily, lest I suddenly lose it, or have being robbed from me, or malignly have it cut off in a castration with a vivid red slash of the sharpest horns. I've slung the cape over my shoulder as I stride out towards the centre of the arena, making a statement to the spectators that I'm prepared to try my hardest in the *porta gayola*, the opening move where courageously I drop to my knees and invite the bull into the arena with no knowledge of how it will behave; but still I'm wary.

I comprehend the 'How are you?' question as an invitation to write down anything that occurs to me, uncensored. Freud used the word *Einfall* for this, literally, what falls into the mind when conscious control is loosened, and unconscious mental processes are allowed to take over so that the full-throated voice can join in the singing of life's symphony. The freedom of pure being is what it engenders; that's been my experience. The strong masculinity of machismo, the swagger of that dance with death in the arena without apparent concern for personal safety, and the total absorption in the verbal play of the job in hand, all of these stylish male qualities are in evidence as I settle my pumps into the sand, and with the arched back of a matador, calmly bring forward my position, confidently exposing my groin to gain ground.

I express thankfulness for having the question in the first place, and its implication of teasing out entanglements, as I settle myself into the wooden carver chair in front of the desk, and take a sip of the strongest coffee, before I begin to tap at the keyboard of the computer, writing out whatever is on my mind. In recounting the happenings and interactions of my days along those meandering byroads of free association that I remember from my childhood in Castlebar, rather than by taking the direct motorways of reasoning and the way that I live now, I'm also recording who I am in a more fulfilling and complete manner. The circular thought processes resemble the delicate way that I lick at an ice-cream cone, turning it round and around to reveal the different layers to my tongue, a habit almost unbeknownst, until eventually I find myself sucking up the core.

I can be shaken by the sudden truth of what I can uncover through typing a slip of the tongue, or by bringing out a phrase which leaves me hoisted on an ambiguity, or blocked by a pause, a forgetting. All of those crumpling, melting accidents that fall down along the side of the cone in drops leave stains upon my clothes. I always terminate the keyboard session early after such a revelatory windfall and walk away from the desk, out onto the sunlit terrace to gaze at the distant sea, readjusting my eyes, fixing the bounds of what I say with the mistake. Truth is written up there behind me on the screen in a burst of flaring light, until finally the computer dies, and fades into sleep mode; but always the vision returns to haunt the imagination. Although my peregrination, my journey abroad wandered from what was right, what I've written is something I never could have envisaged, that never would have existed in time before now: it's new, it's a sly visit from the future, and beyond price. Just as the reader acting in my place will substitute his own future when confronted with a past that was created in this book. He too will live eternally, creating more amalgams which walk invisibly among men like the angels who inhabit a dream, a reality I've come to honour from my work as a psychoanalyst.

Gerald Byrne, an artist friend who's a self-taught master of his craft, told me over coffee in his ultra-modern kitchen in Dalkey, that when he's working on a painting *en plein air*, gusts of wind buffeting the canvas, or a sudden squall of rain, cause unintentional markings, a desire or a feeling from nature that he incorporates without repair into his finished work, to honour the unplanned and inexplicable aspects of life that affect him, as much as do the planned and intentional ones. The remembrance of my friend's casual remark continues to lift my spirits, and I feel confirmed in my own strange, aleatory, creative method which also depends on the throw of a dice.

Now is a three-lettered word that I experience joyfully, shining up there on the computer screen in Spain, like a triptych painting I'd seen in Germany. In Weimar's Herderkirche, I'd stood in wonderment before a famous Crucifixion, which is surrounded on either side by scenes from the Old Testament dealing with God the Father, and the New Testament dealing with God the Son. The guide explained that the painting was begun by Lucas Cranach the Elder, and brought to completion by his son, and the father's substitute self, Lucas Cranach the younger. I saw two wing panels depicting the past and the future folding over that larger central one: they apply to the time directly preceding and to the time directly following this central, present moment of mysterious redemption, when all of time is changed in an instant by the direct intervention of God.

While the painting reflects a sixteenth-century framework of ideas and beliefs through which the Cranachs interpreted their world, I reflected that the central moment of pure being, the *now*, that fragile pointillist point which they venerated, is all that we have; although more often than not, I'm occupied elsewhere, off somewhere else, preoccupied in the margins of the painting, out on the edge in a different time zone. I've been made more conscious of the value of this gift of immediacy, this moment of pure being, since it was nearly taken away from me by the cancer. I turn in my chair and lift the heavy dictionary off the back of the couch and consult volume two. I discover that it was from the open wide wingspan embrace of the earlier word *now* that issued the later formation meaning of the word *new*, meaning what was recently brought into being, or *nowish*. It's a father and son concept that melds again into the variant *now* in the sense of *newish*.

Out on the terrace in tee-shirt and shorts, the sun stings the flesh of my face, and scorches my arms and my legs. Down below, beyond the parched land, the sea is glittering in the sharp morning light. I've come to realise that every word shines with this same, wavering angelic light. Words are shape-shifting and mercurial. They can change perspective as they resonate endlessly across the generations. But always they're grounded in the momentary present tense of the speaking voice which I can hear in my head, or in the written voice which I read from my computer screen, as I advance to gain ground on myself by giving a clear and detailed account so that I can feel justified. The panoramic view from the terrace of the Mijas mountains on the left, all the way around to the Rock of Gibraltar, hidden now in the August mist, not yet burnt off by the fierce rays of the summer sun, nourishes my spirit with its peace and tranquillity. Down in the plain, the rising heat is visible as the finest, almost inconspicuous mist. A declaration of righteousness will ensue from having written out the poem of my life with as much truthfulness as I can muster, so that it expresses God's creation. The hope implicit in the 'How are you?' question is that like the Cranachs, I too shall create a work of art which has merit, and saves. I turn and go back inside the pleasant coolness, to write some more.

On the computer screen, words become the intricately worked ornamental screen glittering with gold leaf above and behind an altar where today I take communion. Whenever I worship there, I read the portrait I'm painting like Hebrew from right to left, and mark the passage into existence of a particular word, a phrase, even a sentence. Writing has inverted how I experience time, where events now happen for me in reverse. The words that I create at the computer read from an invisible state of potentiality in the future, right through a coming to be on the computer screen in the present, and after that composition, they move on into the final state of a printed existence on paper in the past. Like looking in a mirror, I face myself in this present moment of being, with the future and the past to my right and to my left. The mirror has reversed how I live my life from day to day, where it will be the future, and not the past, which will come for me in the end of time. So that when I confront myself in the moment of writing, on either side of me there's both a past and a future together, and there's no difference between them: truly, the *now* is a moment of the purest being, whose ripples extend outwards into a circular eternity. As a child, I used to solemnly recite a bedtime prayer to the four evangelists:

> There are four corners on my bed
> There are four angels round my head
> Matthew, Mark, Luke and John
> God bless the bed that I lie on.

More properly, it echoes the ancient Hebrew prayer to the four archangels: 'In the name of the Lord God of Israel, may Michael be at my right hand, Gabriel at my left, Uriel before me, Raphael behind me, and the *Shekhinah* of God above my head.' *Shekhinah* is the radiant presence of God, a form of feminine joy, a *jouissance* that's connected to prophesy and creativity.

Over time I've come to realise that the priestly power of the writer derives from the fusion of the *now* with the *new*. I raise up a chalice encrusted with precious jewels overflowing with the fruit of the vine before the painted retable, and hold upright between my thumb and forefinger a host of unleavened bread above the golden cup, as I pronounce the mysterious words of transubstantiation, eternal words of great age which are never to be brought to an end. This is a holy Sabbath meal. In the primitive past of Genesis, God spoke the world into existence: his voice created the world. As I type on my keyboard, I'm aware of bringing forward that creation, speaking words that are unconsciously inspired by His breath and giving them form, writing them down and into existence. God sometimes wrestles me to the ground with the turbulent emotion that unexpectedly leaps upon me from what I've written, arching out of the dark like a lithe and unruly archangel. Held warmly like a protesting child in his firmly loving embrace until I yield, I realise the disturbance will have landed me into the truth. It seems strange to read it up there before me in all of its blinding glory, an alien being of light, eminent above all others, a new perspective at odds with the established ego view that I've had of myself until now.

At the end of the session, I read and re-read what I've written. I give it the time for seeing, yet more time for understanding, and then accord to what I've written the length of time required to take the many shining facets of this new information on board in order to act upon them, and finally, to do something about it. The confrontation has assigned impossibly widespread limits, which call for a re-arrangement of the parameters of my being to incorporate what has just been announced: 'Be it done unto me, according to thy word!' When I leave the study and enter the loggia of the terrace, I'm like a participant in a Fra Angelico fresco. Although who I am may look the same, I've become a different person, substantially changed, a humbled virgin possessed of God, having been ravished by the impulse of his muscular archangel. He bore me apart, covered me by the powerful propulsion of his stripy wings. How I am transported now in a new and unconscious direction, which is other than the old destination I'd consciously set for myself.

I always marvel that the words are already there to hand. They're a given, and don't have to be newly coined. Like ghostly presences, it's possible to pluck them out of the air and have them materialise on the tongue or on the screen. They have their own personalities, directing thoughts along specified pathways unless they're combined in a poetic way, which causes them to break open and effloresce. Then they can better encapsulate the overflow of the spirit, because like the dry stone walls in the west of Ireland where I come from, the gaps in precision give a freedom to whistle through like the wind and approximate, without collapsing the edifice. There's room to manoeuvre, building up the stones by hand one after the other, choosing them carefully for their outward form, creating a necklace of liminal shapes across the landscape that protects and exposes, conceals and reveals, that both lies and tells the truth at the same time. The apparent distancing involved in this poetic approach places more creativity into my hands. It allows me to express myself more fully that ever I could through prose, where I'm subjected to the channelling effect of the words on offer, and limited further by the set order in which these words have to be spoken, always with an eye to the future conclusion. By combining them in a manner which disrupts the normal sequencing, whereby some of the words in a sentence are no longer arranged logically or even comprehensibly, it's possible to allude to unpredictable concepts that are outside the scope of the conventional, outside of space and time. I communicate in a new and more complete way, and say things which I've never said before, never could have dreamed possible or true.

There's another way to achieve the same result. When I work psycho-analytically, sitting composed in the capacious black leather armchair out of sight behind the individual lying on the couch in my consulting room, I listen very carefully to the word for word meaning of what the person is saying, limiting my understanding to the explicit and primary meaning of the words they're using: *à la lettre* is the French phrase, I take it literally. That way I'm able to capture the truth, and hear within them the dream which is determining the identity of their being, and ultimately appointing their destiny. I hear an aspect of what's being worked out inside according to a set pattern, the string in the necklace which is holding the stones together, the gaps in the wall through which their spirit whistles. But for myself, I find it impossible to speak freely using the stream of consciousness technique, while at the same time attempting to listen to myself with the concentrated direction of mind that's required in order to punctuate my own discourse, and draw my own attention to the surprising truth of what I'm saying. The way around this is to write it down. And I've the cancer to thank for catapulting me into the life of an author, and an ongoing analysis that's causing my life to grow.

At the end of a morning's work writing a book at my desk in Spain, the warm wind wafting over my skin from the wide open windows, the light outside the room begging to participate, I can look back on a text that I've written as if it were produced by someone else. There are times when I've no knowledge of having written it, and certainly no recognition of the way in which it was wrought and worked out. From my psychoanalytic background, I can see clearly embedded in the prose the unconscious forces that are directing how I write. I can see clearly the desire that animates what I've written, and identify as nearly as possible what it is that's writing me, the voice that carries what I want to say, the true voice of the self.

That voice comes from within the heart, and it's the medium through which I can go out beyond the limits of my body and touch another person. It's so deeply personal that at times I'm conscious of skin on skin, as I rub the tips of my fingers over their nakedness, and then embrace them: it's akin to having sexual relations with the person to whom I'm speaking. My voice seduces. The intimacy of the tone I use, confined to one person, is the link that binds us together, and warns other people off. It's also the channel for expressing my desire, the hoarsest craving which can be heard in my voice, animating it, and like the poetic writing in my first book, perused for feelings and motives. My voice licks the person from the pubic bone, up over the stomach and chest to seek out the ear, and tastes them with my tongue. That appraisal suspends them within the boundaries of my voice, overpowers them and brings them to me. The voice is naked, vulnerable, obvious, and it demands a response.

I saw the power of the voice in action, when Terry and I arrived in Malaga from Italy without our luggage, and we were standing in the walkway outside the door of the plane waiting for Terry's walking aid. A young Spaniard, powerfully well-built, unshaven, with sleepy, honey-brown eyes arrived up the steps and leaned seductively against the entrance. The scuffed shoes and dirty work clothes he inhabited were in sharp contrast to the unappealing peacock males we'd seen in Italy, with their fitted shirts and tight, white trousers. His deep, softly ruminating 'Hola . . .' rumbled out into the night air like a lasso that ensnared everyone, as he presented himself like an unexpected word to the airhostesses, who were delighted to be surprised by him. They were drawn excitedly towards him in their high heels and elegant Vueling outfits. He didn't change his position, just moved his head with its mop of curling brown hair ever so slightly forward, to be kissed successively on both cheeks, a bead of perspiration coursing down from his temple.

As I cut open one of the books with my face on the cover, and I read in a finished form what I'd written so many months before, I was surprised to be filled with an encouraging wonder. I have marvelled at the strangeness of the thoughts that were written there. When my friend, Hedwig, was translating what I'd written into German, although she teaches German to English students at the Goethe Institute, she found that the way that I constructed the language, the piling together of the words and the building up of the emotional sense to be not easy, '. . . almost as if the realities you were creating belonged to the spiritual world of the divine, somehow independent of the sensate existence . . .'

I was taken aback. 'We had one of those at home, Hedwig, but the back wheels fell off . . .'

'Ach, so!'

I've always known that I must consciously facilitate and collaborate with the unconscious daemon that has inspired my writing, because it dispenses my destiny. The Spanish have an impish word for it: *duende*, which captures the idea of performing like a bullfighter, with the uttermost passion and artistic excellence, right on the edge so that an audience is transported. What emerges on screen is neither an unconscious splurge of material unformed as in the wildest, storm tossed Atlantic ocean, nor the dry, flat land in Tarifa extending the shoreline at the southernmost tip of Spain, a conscious ordering that provides a boundary, and which does justice to the writer's technique. An equitable fusion drawing on both results in a third text which is new and exciting. My alignment is with the words like stars in the sky that I've closely inspected, a universe of thought and activity in which I have my being: *scripsi scripsi*. The linguistic dwelling in which I was led astray and made a fool of, the written testament of my book witnesses to my soul. It's a purlieu frequented like the traversal of a fugue, a reiteration of complex musical themes which only cry out to be sung.

The choral music referenced in my first book, in particular the B Minor Mass, was composed by Johann Sebastian Bach, who pared the quills and ruled the paper in his busy study at the Thomaskirche in Leipzig, which hosted journeymen and apprentices and the eleven children from his two marriages. He fluently wrote out the fugal parts that have resounded through the rooms of three centuries, to surface as a soundtrack that has permeated my successive texts, which are written on a palimpsest, each one rubbed smooth to make way for the next. But from the writer's perspective, Bach's ordered notation has never been erased. And when I pondered how to give voice to such a heartfelt collaboration between Bach's music and a modern Irish libretto, the vast forces of the Goethe Institute Choir, steeped in its Germanic tradition, and the trained voices of my newscaster friends, Eileen Dunne, Emer O'Kelly and Eamonn Lawlor, as soloists, came readily to mind for a concert reading of my book, to be given at the National Concert Hall in Dublin, in September 2010. The joint project transformed itself into a type of secular Mass, grounded in the fundamental agricultural theme of death and resurrection. The chosen chapters of my memoir which tell the story of my battle with cancer, a dance with death in the bullfighting arena of life, are counterpointed by the choruses which comment on and carry forward the emotion involved. The wresting involved in this, the forcing away by a pulling or twisting, was begun back in 1751, when Bach, as a devout Lutheran, composed a Catholic mass for the Saxon court in Dresden.

From my own experience of having been in analysis, lying on a couch and looking out through a window as in the Matisse painting of the Conversation, where the framing of realities gives way successively, one upon another, I can see through my computer screen the individual words that collectively point towards an uncharted world of the imagination. They create further realities that influence in turn the words that I've written on the screen. These realities ask me to change or to alter the words, the better to correspond with the truth that's invisibly pushing forward from behind like a figure elbowing through a crowd, a delicate breath of life that's forever struggling towards the front to have its say in the sunlight. Three times a week, for fifteen or sixteen years, I excavated the psyche before a silent listener. I trained myself to put what was hoarded there on public display through words, so I know that I don't lack the courage to be a pioneering pilgrim; that's been my training. However, I also know that the utmost courage is needed to give the truth of who I am that final push from the wings, and at the same time uphold my being against the backdrop of emotions that are difficult to carry once they've been brought forth and named, another polder of land reclaimed from the ocean of unconsciousness.

The hiccupping of my sobs on the couch would gently be interrupted from behind by a disembodied voice 'Can you put those feelings into words?' I baulked at a puzzling request about semantics that was interrupting my reverie. What does the sound and the suggestive power of the words in a poem mean? I knew from the intensity of language and of imagination that my feelings were a genuine expression that didn't require a commentary, until I realised I was being asked to encase them in words for an analyst, who could only guess at what was going on until I said so, and that even then, the words were porous, and required further elaboration. So my selection of them had to come from the widest possible constellation, and be precise and explicit, but also intimate, reflecting what is innermost. Shakespeare had twenty-one thousand words at his command; Racine used two thousand.

Nowadays, looking through the screen of the computer, the finality involved in naming is also a consolation, because it puts amorphous feelings beyond question, even beyond the refusal of my denial, that ghostly, elegant sight-hound always at my side, which urgently can set off to another place, away, demonstrating a lack of sound obedience training, heedless of commands to return. There was one occasion in Spain after a bitter argument, when Terry had decided he'd had enough, and he called a halt to our relationship. In the face of Terry's cold determination, I was helpless. For twenty-four hours I watched my erstwhile partner run wild with freedom, as he prised open the fingers of constraint and carefulness one after the other that had held him fast. He appeared drunk with the potency of his liberation from bondage. The lesson learned caused me to vow then that if ever Terry were to return, I was duty-bound never to deny him his freedom as the distinguishing attribute of his truthful spirit, but to defend its flourishing with my life.

The naming in the beginning, that mystical, nine-fold repetition of 'God said . . .' in Genesis, has put naming at the centre of literary creation, while at the same time it has given an overwhelming authority to the voice, which has the power to evoke a world out of the deep, silent nothingness. It calls forth a presence out of absence through plucking random words out of the air, and voicing them into the embodied existence of alphabetic signs. Muhammad took that naming a step further when he recited the Koran, because then he was speaking with the direct voice of God. Unlike the reported speech of Genesis, God was present in Muhammad's voice at the instant he was repeating aloud: the house of purest being. In the face of such poetic assertions which are open to experience, I puzzle over how it could ever be possible for an Irishman to become an unbeliever. The word God derives from the Gaelic root *guth*, which means voice. And the Irish greeting *Dia dhuit* invokes God through the warm embrace of saying 'God be with you!' Today's interpretation in a post-Christian context of unbelief preserves at its heart the triumph of the human spirit over the forces of darkness. I have met and been confirmed by the lone voices who bravely sing of hope in the midst of depression and despair, and offer to others fugues of salvation and redemption. These courageous individuals inspired me in my writing, always to enhance, always defend, always to be kind, whilst remaining a heretic in my heart.

Gloria in Excelsis

Like a wise man following a star
I bring my gifts on Christmas day
To the baby in the crib
I leave behind anxiety
Protect the cradled child from life's pessimism
If I no longer believe in a divine redeemer

Surrounded by the smell of pine and evergreens
I light a silent candle for the dead
Remembering the candle in the window
And the long ago welcome home on Christmas Eve

The children's story of no room at the inn
And the superstition of my grown-up sensibilities
Equally excluded from the humble scene within
I bring imaginative possibilities to the framing from without
Of a young mother with her newborn baby
A practical commitment to the business of the present
A careful reverence for life continuing on
Discerning mystery amidst the ordinary straw

This Christmas day has been born in Bethlehem
A saviour
I am my own redeemer

I whisper a prayer and muster help with hope
I say to the midwinter gloom of an empty universe
I am alive thank God
For those with whom I live and love
I can try to make things better
And bring glory to the highest heavens
Gloria in excelsis

Part Six

The Man in the Mirror . . .

I spoke to Robbie and Mary on the phone at Christmas. I didn't ask them anything, because there was nothing that I wanted to know from them. It felt odd, as if I was unable to speak freely, and the conversation limped on awkwardly as a result. My demeanour in holding the receiver away from my ear registered my wariness. They'd have discerned my obvious lack of enthusiasm from the flatness of my voice. It must mean that they won't feel an urgency to ring me again. I'm sorry it has come to this pass, but there's a hardness around my heart, a petrification as if the organic material at my centre has been converted into a fossilized form, rock-like and deadened. Terry has urged me to be careful: 'Make sure that this hardness of spirit isn't unconfined,' as though death were a contagious disease. Death has infiltrated my body, and marked me. The surgeon said, 'We got all of the cancer, except for a piece about the size of my thumb, which was attached.' Like a ticking bomb, I carry Death around inside me waiting for the cataclysmic boom that signals the horror has happened, and Death is now unconfined.

My uncle and aunt's two-handed response to the publication of my book, their refusal to notice, and their subsequent attempt to carry on the pleasantries of life while disregarding what's uppermost in my mind, is all of one seamless garment that conceals the truth like a dustcover. Were I to go along with their ignorance, their passion for the absence of knowing what I've written in the final version of my book, then I'd be like them, emptying out my being of the words that have created me, leaving behind a hollow which could never again be filled, as if I'd swallowed one of my own children. At the very least I'd be an accessory to murder, to suicide, and be consigned to Hades, assenting to live life as *eidolon*, the hollow image. In the Prado in Madrid, I stood in horror before one of Goya's Black Pictures, *Saturn Devouring His Son*. The portrait is of a naked old man with straggling grey hair, whose eyes are bulging out of his head in a voracious frenzy, as he holds up a bloodied, headless baby like a side of ham to the black cavern of his wide-open mouth. The picture is a silent scream of pain from a demented Old Testament prophet, which Goya painted onto the wall of the room he lived in when he was in his mid-seventies, and near to madness. He was expressing himself through the truthful myth of the human condition portrayed in his painting, a vision that I could understand in the place where I'm living. My life story incarnates what's inassimilable, what's been repudiated, and by bringing it into collision with another's foreclosed universe, the impulsion is to reach for a blanketing delusion in order to reconstruct it. I've no purchase there, and my sanity depends upon not letting this happen. Were I to go along with this misrecognition, that organisation of negations and affirmations which makes people capable of knowing what it is to misrecognise, then I'd be colluding with ignorance, playing the game of cowboys and Indians from my past, hiding behind the tree trunks on the Mall in Castlebar with my brother – 'I shot you' 'No you didn't' – and implicitly accepting that I've done wrong. I'd be acknowledging to my aunt and my uncle that they've a right to punish me, and that I'm grateful for their forbearance in permitting normal business to resume. All of this under the seamless blanket of silence, without anything being said. Or maybe the game of cowboys and Indians that I'm playing with them, is a game of make-believe where death has no place, of skirmishing and of circling the wagons with no deadly intention. I'd like to think that I may have just stumbled across the truth, which has the potential to save me.

My own battle with reality, deleting and ignoring and carrying on with suitable rearrangements so that I wouldn't offend or be offended by my suffering, was as insane a dream as that real, rogue cancer cell which precipitated the insult of my truth, a disease which had to be eradicated to save my life. Maybe reality is like that: part of it has to be removed, because there's no way to make it similar; the core resists incorporation. It's the trauma that can't be entreated, or brought to an end by an imaginative speech from me, that resists words so completely because it's unbounded, and runs on forever like a cancer cell, spreading and colonising: what's impossible to imagine. I know that if I signalled my participation by the flicker of an eyelid, the slightest crook of a little finger, my personality would be overrun silently in a coup d'état, and I'd be turned to stone, and become catatonic.

I reproach myself bitterly for being abused, and for inhabiting the relaxed, funny, unguarded part of my personality that's childlike in its trust because it feels 'you're at your granny's'. I question what part of my story was so harshly unpalatable that it engendered unrelenting hostility: the child who was beaten, or the child who was sexually abused, or was the problem that I broke the comforting silence of the status quo and told my truth? It was difficult to own my story, to shoulder the full burden of it, to dispute with myself about whether it was mine, recognising a degree of distancing through the possessive case, or whether this story was me, without the obfuscating protection of being separate. What I was afraid to feel in the past is the undertow washing back now into the present following the breaking of that wave. I received a letter from Declan in Dublin, who said, 'People have read your book and said it is too stark, too true, too much. And now that I've read it, I have learned more about them than you, and question what they say about all other matters.' If only I could've been helped to carry the truth by the freely given encouragement of more people like him, who can recognise and value what's true. Instead, I made an approximate equation woven out of words, a verbal ambassador who's my authorised representative, but his credentials weren't received.

As memories of sexual abuse randomly re-present from the archive of my memory, I've come to question my complicity in the events, even though I know intellectually that I was just a child who firmly believes that he's to blame. Different men had covered me. They breached hidden boundaries with no unpleasant consequences ever accruing to them, unlike to me. They passed me around like a grubby, ten shilling note, each of them linked to the other through their access to my body. I fell into those incidents, and the repetition of the abuse coming at me from outside seems to imply a seeking again after something, scenting it out like a hound. Even though I was fearful, I learned what to expect. And yet, I took torturous routes home after school, to avoid passing by the doors of my abusers. Still it would happen that when I turned a corner, out of sight for a moment, I'd be solicited, ushered obsequiously into the shadows and always with the same whiff of peril, of trembling and terror, but with somebody new, nevertheless. Nothing was ever said, at least by me. Each of us used the cloak of silence – the fact that my child's eyes were the only ones which saw, that boldly held the men's gaze until they looked away – to conceal their nefarious activities. And I was used by them shamelessly, until I emerged on my own back into the sunlight.

I want to take a shower to wash them away from me. When I was coming out as a gay man, after I'd willingly had sex for the first time, and I remember it as a joyous seduction, I drove home dazzled by the early-morning sunlight, and stood under the shower for over an hour, letting the lukewarm water flow down over my forehead, through my hair and over my skin, soaking me, washing me clean, cleansing me as I thought, from the surprising happenings of the night before. Now I understand why I couldn't move for shock. I bring it up against myself that I'd allowed them inside to do this to me again, from the Latin *al-laudare*, to praise, by presenting myself to them, like my story was presented in a book. People have an animal instinct that can smell out those early woundings to the spirit, as sharks in the ocean smell blood. And some of them cannot resist entering through the opening to run amok in a feeding frenzy and have a go, to cry havoc as a signal to seize plunder, simply because they have the opportunity. They cut off moral considerations, and decide to take it.

I was sitting with my laptop at an art-deco table in the large, wood-panelled library of the Elephant Hotel in Weimar, an intimate baroque city, which is the spiritual and intellectual heart of Germany, when I deliberately scrolled through all of my manuscript over a period of three days after New Year, and deleted every reference I could find to my uncle and aunt. I reorganised the text as if they'd never existed. That was the time when they died to me. I killed them off as characters in my narrative, and watched impassively as my cursor swallowed up the letters that were giving them life, emptying out obligation from the sequences of my words. The deleting wash renewed and refreshed the text, made it leaner. I was unable to detect any awkward connections or impoverishment as a result of my action. The re-weaving holds no reproach for one who knows.

The first Civil Partnership ceremony I attended took place in the heart of the county Wicklow countryside, in the garden of Ireland. It was a glorious day in late spring, when the hawthorn bushes in the hedgerows were pushing out into the winding narrow roads, dappled under a canopy of fresh green leaves. The strong sun shone out of the clearest blue sky, and everything glistened in the light. At the ceremony they'd planned in the tiny chapel, which was striking for the warmth and goodwill from the one hundred and fifty glamorous guests, all of whom had made spectacular efforts with their outfits, we were surprised to be taken up by the swell of emotion. Everyone was so supportive of the happy couple. We continually burst into applause during the ceremony, and we were aware that we were participating in a little piece of Irish history. Ireland at last was facing up to the truth of human relationships. The generosity of spirit continued on into the reception afterwards. Jarlath, one of the grooms, gave a graphic speech in which he not only thanked his family for raising him, but also the people of the village in which he grew up, who had always looked out for him. He teetered on the edge of sobbing.

On the way home in the car, sated with what was a memorable day blissfully near to perfection, Terry casually remarked with a psychoanalytic eye, 'I think Jarlath has a bit more maturing to do . . .'

'In what way?'

'All that seductive come-hither business about the home-place in the West of Ireland needs to be left behind.'

We'd been made aware that in a phone call just one week before the occasion, Jarlath's mother had omitted to tell him whether she and his father were going to be present. On the morning of the ceremony, she bumped into Jarlath and Blair in their dapper cutaway frock coats in the hotel, and Jarlath was mightily relieved to see her there. In a deflating put-down, she enquired, 'What are the two of ye doing dressed up like that?' We found out later that Jarlath's father had had to be confronted by his own sister in order to get him to put back by twenty-four hours his trip to the States, to watch the local GAA football team play a match in New York on the following Sunday. Plainly, his parents didn't want to be there, despite and perhaps because of the prevailing mood of celebration. So the groom was in two minds about how he'd express himself before his well-wishers without publicly embarrassing himself and his parents, and I felt that he'd traversed the obstacles very well, and come up with an inclusive form of words which was truthful, and which expressed the warmest feelings of his open heart. He was not unaware. I know that privately he'd acknowledged to his partner after that phone call with his mother, 'As their eldest son, I deserve better!' It was a searing indictment. Nonetheless, I could see Terry holding strongly to the view that early attachments should be definitively left behind if you're to mature appropriately, and not be held in thrall to a sentimental positioning from the past that's rooted in childhood. The hankering impedes psychological growth, and doesn't reflect present realities.

In my own case, unlike Jarlath, I'd always felt menaced by that call from the past, which releases a stab of fear in my stomach whenever I'm made aware of it, because I know the experience of family to be ambivalent. The adjective 'ambivalent' is actually a psychiatric term. It was coined by Eugen Bleuler, when Carl Jung was his assistant at the Burghölzli Mental Hospital in Switzerland, so it's a relatively new word, less than one hundred years old. Bleuler formed it from the Latin prefix *ambi-* meaning both, in two ways, plus *valentia*, strength, vigour. I see now that 'ambivalent' is an obfuscation I've clung onto, rather like those clients who come to me initially proclaiming that they're bisexual, until eventually after work in depth, some are able to admit to themselves and to me that they're gay. Ambivalence also masks hostility, which has served to darken over the truth of the pain I've known in my body. What I haven't known is how to deal with it. Like Jarlath, I too have always deserved better.

I would have expected that murder, the secret killing of a person, to have perturbed my spirit. I remember the first time a particular client came to see me. His appointment was the last one that evening, and it was already dark outside when he walked into the consulting room. He sat opposite in the leather armchair moving his head about unnervingly as if it were separated from his spine, and perched atop his neck. He didn't speak at first, just kept wobbling his head, sometimes rolling his shoulders. Then he looked at me in the eyes and said, 'I've committed a murder.'

I didn't move.

'Are you afraid of me?'

I said nothing; just held his gaze.

'You should be. There's nobody in the building, except for the two of us,' all the while staring at me intently with ice-blue eyes.

I felt a frisson of fear, released into my stomach like acid. But still I said nothing. He looked away, and then he began to weep. It turned out that he'd been badly damaged as a child. He'd suffered greatly at the hands of a brutal and alcoholic father. When he was old enough, he'd turned on his father and killed him during a row, and he did time for his crime. But my client was crippled with remorse: he felt heartfelt regret for the wrong he'd done in taking his father's life, and for not allowing the man to remain alive, and perhaps repent of his behaviour. He was haunted by the fact that he'd robbed his father of possibilities, which have the potential for development. He'd believed he'd killed the future, whereas while undertaking the work of analysis, he found out that he, in fact, was the future.

As a psychoanalyst, I'm conscious of the privilege people accord in telling the story of their life to a listener, particularly where there are secrets. It can be an unruly and non-sequential drama, highly emotional, when characters in conflict come alive in the calmness of my consulting room, and wrestle around on the floor to win the argument. I treat them all with understanding and honour, and support the various voices of those hesitant speakers as best I can in their struggle to be well, for they know that my psychoanalytic assessment comes from a sitting alongside them. While the therapeutic approach is rooted in my professional training, it's a stance that I've always tried to take towards others, an attitude of well-wishing that I expect in return, because life is difficult at the best of times for all of us.

Maybe my mistake in relation to my uncle and aunt was to have believed they'd judge my work with considered, critical, literary distinctions to achieve a balanced viewpoint on a work of art. They've judged my book through the lens of different criteria. I presume I'm the subject of obloquy because of what I said about my father, and Robbie's older brother. My own uncertainty and unease surrounding publication was about holding on to the secret of alcoholism, which for me is centred on the figure of my father. Like all family members who suffer from alcoholism in Ireland, my father has been sentimentalised into a romantic figure, and patronised into harmlessness, who beat me savagely when he was drunk. My uncle and aunt don't want to have that said, so they've closed off the future, where I could re-work the past.

I'm also aware that the battle between us is the earliest one for supremacy, played out now between the last survivors of my father's generation, and those who are younger, coming up behind. By their silence, my uncle and aunt intended to render me impotent and supplanted, paradoxically, the two outcomes which cancer has already achieved. The disease tripped me up and robbed me of physical potency. After that stumble, I was forced to pursue personal growth and development in a different direction, through writing. Like a hunter sighting prey, my shouts have propelled me to hunt down and explore my new family of words for their definition and determination. The experience is without emotion, in that I don't feel lambasted by the words in a dictionary. Yet, words too have a history, and also have a loyalty to their ancestors, but they're amenable to change, and supportive of my individuality. And the language I used as a child is different to the vocabulary I employ now. And yet, by removing from my uncle and aunt the endless possibilities of living in a book and entwining their life stories with mine, I've fulfilled once again what was familiar to me from before: become an only child, a foundling, a child found deserted, orphaned, who'd grown up in the house next door. The continual supplication of wanting to be accepted back as a member of the family was what confounded me, whereas the absence of words sent back and forth between us entirely pointed out the truth. I have the sense that in erasing them from my text, I was carrying out or satisfying a determining prophesy, and interpreting correctly the will of the gods.

The brilliance in my book has confined to the dark margins, an estrangement from others who lack faith, who cannot see or wouldn't hear, and who choose to remain in ignorance. My writing has vexed my uncle and aunt, annoyed and provoked them so that they feel they have to react negatively. Perhaps this experience means that despite the appearances, and the hurt from once being thrown back and abjectly cast aside, nothing good is lost, or ever can be, least of all, in oneself. Nothing passes away so entirely, that it's unable to be found or recovered. For an exile, yes, it can be an ambivalent lifeline to have to live with the hurtful echoes from another time with which regrettably I'm familiar, and see them conjured up in the present like ghosts stepping out of the past. But it's past time to decide when it was that I first belonged to another place, or to another person, and became alienated from who I was, so that I can finally terminate the torture I once accepted by setting my own boundary, and like the child, say, 'No! I say no!' I've more than paid the price for my release from captivity, even though others have dogmatically presumed to set the ransom terms for me. Capitulation: draw up surrender terms under headings which terrorise into silence first, then exile, and finally death. I withdraw relevance from them, and set myself free through accepting the discipline of a writing ritual. The words in my first book shall continue to bring this about, improving and developing my being, and finessing the truth on which I take my stand: I am who I am.

I visited my ninety-three-year-old mother on Saturday. She was having a good day, and she broke the surface of consciousness to shine with the sunlight of her love when she recognised me. During the visit, Mum leaned forward out of her chair, and she tried to rub out with her hand the furrows on my face above the bridge of my nose. I laughed with surprise, 'You want to get rid of my frown, Mum: I'm getting old . . .' but still she persisted, pressing and flattening with the balls of her fingers the skin on my face, confounded, wanting to make everything right. Later on, the clouded sky cleared momentarily again, and she sought out my eyes with hers, and held me in the clarity of her gaze. 'Michael, I have something to say,' she began. 'I have . . .' she stated, and I awaited the import of her words. 'I don't know what comes next . . .' she faltered to me as her eyes filled with tears, and instinctively I took hold of both her hands, and held her. She grasped onto me tightly at first, and for a moment we shared in the calamity of what was happening to her. My heart broke open before her. Then she faded back into her chair as the beams of light disappeared into the open ocean of her forgetfulness, and she inexorably slipped down slowly beneath the calmness of the sea. When it was time to head back to Dublin, I kissed her on the lips. 'Good bye, Mum: I'll come back and see you again.'

'Thank you,' she replied, automatically polite, but she didn't take her eyes off the television.

Driving home, I marvelled at those precious moments of clarity, when my mother was able to let me know that she had something in her possession that she wanted to share with me. She was quite definite about this, and she repeated the words: 'I have something to say . . . I have . . .' When she searched through the archive of her memory for what followed on, she couldn't find a continuity there: 'I don't know what comes next,' she explained. The something she has which was to be expressed, a word or a phrase, eluded her, and then the briefest time in the present for imparting it had passed, so that what she was talking about remains unuttered forever, never to be communicated. She was certainly making a statement that referenced her future: 'I don't know what comes next,' she said, but her tone was more factual than apprehensive. The complete statement of what she actually said was, 'I have something to say . . . I have . . . I don't know what comes next . . .' This was, in effect, a pictorial representation of her forgetfulness, a painting with words which told a narrative. She was in possession of something; there was something that she owned. But in her mind she'd stumbled across a nothingness where there should have been something, an absence which is impossible to convey with words. That private and unintentional communication sheltered the two of us in an interlocking embrace. I can understand what it feels like to be incarcerated in a prison surrounded by fields of absence, unable to bridge the gap and communicate directly with the outside. It's a hopeless situation to be thrown back upon your own resources when all connections are down. It's as if you're striving to commune with those who're already dead, whereas the person who's actually dead is yourself. It's fearful to realise that you're the man in the mirror. As a child, I was taught in religious knowledge class that there's a fixed and unbridgeable gulf between us and those who have died. And while they can see us, they're unable to communicate with us.

New words are required to express the ineffable, the unspeakable, and to be turned away towards the future as well. This impossible task is required of me: I have to name what my mother has. I have to piece the puzzle together like a detective, to pose or to put in a certain position, to propose, suppose. 'I have something to say,' she said twice, 'I don't know what comes next . . .' as she interrogated her memory. That betwixt and between is now from a mother to her son, and from a son to his mother. I have to name in that liminal space, because she's unable to. Because of my mother, I'm obliged to become a writer, and to inhabit that calling, and somehow to reference the future.

On a Sunday evening, I still think 'I must phone Mum' and realise with a dunt that she's no longer at home in the Mall to take the call. She's no longer there at the centre of the family to weld us together, her pledge of responsibility in the case of a familial default. The catastrophe of the concluding act of the drama, that *fracaso* which develops if the *torero* has failed to impose his will on the bull during the initial cape-work, is becoming clearer. And yet through this new gift of discernment and clarity from writing out the words and seeing where I can find my bearings, I'm being led to accept that the wrongness, which I don't want, is the truth; and like everything else in my life, it must be assumed, and heroically borne. After some inspired cape-work with the *muleta*, I now stride out into the very centre of the arena for the *suerte de matar*, the kill. It's a battle that has begun in the evening of my life, at five in the afternoon.

My mother is seated at the piano in the nursing home, effortlessly playing a medley of Al Jolson songs: 'Swanee', 'The Camp Town Races', 'California Here I Come'. One song follows the other, tumbling out, expressing joy. She has a smile on her face as she inhabits this world of musical feeling. Then to my astonishment, she switches to 'Black and

White Rag', and 'Twelfth Street Rag'. We used to listen together to Winifred Atwell play these pieces, tuned in to Radio Luxemburg, waiting for Dad to come for his tea. Mum looks across at me as if she knows what she's doing, sharing with me these memories, handing me a present, as much as to say, 'I'm still here. Listen to what I have to say in the music, Michael, listen to the music, which was always our language.'

I join her at the piano, and pick out a duet on the high notes. It's the piano music which can continue on.

Part Seven
Terry's Mother

Terry no longer receives birthday cards in the post, because his mother and all of his immediate family are dead. On the morning of his last birthday, he was delighted to receive a large letter addressed to him at home: 'Isn't this great!' he exclaimed, as he eagerly tore open the envelope. He unfolded the page, and held the letter in his hand. He was staring at it uncomprehendingly. Eventually he said 'It's from the Health Service Executive. "Dear Mr O'Sullivan, we are searching for the son of Sarah and James O'Sullivan . . ."'

I continued to watch him carefully: 'That's you.'

'We would like you to contact this office.'

'What does it mean?' I asked.

He looked at the heading address. 'It's from the tracing office.'

'The tracing office? Maybe somebody has died and left you an inheritance.'

'I've a feeling I've got family I don't know about.'

I was astonished. 'But how could that be?'

'A cousin down in Laois was trying to get in touch with me a month ago, and I hadn't been able to contact him; I've a feeling this must be what it was about.' He glanced at his watch 'There's a number here – a woman called Martha – I'll ring her after nine.'

We continued to speculate about the import of the letter, and what it could be about to carry into Terry's life on the morning of his fifty-ninth birthday. From our work in analytical psychology, we know that anniversaries are important dates not only in the lives of the individuals concerned, but also in the wider collective unconscious of the family. They order events to come forth in due time, in a synchronous relativisation of time and space that cannot be explained causally.

Terry took a morning off to travel across the city to meet with Martha, as she had requested. In her office, he received the definitive, bewildering news from her that he had an older half brother, now in his seventies, who had recently arrived in London from a lifetime spent in Canada. Martha treated the matter with great sensitivity, mediating the fact that this man now wished to get in touch with Terry, his remaining family. Terry was very shocked. 'He's not my family,' he stated unsteadily, 'all of my family are dead.' For whatever reason, the man's existence was a secret that Terry's mother, Sarah, had taken to the grave, although Terry suddenly recalled a bitter row down in the home-place in Laois when he was little, and Sarah's twin sister, Aunt Nan, had called his mother 'a whore'. It was likely that his aunt knew, because the sisters had always been particularly close. In the ensuing discussion with Martha, it emerged that the man had been raised in an orphanage in Cork, always believing that his mother was dead, and afterwards he'd emigrated to Canada. It wasn't until the institution by the government of the redress board that he learned the truth: Sarah had been eighty-four years old when she'd died. The man had brought his family back on a visit to Ireland some fifteen years before. They'd stayed in Dublin's Shelbourne Hotel, which is less than a kilometre from where Sarah was living in Hatch Street.

'Wasn't my mother a warm and generous person?' Terry asked me, despairing. 'I know that she was undemonstrative: she'd never volunteer a kiss, but I believe she was a loving mother. She was non-judgemental and very liberal in her outlook. She always took the part of the underdog. When my cousin Maura was fighting with her mother, she'd travel into

Hatch Street to confide in Aunt Sarah, who immediately got on the phone to defend her. I just can't reconcile the loving mother that I've known all of my life, with the callous treatment meted out to her son.' And the man was indeed Sarah's son: Terry had viewed a copy of his birth certificate. He'd been born in the Stella Maris nursing home in 1935, three years before Sarah met and married Terry's father.

'Look,' I said, 'you don't know the circumstances surrounding this man's birth.'

'But to surround the man with silence . . . I can't get over it!' Terry shook his head. 'I can't forgive her that.'

For several weeks following that meeting with Martha, Terry was destabilised emotionally. The foundational premise on which he'd constructed his life had been undermined. He no longer recognised the picture he had of his mother: 'Not my mother . . .' he said, incredulous, denying, sometimes laying the emphasis on the 'my', more often on the 'not'. Day after day, Terry combed through the archive of his memories to find reassurance and a place of security, but as the search continued he became more and more anguished. Far from the expansion he sought, there was a narrowing of perspective that pressed in upon him, and the distress with which he was afflicted, the pain and the sorrow brought anger in its wake. The comforting unity of the family he'd grown up in – father, mother, his eldest brother, Joe, and Eileen, his older sister who protected him as the youngest – had been irremediably altered by the sudden intrusion of this interloper, who'd introduced himself into social circles where he doesn't belong: 'He's my relative, not my brother. I didn't grow up in his family, just as he didn't grow up in mine.' The fact that his mother hadn't entrusted Terry with this information during her lifetime hurt him grievously. 'She'd have known that I wouldn't judge her. I think the only time that I slapped my mother was when I charged her with not really wanting me, and she admitted that she didn't. I wonder now was that a transference from not wanting her first baby? Or maybe not?'

Over the years, he and his mother had coped with the blight that living with an alcoholic father, and a sister who suffered from manic depression, had brought to the door of the family home in Lower Hatch Street. They grieved together when Terry's eldest brother Joe was killed in a car crash. 'He crashed his car into a lamppost on Upper Leeson Street (I remember it was one of the first BMWs sold in Ireland), and he ended up entangled in the railings of the house, from where Joe had to be given away to be temporarily fostered for his own safety. My father was a significant threat to his firstborn, an established phenomenon in some alcoholic men. He'd threatened to throw him out the window onto the railings below, and my mother wasn't able to protect her baby. And then I was forcibly taken away from my mother's lap by the nurse, to spend two years in hospital when I suffered polio at four years of age.' He reflected, 'That was the law of the land, which you had to abide by. Still is,' he added, trying to understand a fracture that seemed to be repeating in his family's history, aiming towards a conscious acceptance of the horror. 'They held onto Eileen because she was my father's favourite.'

Sarah was an enterprising woman, who worked successfully all her life to provide her three children with the best, private education. The continual dramas caused by her husband's violent alcoholic behaviour and her daughter's illness didn't prevent her from always trying her best to create 'a happy home: I want everyone to be happy!' Terry still suffered from residual guilt that he took himself out of that situation in a mighty bid for freedom, to set up home with me. Since their deaths, at least he wasn't compelled by the anxiety that a phone call from Hatch Street could trigger. 'After Eileen's death, which was the last one, I remember taking off on a flight to Spain, and realising that I didn't have to ring anybody about it, and that I didn't feel guilty. It was the first time that I knew my sense of obligation was officially retired.' He was angry with his mother for leaving her baby on his doorstep, this time from beyond the grave. She'd made certain choices in her life, for which he couldn't be held responsible. And he was also angry, however irrationally, with the half brother he'd never met, because he didn't want to have to deal with him. He was feeling stalked by the ghosts that had once haunted Hatch Street, 'the madnesses of my family' as he termed them. From the terror he was now feeling, they seemed to have kidnapped him once again.

Terry was immensely sad for what had befallen his mother when she was barely twenty-one years old. The Ireland that she lived in immediately following independence from England was a cruel and repressive place, where the religious orders of the Catholic Church had moved into the big houses to take the place of the ruling landed gentry. They set up novitiates and schools and orphanages in them, which sometimes became places of cruelty and sexual abuse, from which Christ was excluded. When Sarah found herself pregnant, she lost her job in the civil service, and was also banished from the tranquil farm in Laois where she'd grown up, condemned to a life of exile. Terry deduced that the man who'd made her pregnant came from a nearby farm, because in her speech, his mother always had expressed a soft spot for this particular man down through the years. Terry had heard that he went off unexpectedly to join the priesthood, perhaps absolved in confession of his sin of the flesh, and his name doesn't appear on the baby's birth certificate. Terry said that from the photographs he'd viewed in Martha's office, the stalwart man in his burly build must look very like his father, more so than resembling his mother, although he does have her chin. He was surprised to see that Sarah had called her baby Redmond after her only brother. He was the eldest in Sarah's family, but he'd died in his early twenties.

Sarah nursed her infant for six weeks, at which time she was sent away from the nursing home. And in a pitiless move, the case notes reveal that she had to be prevented from attempting to make visits to see her baby afterwards. The 1930s was an era of deference and of obedience to the authorities in the new Irish state, and despite Sarah's repeated best efforts to make contact with her baby at the time, she'd ultimately complied with what was demanded of her, and she never made contact with Redmond again, so that the child had to make his way in the world all alone, without the support of a family.

'Isn't it awful to think that she never heard her own child speak?' Terry surmised, 'My mother must have been terribly ashamed of her pregnancy never to speak of it. Or maybe the pain of having to give up her baby was so severe that she just had to cut off from her emotions. Or maybe the truth is a mixture of both? What I find hard to understand is why my mother didn't trace her son in the more liberal era of the 1980s and '90s, particularly as my dad was dead by this time. Although he surely would have known: when he was drunk, he used to call me a "cur" and a "tinker's breed". It all makes some sort of grotesque sense now, although the meaning of what happened escapes me entirely.' As Terry began to settle, he was full of empathy for his mother. 'Those were the impossible choices that Sarah had made, and lived by.'

Martha was encouraging of Terry to make contact with Redmond, who subsequently wrote him a short letter, enclosing some further photographs. His life had paralleled his mother's to the extent that both of them had married alcoholics. Terry's mother had married his father on the promise of him giving up the drink. He lasted as a teetotaller for a fortnight, and she remained married to him for forty years. 'At least Redmond had taken the further step of divorcing his wife. Our lives in Hatch Street would have been so much better if my mother had had the courage to do the same: the courage to face up to the truth on many levels.' Terry took Redmond's letter and his photographs with him on that ill-fated holiday to Italy, from where he expected to have the leisure to write him a considered reply. They were stolen, together with some photographs he'd assembled of his mother, in the robbery of the hire car at Fiumicino airport in Rome, the eternal city. So he decided to let the matter drop.

Fully a year later in Spain, I was working at my computer, swimming in the 27 degree heat of a very early August morning. It wasn't yet light. All

'Terry forgot the intrusive camera setup. He'd turned to me to enquire happily
"Well, Cook, how's the barbeque doing?" and then turned back to Conor.
Click, click, click: "Yes!"' (Conor Ó Mearáin)

'Aengus and Anne
were happy on that
afternoon, waiting for
a doctor to give them
some steer about the
symptoms he was
suffering.'
(Justin Farrelly)

'Anna sat on the wooden bench holding a fan in the colours of the
famous bullfighter, Manolete.' (Conor Ó Mearáin)

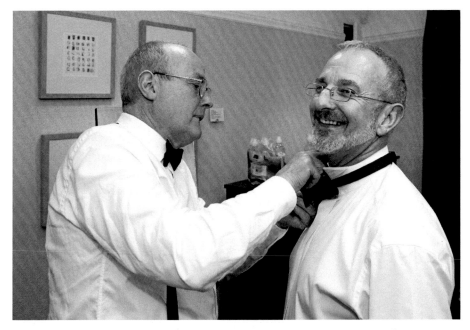

At the National Concert Hall, Eamonn Lawlor lends a hand. (Conor Ó Mearáin)

'. . . the trained voices of my newscaster friends, Eileen Dunne, Emer O'Kelly and Eamonn Lawlor, as soloists, came readily to mind for a concert reading of my book, to be given at the National Concert Hall in Dublin . . .' (Conor Ó Mearáin)

At the National Concert
Hall, watching the *At Five
in the Afternoon* rehearsal.
(Conor Ó Mearáin)

'My mother is ninety-three
years old, and she dwells now
in a house of pure being.'
(Keith Heneghan)

'Helen had arrived at a conclusion. "Now that it's been done you can use the
photograph in the new book if you like," she stated.' (Conor Ó Mearáin)

'Terry then signed the register, followed by Barbara and Tiernan, who used the special Italian Delta pens for the first time that we'd given to each of our witnesses as a gift.' (Conor Ó Mearáin)

Not-a-wedding guests: Aengus Mac Grianna, Emer O'Kelly, Eamonn Lawlor, Eileen Dunne and Colm Murray. (Conor Ó Mearáin)

'We'd prepared Helen by telling her that I didn't intend to use the portrait in my new book. Some of the other photographs that we'd taken paparazzi-style through the bustling streets of Tarifa earlier on that carefree August day were brimming with life and movement...' (Conor Ó Mearáin)

'... Anna wears her heart on her sleeve. When she deems a person her friend, she impulsively gives her all.'
(Conor Ó Mearáin)

'Conor tries to capture through his lenses this revelation of being, a point in time which affords him a glimpse through to eternity.'
(Conor Ó Mearáin)

of the windows were open, letting the slight breeze move over my skin and circulate throughout La Mairena. At that time of day before dawn, it's easy to be spooked in the stealthy silence. A gust of wind can billow the *toldos*, the awnings over the terrace, so that they creak harshly, or a door will slam shut, even throw a piece of furniture about like a poltergeist: nature is on the move. I thought I heard a footfall, and turned to make out a figure suddenly stand motionless in the darkness at the far end of the room. I got a surge of shock.

'I'm sorry if I startled you,' said Terry, 'but I had a terrible dream.'

'What is it?' I enquired gently.

Terry approached me until he stood in the circle of light spilling out from around the desk. 'My brother Joe was in it, and I was very anxious lest he find out accidentally that he was no longer the eldest in the family.' He sat down heavily into the couch.

'What do you think it means?'

'I wanted to be the one to tell him: controlling the mess in Hatch Street, which was my usual position in the family. There's obviously a part of me, since I'm now the oldest surviving member of my family, which is grossly offended, outraged really by the news that I have family I knew nothing about, that I'm the eldest survivor no longer. There's also something there about a loss of status, a loss of rank from the position of being keeper of the flame, the protector, the educator, almost being in the fatherly position, really: they looked to me to save them, and I failed . . .' He reached for the television zapper. 'It was a very vivid dream,' he said. 'I think what it means initially is that it's time I wrote that letter to Redmond.'

Over the next few days, Terry talked about his feelings. The dream was on his mind, and we clarified in those ongoing discussions what Terry wanted to say to Redmond. He analysed the dream in greater detail, allowing it to work through his consciousness so that he was able come up with a position which honoured the truth, and the life he'd had with his family in Hatch Street. While the dream proposed a position desired by his eternal unconscious, he was very aware that there was a third position to be arrived at, which also partook of what he consciously wanted, so that justice could be done to both presentations. He parsed and discussed every word.

'Dear Redmond,

'It was a shock to hear from you, because your mother never revealed her secret to a soul.'

Terry begins his letter factually. Despite Sarah's silence surrounding the birth, he was acknowledging that she was Redmond's mother. In the same breath, he was keeping himself outside of that particular mother/son configuration.

'Nobody can condone what happened to you at an abusive time in Ireland's history. I'm finding it hard to reconcile the cruelty you experienced, with the unwavering kindness of the mother I knew.'

Terry is sympathetic towards Redmond. He's saying that eighty years ago, the zeitgeist, the attitudes of people in Ireland were repressive and punishing and shaming. Even so, he makes the big statement that he can't condone what his mother did to Redmond in abandoning him to an orphanage, and he labels his mother's treatment of Redmond as cruel. However, he also defends his experience of his mother. He didn't want to say that he can't reconcile these two conflicting sides of her; rather, with Terry's penetrating understanding of human nature, what he said was that he's still finding it hard to reconcile them.

'She named you Redmond after her eldest brother, whom I know she had loved.'

In concluding that opening paragraph, he goes on to reassure Redmond that through his naming, not only was he acknowledged as the first born, but that his mother had loved him.

'I believe you were told your mother was dead. When you discovered the truth recently, you must have been full of expectation.'

The nuns lied to the orphans of Ireland on behalf of the state, torturing them further by telling them that their mothers were dead. Terry could see that if you were made to live out such a lie, then you'd be very angry at that abuse of power. His mother had lied to Terry by omission in not telling him about Redmond's existence, and he was furious with her about that.

I'd pointed out to Terry, 'If you've lived all of your life as a solitary with nobody there to lend support, then the natural expectation from finding family after such a lifetime, is driven a desire which is unmediated by reality, and unboundaried.'

Terry was acutely aware that these two reactions of anger and expectation are without limits when evoked in a child. They can never be satisfied, although they can be tempered over time and brought into alignment with the present reality of the adult. It's a position Terry had been caught in with his family for fifty years due to the inadequacies of his father, and Terry is adamant that he no longer wants to live in such a bind: he values his freedom, which was late in coming. The encounter with Redmond had the potential to be fraught. 'I wish my sister, Eileen, were alive. It's too demanding a burden to be landed upon the sole remaining relative, without the support of other family members there to absorb it.' Terry was gaining a deeper understanding of what it means to be orphaned. He was also grounding himself in his understanding that he, too, has rights in this situation.

'I have to deliver a lecture in London before Christmas, and we could meet up then if that timing suits you.'

This next paragraph sets a limit to the effort Terry was prepared to make in his acceptance of Redmond. It was a business that required his attention. Terry didn't want to open himself up to collecting long-lost relatives he didn't need. Apart from his beloved cousin Maura in Dublin, Terry isn't in touch with his relatives in Laois. The purpose of the meeting would be to give information to Redmond about his mother, and also his father, although information on the latter would have to be speculative.

And he was wary of offering information in a letter, since he didn't know how it would be received: Redmond was a stranger to him. From his psychoanalytic experience of dealing with these matters, Terry anticipated the differences in each other's upbringing and outlook on life would prove too great to forge an alliance.

'The least you are owed is information about your mother, and I shall facilitate you briefly in sharing what I know. I don't want to cause you further hurt, but opening up the family archive poses many complications. My mother married an alcoholic, which brought difficulties that I believe you can understand. The final decade up to the death of my sister was another trying time for us. When all of my family had died, as well as suffering grief, I was relieved.'

In this section, Terry is acknowledging Redmond's legitimate hurt, and he's making his attempt at healing a wound, which he knows is impossible to salve. There were aspects to Terry's family life that he has found difficult, and doubly difficult being forced to confront them again in these circumstances. He suffered anxieties and responsibilities down through the years that Redmond had been spared. Terry deliberately understates the damage that living with an active alcoholic, wife or father, causes to the family through wryly acknowledging their shared experience. Terry also implied that his sister was troublesome. I know from listening to him that there were times when life in Hatch Street was hell on earth. In his mind, these two experiences add up to a lifetime of family hurt. In stating that he was happy to be freed from the obligation he felt towards his family, Terry was implying he didn't want to revive another familial situation with Redmond, who was a shadow stalking him from out of a dream.

'Today would have been Sarah's 97th birthday. Did I ever really know her? I know now that she made decisions about her life which had nothing to do with me.'

The revelation that Redmond was Sarah's son has fatally undermined the image Terry had of his mother, a violence that appals him. He accepts no responsibility for the choices that she made at the time, about which he has no personal record. Coincidentally, the letter to Redmond was being written on Sarah's birthday, so that in keeping with anniversaries which register in the collective unconscious, she too was having a hand in the direction of this process: Redmond would be receiving a letter inspired by his mother. In a very real sense, Terry was giving her voice.

'With every good wish, Terry O'Sullivan.'

He ended on a formal, but warm note, wishing Redmond well. This was an important statement, because Terry could have reacted differently. The period of reflection caused him to regard this situation in the way that he specified in his letter. However, Terry is conscious that this is the first letter that Redmond will have received from a family member, and his intention is to be kind. At no stage does Terry refer to Redmond as his half brother. The fact that he names himself signing his full name re-emphasises the fact that up to a year ago, Terry was a member of different family. It further demonstrates his intention that Redmond's existence isn't going to alter the position that has prevailed for the past sixty years, although in truth, he doubts whether that will ever be possible.

Terry has meditated deeply on the nature of family. The experience he had of growing up in Hatch Street has had to be re-imagined by him. The feelings from that time have been submitted to a process of thought that has grappled with the concept of the stranger, who is an unrecognised part of himself. In the dream, a stranger can pose a threat, but it also brings new or unused qualities whose potentiality can be mobilised to help the dreamer. And Redmond, whom he has never met before, is a character that has come to Terry in a dream, or even a nightmare, calling for his attention. He brings with him a more penetrating understanding into the emotional restraint of his mother, who suffered the unbearable hurt of being separated from her child shortly after birth.

Terry recalled that on her deathbed, there was a moment of closeness where they both had trembled on the brink of truth. He had posed a question to his mother: 'Is there anything you want to tell me, Mum?'

Sarah had hesitated. He could see that she wanted to tell him something, and at the same instant he realised she was so heavily dosed with medication, it would have been unfair to take advantage of her vulnerability, so he pulled back. He moved her on to other matters, not realising that there was a revelation to be disclosed by his mother, and the moment had passed. He told me he'd often wondered what she would have said had he been prepared to wait, and not bring matters to a premature conclusion. He also speculated whether the hesitation was, in fact, his own.

Terry didn't hear his mother's answer at that time. She has spoken now, some years after her death, as if the past and the future are equivalent, and somehow part of the present moment. By way of his response, Terry mobilized within himself the resources he needed to deal with the birth of Redmond on the day of his mother's birthday, a birth which had been announced on his own birth date.

It would be invidious to term Terry's early December meeting with Redmond in London an anticlimax, because for both of them, it was a momentous event. Terry had steeled himself to meet Redmond for the first and possibly only time to tell him about his mother, but Redmond had arrived armed with photographs to tell Terry about himself. It was as if the absence surrounding his birth had made Redmond determined to insist on the actuality of his existence. The many photographs from various periods of his life in Canada and in Britain that he spread out across the table in the hotel lounge were an additional, visual proof of that. Terry recounted, 'He didn't ask much about Mum: I don't think he knew the questions to ask. Don't get me wrong: he had excellent verbal skills. He informed me that he'd had no firsthand experience of having a mother, or of growing up in a family. If you've never had a mother, how would you know what questions were the right ones? For over three quarters of a century he thought that his name was Patrick, until he was given his birth certificate and read his actual name for the first time a year or two ago.

Redmond has lived his whole life as someone else. It was a very sad, a very tragic situation for all concerned, and I felt deeply for him. He had an idealised picture of his mother. At one stage he said that it'd be nice if Mum was here to witness this event, and I said if she were here I'd want to kill her!'

Redmond was shocked, and said, 'Oh, don't say that!'

And I said, 'It's alright: it's just a figure of speech . . . But still I'd like to kill her!'

The following morning, when Terry got into the taxi to take him to Paddington station, in the ten minutes it took to get there, I was surprised to observe that he told the whole story of his mother and of Redmond and his reason for being in London to the driver. As I was hauling the case along the platform towards the Heathrow Express, without me saying anything about what had just occurred, Terry turned towards me, stopped and took a rest. Waving his walking stick towards the heavens, he explained, 'It's like throwing confetti into the air: let the wind take the words where it will . . .'

I understood then that he was handing over the encounter with Redmond into the maternal care of the metropolis, which seemed appropriate. For Terry had known his mother, Sarah, all his life, but he hadn't ever met Sarah, the woman, until now; she'd been a stranger to him, until she pulled aside the curtain of her reticence, and inhabited her rightful place, which was now complete: a filling up of pure being. And as we sped out of the darkness in the station and into the light, the air seemed to be alive with falling particles of dust, or seeds blowing in the wind, or maybe they were droplets of mist or hail drifting down like the lightest snowfall changing the appearance of everything. We didn't speak of it again.

Part Eight
That Dingle Day

'Dingle no longer exists by law.' Those words of a former Minister for the Gaeltacht, the Irish speaking area, expressed the sense of dislocation we felt three hundred kilometres south-west of Dublin city in County Kerry, as we wandered in the wind through the streets of, what was officially known after a local plebiscite five years ago, as *An Daingean*. Dressed in dark suits and ties, swishing overcoats and shiny urban shoes, the solitary winter visitors drew bemused glances from the locals, layered in woollens. We bought two ice creams at Murphy's ice cream parlour, passing time, waiting for the funeral of my publisher, Steve MacDonogh, to start. The incongruity between the business of living and the waking of the dead sparked a memory. When Terry's cousin had died in Laois, he and his mother were late into the house, and the recitation of the rosary was in full swing when they'd arrived. As the prayers swirled around them, Sarah made her way through the throng over to the coffin, knocked on it to make sure it was made of oak, and then stood transfixed: 'Is that an apple tart I see on the table there?'

'Shhh Mammy,' whispered Terry, indicating the body, 'remember Kathleen!'

'Oh, she won't mind: she's dead, and I'm famished!' said Sarah, valuing the living over the dead, and heading directly for the table.

The death notice in the newspaper had said that Steve's body would lie in the funeral home for two hours, between three and five o' clock, before its cremation elsewhere. We'd driven past the utilitarian building standing proud on the outskirts of the pretty fishing village, on our way in from the county-town of Tralee, where we'd lit a candle for the happy repose of Steve's soul in the Dominican church a few hours earlier. Less than two years ago, at our first meeting in the Merrion Hotel in Dublin, during one of the only extended conversations we'd had with him, Steve had mentioned that he was the son of a Protestant clergyman. He also alluded to the fact that when he'd published the memoir of Gerry Adams, the republican leader, it had caused trouble for him with members of his family. 'Somebody had to do it,' he'd said. 'Freedom of expression must be upheld!' The manuscript of *At Five in the Afternoon* had contained a chapter about my great-grandfather's fight for Irish freedom in the 1880s, at the time of the Land League. So maybe that was one of the reasons Steve had warmed to my book.

While we were standing in the way of the wind and whipping white foam of Derrymore Strand, scattering Terry's sister's ashes over Tralee Bay some two years previously, Steve had phoned us, offering to publish the book. 'You're a wonderful writer,' he'd said to me in the only time that he'd betrayed his feelings, 'but your book is all over the place. Would you be prepared to work with an editor?' I'd been a Senior Producer/Director in RTÉ for over a decade, so my experience of editing the beginning, middle and ending of every programme I'd ever worked on was extensive, and I took umbrage at his criticism of my skills. 'I'll think about it and get back to you,' I said to him loftily with the confidence of the novice, 'but thank you for your offer, which I appreciate.' And I clicked off the mobile phone.

Terry was looking at me aghast.

'What?' I asked him.

'You've sent that manuscript to thirteen publishers already, and it's taken over a year to get to this stage,' he said.

'So? What d'you think?'

'I think you should get over yourself!'

I rang Steve back immediately to say that I'd be happy to work with an editor, if that's what it took to get my book published. I could appreciate submitting to unexpected requirements from my experience of working in the allied field of television production, where the necessities for getting a programme onto air were various, and often surprising. As we consigned the small packet of Eileen's ashes to the waves in the birthplace of her beloved father, having first had to break open the sealed wooden casket with a car jack ('She was always stubborn,' remarked Terry), we gave thanks to his sister for having looked after us, and having found for us someone who'd finally agreed to publish the book, as the wind blew her ashes over the frothing waves, and her spirit moved like a queen across Corcha Dhuibhne and Uíbh Ráthach, before a gathering of the souls of the dead screamed out over the Beara peninsula. Now we were back on a visit to Kerry once again, where Death still seemed to hold sway.

My book was shortlisted by the Irish Book Academy in two categories of the National Book Awards: the RTÉ Radio John Murray Show Listeners' Choice Award, and Best Non-Fiction Book of the Year Award. Despite my misgivings, Terry and I felt obligated to attend, not only because Steve had bought the tickets and invited us to the gala dinner as his guests, but primarily because of his shocking death the week before-hand. My book was the only publication of his Brandon imprint to have made the shortlist. I heard he'd been visiting Morocco, and that on his way home to Dingle, he'd been driving erratically through Limerick city, when the Gardaí had pulled him over. They realised at once that something was badly wrong, and Steve was admitted to hospital, where he went into a coma. Subsequently, he was airlifted to Cork University Hospital. One lunchtime, midweek, I received a phone call from my literary agent, Emma, who seemed to be in a state of shock: I had to ask her to repeat what she was saying because it sounded so garbled, so incredible: 'Steve MacDonogh has died in hospital of a brain haemorrhage.' It was hard to take in such unthinkable news. Steve was a relatively young man, barely sixty years of age, younger than me. He was in charge of my book: it was his production. Suddenly, he was dead.

I'd found Steve to be an intense and shyly reticent man, who had protective boundaries in place. When he spoke in his hesitating, guttural voice, the words seemed to be wrenched from him. He gave the impression of being watchful about what he was saying. I was unable to read the absence of emotion I experienced in his presence, other than to conclude that he neither liked nor disliked me, and I was unnerved by that neutrality. It was my writing that he was interested in, and I found such a compartmentalising split difficult to handle. I believed that my soul was written out into my book, that the words therein were expressive of my being. After the initial flush of support around publication, there was little contact between us. The tragedy of his awful, sudden death confirmed me in my feeling of having been cut adrift.

Over the course of that day, the shocking jolt of hearing about what had happened to Steve brought into focus random thoughts about the vigour with which we live our lives, as if there's no tomorrow. While the big question about the meaning of life seems to be answered by the simple, existentialist practice of living it, I was cast down, afflicted by obsessive thoughts of whether a particular life – Steve's, my own life – mattered that much in the end: whether it had any value whatsoever, other than to swell the chorus of the living. I was visiting my brother Kie in his hospital room where he lay dying from cancer, and he'd said, 'Nobody will care when I'm dead.'

I argued back instinctively, 'Your family loves you,' which seemed to be a non-sequitur, almost as if love were some sort of protective tether that could fasten him to the living. We stared at each other in silence, overwhelmed by the fright of our helplessness, and the import of our doomed love one for the other, still unexpressed. That was fully fifteen years ago.

The Dingle day was to hold many surprises. At three o'clock in the afternoon, a hearse followed by a line of cars drove slowly down the hill from out of the green, patch-worked countryside, and pulled up in front of the funeral home. The low light levels in November, the cold, foot-stamping feel of the weather that day, contributed to the dismal mood of the groups of people chatting in hushed tones who were scattered round about. A people mover following directly behind the hearse had peeled off and turned into the car park by the sea where Terry and I were standing in the way of the wind, and came to a halt. Several people got out, including a tall, strikingly beautiful young woman in her early thirties, with a luxuriant mane of well-cared-for black hair. She was wearing high-heeled boots, and was glamorously clad in expensive black suede and leather clothes; she carried a young child in her arms. Our friends, Jen and Garrett, had met Steve before in Morocco, so we'd known he had a place there in the hills beyond Essouira, where my writing hero, the sainted Jean Genet, lay buried in the Spanish graveyard. The death notice had mentioned his wife's name Maryam, and also referred to his daughter Lilya, so I guessed that the woman who looked like a model was Steve's wife from Morocco, and the pretty little girl would be his two-year-old child, who was clutching a soft toy in her hand.

We all made our way towards the funeral home, and crowded together under the covered terrace at the front of the building. A local fife and drum band had materialised as if conjured up from out of the depths, and they began to play a lament. A man in a raincoat standing in front of them held aloft the tricolour, which swayed fitfully to the swirl of the music, in the breezes blowing in off the sea. I could see that the northern politician and President of Sinn Fein, Gerry Adams, was one of those who were lifting the coffin out from the hearse.

People were filing into the pews to the right-hand side of the door, and the open coffin was on trestles in an alcove to our left: I could glimpse Steve's waxy face pushing up above the parting in the white, lacy covering. It felt icy cold in the funeral home, even though people were crowding in together. When eventually we were all packed inside, the undertaker called for our attention, and he invited any person who wanted to say anything, to do so. A tall man then stood up beside the coffin, and he began to talk in a strong, clacking Belfast accent. Because there was no microphone, it was difficult to follow what he said, and the eclectic gathering of locals and hippie blow-ins, and the visitors who'd come down from Dublin, were carrying on snatched, murmuring conversations all around me. It was Gerry Adams who gave the oration. He spoke for about twenty minutes, and he talked about his friendship with Steve, which I hadn't known about, and how he always stayed with Steve in his house outside Dingle whenever he was in the Kerry area. Adams resumed his seat at the foot of the coffin.

As we were about to pass him by on our way to sympathize with the relatives, 'What are you going to say to Adams?' I whispered to Terry.

'I'm going to say, I'm sorry for the loss of your friend.'

Steve's relatives sat uncomfortably on straight-backed chairs all along the wall behind the coffin in a sombre line of black, silently observing the happenings in the room. His brother was also called Terry (which must have accounted for the fact that Steve always took Terry's phone-calls) and his sister Deirdre was there, and sitting out at the end in a corner by the exit door was his ninety-two-year-old, sprightly mother. They were all English people, and they replied animatedly and warmly in very middle-class accents to our expressions of sorrow. Steve's Moroccan wife had spoken to me in French as I sympathised with her. I wondered what the evident, refined politeness of their background had made of the bleak, humanist proceedings in that icy funeral home. I missed the traditional ceremony of a blessing, and hoped that Steve's relatives would have their own, more personal leave-taking in private, elsewhere. Everything grated on the senses, even a woman's thin voice that had pierced the chill with 'The Parting Glass' some moments before. We met Máire for the first time, who'd worked with Steve in the office, and we embraced her warmly. She appeared marooned by the tragedy that had overtaken her. Suddenly outside in the wan glow of the evening sunlight, I was approached by the undertaker, who welcomed me to Dingle, and apologised that he hadn't realised he'd have need of a microphone. I met the designer for the first time, Brendan Lyons, who said that it was he who'd typeset my book, and I was delighted to congratulate him on his wonderful achievement. We chatted together about Steve's reticence, not only about everything to do with his private life, but also about how uncommunicative he'd been surrounding the success of my book, a lacking which had frustrated me, but which his underlying ill-health had now made comprehensible, if that was indeed the reason.

One morning very early the previous March, I'd woken up distressed, knowing that I'd wet the bed. Since the prostatectomy operation, I don't have the same control over my bladder, and this sometimes happens. Terry was sleeping, so I left my soaked mattress as it was, exited the bedroom and went in to the computer. I wrote a bad-tempered email to Steve, pointing out that I was staying in Ireland travelling the length and breadth of the country promoting the book, while he was going to Morocco on his holidays, and sent it off. When Terry saw it, he was very angry, and said, 'You're going to have to apologise. The last line is unconscionable. It's unprincipled and immoderate: unworthy of you.' Terry sees my behaviour in relation to others forensically. Like the good analyst that he is, he'd spotted something that I hadn't seen, and I've always respected the keenness of his insight. He dialled Steve on the mobile, and when he answered, held out the phone to me. 'Steve, I need to apologise to you unreservedly.' Later on that day, I ordered a case of French wine from Mitchell's to be sent to him, to underline my repentance. Terry then took the phone when I left the room. He told me later that he'd explained to Steve about the wetting of the bed, and how it had thrown me into a paranoid place; in truth, I hadn't recognised the ongoing physical and emotional impact that cancer continues to have on my life. Steve rarely replied to any of my emails again.

Terry had a difficulty about wearing a dress suit to the National Book Awards. Primarily, it derived from his republican background. His father was a member of the Old IRA, who'd been on the first hunger strike in Tralee jail at the time of Ireland's fight for independence. Terry talks about the time he accompanied his father to a Fianna Fáil *cumann* meeting, at which the disgraced former Taoiseach, Charles Haughey, was speaking. As his father aged and his deafness increased, his dad used to wear a hearing aid, which he'd turn up loud so that it squealed. In the sudden silence that followed the interruption in the room, Terry's father said at the top of his voice, 'You see that man up there on the podium, you mark my words, he's going to be the ruination of this party!' Terry belonged within the pure stream of republicanism espoused by those founding fathers. So he had a dark suit made at Artesanos Camiseros in Marbella, which looked the part from a distance, but which in a practical advantage, could be used again for everyday occasions.

I'd often watched the Oscars ceremony on television, with the camera focussing in on the various nominees for an award, and I'd wondered what was going through their minds as the presenter opened the envelope to announce the winner. At the Book Awards, I found that managing to smile during the nomination process was easy, because I was relaxed in the knowledge that I'd been shortlisted by the Academy of booksellers, librarians and book-lovers, and for safety's sake, I'd also my two acceptance speeches hidden in a leather folder down by the side of my chair in case I won. I'd heard the six reviews of the various books on radio, and I was gratified that mine had been favoured over the others for its literary quality, so Terry and I held out the highest of hopes. Holding that smile to mask my disappointment, which was a physical reaction flooding my body like being hit by a giant tidal wave when I wasn't announced the winner, took me by complete surprise, and it proved impossibly difficult to feign the untruth.

Emma, my literary agent, who was sitting beside me whispered comfortingly in my ear, 'How are you?'

'I'm feeling gutted,' I smiled back through gritted teeth, like a ventriloquist, with my generously applauding hands masking my face as I watched someone else walk across the floor and up onto the stage to accept his award. When I was on the RTÉ John Murray morning radio show to talk about my book before the Listeners' Choice competition, and I said that voting for books wasn't the same as voting for your favourite act in the television talent show *X Factor*, John had contradicted me, 'Oh, yes it is!' And he was proved right. Being thrust into that level of public competition turned out to be another unforeseen step on the torturous climbing route over the mountains of not only writing books, but having to publicise them by every possible means as well.

When I was talking about Steve's death to a thoughtful, well-read young American woman, Sarah Bannan, who said that she'd liked my book, and was seated to my right-hand side at the Book Awards dinner, she volunteered she too had been there in Dingle at the funeral. It emerged that she was the Head of Literature with the Arts Council, and that she'd had dealings with Steve in the past. Nevertheless, she too found the funeral to be revelatory. Sarah said she'd played with Steve's little daughter, Lilya, who took a shine to her watch. And the little girl was so fascinated by it, that Sarah felt she couldn't take it from her when she was leaving. 'It wasn't that expensive,' she assured me, gaily.

We were relieved to regain the warmth of the car after those happenings in Dingle, and we headed out on the road back to Dublin, with the Gerry Adams massive Volvo estate driving immediately behind us. Terry was keeping an eye on it in the wing mirror. We barely spoke, lost in our thoughts about Steve's secret life and the surprise of his funeral, until we abandoned the motorway for a bite to eat in Matt the Thresher's public house, and the Gerry Adams Volvo had swished us by, disappearing into the silent blackness of the November night, with the rest of the holy souls.

Part Nine

Anna

Bernard, the French hairdresser, says, '*Anna a le coeur sur la main*': Anna wears her heart on her sleeve. When she deems a person her friend, she impulsively gives her all, whatever the cost to herself. Anna met her Scottish boyfriend, James, at a time when she was vulnerable, and recovering from breast cancer. He was twenty years her senior, and said he'd been attracted to her from when he first laid eyes on her as a young seventeen-year-old wearing hot pants, while he was staying with his friend, Richard, in Mijas.

'I've never worn hot pants,' she said, wonderingly. 'Shorts, yes!'

She took him in, changed his polyester shirts for cotton ones, bought him an expensive Rolex watch, and brought him to the best restaurants on the coast. While James helps out around the house ('our house' he calls it), most of his money goes towards supporting his family back in Glasgow, and his wife Linda, whom has talked of divorcing. As the relationship cooled, Anna complained effusively to Terry and me that James was tracking her comings and goings. She said he denounced her for supposed infidelities with men from her past, and she was finding these bitter condemnations debilitating. 'Another unlovely quality,' Anna said, 'is that James is constantly accusing me of preferring others' company to his.' Whatever the sad truth of a relationship in trouble, a supportive tie which suddenly becomes imprisoning when examined with a disappointed eye, I knew that the suspicions regarding her friends were justified, because we could see that as Anna felt her freedoms being curtailed, she was becoming increasingly unhappy. A private conspiracy had developed around her, how best to get her away from this man, who apparently had captured her.

Anna's heart developed a serious problem. Sometimes it beat so violently, up to one hundred and forty beats per minute, that she became exhausted physically and emotionally. The doctors in Malaga diagnosed that two valves were faulty, the one at the back that took the blood in, and one at the front that let it out. Her friends worried for her that one day her heart would stop beating, and that they'd lose Anna. A star would be extinguished in the firmament, and her joy in life and the abiding affection that Anna's beautiful soul brings to her friends, would vanish without further warning into the void. So they entreated her to take better care of herself, not to be so driven, to put limits on the long hours, seven days a week that she devoted herself to the restaurant and to the many people in her life, to take some time for herself and lead a more tranquil life for the sake of her health. Whenever we're down in Spain, Terry and I have her to stay with us in our apartment for some relaxing overnights, and we look after her as best we can. But as Bernard, with a Gallic shrug, scissors in one hand comb in the other, concisely put it, 'Anna is Anna!'

When she arrived in through the door of La Mairena over an hour late for dinner, flushed in the August heat and still talking animatedly on the mobile phone, Terry planted a kiss on both her cheeks, and greeted Anna appreciatively with, 'I don't know anyone who can wear white as well as you!' She had on a simple white top over a pair of well-cut dark navy slacks, which set off the expensive pair of Bally pumps she was wearing. Anna folded up the phone, and said, 'There were three women in the restaurant for lunch today, who told me I needed to change my bra because my tits were sagging.'

Anna's first language is Danish, and she can sometimes take your breath away with her choice of colloquial words in English, and her manipulation of the overflow from many languages.

She read my face as I kissed her. 'Tits, yes? Breasts, my breasts are sagging.'

Terry reassured her, 'Your breasts look great. And I hope you told those biddies that after surviving breast cancer, their comments are wholly irrelevant. You're above ground, and we love you: that's all that matters.'

Anna is wary of women, and well understands their potential for spite. She told us that her adoptive mother in Denmark used to say to her, at seven years of age, that she'd send her back to where she found her in Austria if she didn't behave, which emphasised a fatal doubt about whether she was wanted and acceptable to others. Anna's struggle ever since has been marked by fears of abandonment, a dilemma about security, which is an assured freedom that was robbed from her at that early age. It has prevented her from daring to speak up. 'One of the women knew that I underwent chemo to save my breast.' And she added, 'She was the one who told me they were sagging.'

About a year ago, there was a fish promotion on at El Corte Inglés in Puerto Banus, and *dorada*, gilt-head bream, which is a flat white fish, delicious when fried in the stable oil from the *hojiblanca* olives which are grown to the north of Malaga, was selling for one euro apiece. Anna got all excited and she rang Fernando with the news. Sometimes she lends him a hand with his catering business during the summer months.

He told her, 'Buy three hundred!' He cautioned, 'But make sure that they're cleaned.'

Anna was waiting at the store when it opened at ten o'clock the following morning, and she ordered all her fish. The staff behind the fishmonger's counter were taken aback: they'd expected each customer to order a few fish, a number they were geared to handle. But for such a big order to be processed and cleaned, they told her she'd have to come back to collect it at two o'clock. When she returned in the afternoon, the fish were in several crates on a large trolley, and sure enough, they'd been topped and tailed. So with the help of some muscular young assistants from the store, she loaded the containers into the back of her Range Rover, piling them high one on top of the other, and set out for her home in Elviria, where Anna would store the fish in her walk-in, industrial freezers, until they were required.

She got an urgent phone call from Fernando: 'I've been let down by a chef and three waiting staff at a wedding I'm in the middle of catering for here on the outskirts of Marbella.' He pleaded, 'Anna, could you come at once and help me out? And bring the crates!' He sounded desperate.

So Anna packed up the jeep, and at high speed drove off up into the narrow winding laneways of the countryside in the Marbella hills. She arrived amidst the chaos of a makeshift kitchen, which had been set up in the stables, as a sous chef overturned a large container of pepper sauce for the entrecôtes onto the floor.

'That's all there is!' yelled Fernando in shock, and Anna grabbed two square plates and started scooping up the spreading mess into the plastic container. She warned us later, 'If there's outside catering for more than fifty people, never, under any circumstances, attend the event!'

Anna began manhandling the crates of fish into the kitchen.

'Where's the meat?' asked Fernando. 'The crates of meat, Anna, from our store in Malaga . . .'

Anna got back into the jeep, and the smell of fish was very strong as she headed down into Marbella, before taking the *autovia* home to Elviria. The jeep had been baking under the hot summer sun for over an hour, but she didn't worry unduly: the fish were fresh, they'd been encased in cubes of ice, so she knew they'd be fine. When Anna arrived at her house, she manhandled the crates into her freezers again, drove to the store in Malaga, collected all the crates of meat, and went back up to the catered wedding. It was after four in the morning when Anna got to bed, utterly exhausted. The next morning she had to go into Malaga early to collect a watch from her supplier for a friend, but she smelled fish even before she arrived at the jeep. When she opened the passenger door, liquor from the fish that must have sloshed out of the crates as she travelled at speed over the hills, spilled out onto the gravel: the stink was stomach-churningly pungent.

There was nothing for it but to strip the carpeting out of the jeep, and to scrub down the interior, which she and her boyfriend, James, did together. Anna was chuckling. 'People passing by in the street could smell the bad fish!' And she turned towards us, suddenly serious, 'Isn't it amazing how an action you take that that you fully intend will be a good one, like me getting the fish for Fernando, can revert in some way, and cause something unintended that is really distressing?'

When Anna collected us from Malaga airport a month later, there was still the lingering odour of fish in the cabin. It was roasting hot from the heat of the engine, and we had to shout above the din of the driving: we were surprised to realise by how much the carpeting in a car dampens down the noise. She and James scrubbed the carpets with washing powder day after day, laying them out on the lawn to dry. They soaked the material in huge industrial basins, they stamped on it as if they were pressing grapes, they went over it by hand with a scrubbing brush centimetre by centimetre, but they didn't manage to get rid of the smell entirely. It was fully six months after the mishap before the carpets went back into the jeep, and although the after-effect can still be detected, over time the odour of rotting fish which assaulted the senses has lessened in intensity.

Anna is a superb organiser. She's designed the look of the most elegant restaurants in the south of Spain, and nurtured the emerging talents of several of the top chefs there. The Madrid businessman, Vicente García, has brought her in to manage his Restaurante Alborán in Elviria, bombarding her with emails and telephone calls until she'd agreed to his entreaties. Despite the inevitable personality clashes, she worked with the existing staff from early morning until late at night every single day for the twelve weeks over the Christmas and New Year period, and turned the restaurant around. Carlos, the accountant, showed her that for the whole month of January last year, the restaurant had taken in very little, with few bookings:

this January under her stewardship, Alborán had on average thirty covers for lunch each day, and the place was fully booked for dinner at the weekends; this was in addition to the considerable savings she'd been making on food and drink through introducing the new bistro menus, and buying wine in bulk. For the first time ever, the Restaurante Alborán has been turning a small profit, and Vicente sounded really pleased. At the relaunch in December, he singled out Anna for unstinting praise: 'She's like a sister to me,' he declared, 'family on whom I can rely!' But for Anna, it came at a cost.

A woman sought her out that night, an American. 'Don't I know you from somewhere?'

Anna was perplexed.

'Have you ever been to the United States?' she asked.

'My husband Carl and I had a home in Palm Beach, Florida.'

'But we live in Palm Beach, on 23 Coronado.'

'We lived at number 27!'

'You're Anna Timmermann,' she said triumphantly. 'I could never forget that face: you're the image of Ingrid Bergman!' And she immediately rang her mother in Florida to tell her of the coincidence.

Vicente was impressed. When the accountant told him that Anna had paid money out of her own money to cover the launch, Vicente reached into his pocket, and handed across to her about five hundred euro in notes. 'I'm afraid that's all I've on me,' he said, apologetically. Unthinkingly, Anna carried the shortfall.

When Anna recounts her dramas, the language she uses seems to draw its energy from other happenings in her life, so that the references are non-specific and could be lifted up and placed elsewhere on the time-line, since they're applicable to more circumstances than the one she's describing. Anna speaks in parables, which give the emotional flavour of her inner life. What's thrown alongside the surface story cross-references the various complexities, and affords an insight into what Anna hasn't fully admitted to, and into her efforts at dealing with the difficulties in which she finds herself ensnared, and her increasingly desperate attempts to bring them to a successful outcome as they escape from her control. Although she rarely speaks about James now, the developing breakdown of that relationship permeates Anna's everyday life, and is a background accompaniment to her each waking thought. It's been affecting her mood, and at times Anna has appeared morose. After having recovered well from breast cancer, she's developed this serious problem with her heart. 'I'm under a lot of pressure,' she'd say thoughtfully, without expanding on what happens when she goes home to James in the early morning. Undoubtedly, he's very concerned for her, pointing out that nobody can continue working at the pace she sets for herself, seven days a week from eight in the morning until three the following morning, and that she's not getting any younger. But the recriminations she alludes to that recommence behind closed doors are oppressing Anna, and she's indicated that they're not helping her.

She made an incredible statement. 'I've seen the accounts, and Vicente pays everyone else on time at the end of the month, except me!'

We were horrified for her.

'I put off discussing a contract,' she explained, 'so I suppose I could walk away.'

'Anna, of course you can: your health has to be a priority.'

On Saturday night, a doctor had to be called to the restaurant when Anna's heart went out of control, and he gave her Valium. 'I felt so calm within twenty minutes,' she giggled.

'Did you go home to bed?'

'It was after three by the time the last customers left.'

Although Anna talked to Vicente several times a week, she felt unable to ask him for the money that she felt was owing to her, and she was unsure whether the fault was entirely hers. 'I'm very like Helen down in Tarifa, who knows how to make do with very little. And in her case I can understand the process involved in giving unstintingly to the other person without any expectation of a return, but I need the money, and not another proposition!'

'Good for you, Anna!'

Vicente had phoned her to say that he'd a proposal to put to her, and he sent her a ticket to come up to Madrid. But Anna was running out of cash. There was no electricity in her house at Elviria, because the electrical company put in four new poles to upgrade the private party-system that she and two other houses were on, and since the owners of the other two houses lived abroad, the company had presented Anna with the bill for nine thousand euro. She assured us that when her neighbours return, she'll get their share of what they owe, although she admitted that her track record in this regard wasn't the best. In the meantime, she didn't have that sort of money, so the company had turned off her electricity until the bill was paid. 'To tell you the truth, I'm not much bothered, because James has to go along to the internet cafe in Elviria to get his computer to work. More importantly,' she said, grinning, 'the machine that James uses to help his breathing when he sleeps runs on electricity, so he has to go up to Mijas to sleep in the home of his old friend, Richard. And the enforced separation is good.' She said, 'It's been suiting me!'

Anna said shamefacedly, 'Don't tell anyone about me not being paid on time!' She'd dressed up in the clothes she felt comfortable in: a fashionable three-quarter length grey cardigan tied at the waist that she'd bought in Clifden on a laughter-filled visit to Ireland, a pair of dark brown Bally shoes paired with a fawn cashmere coat, and the Bally postman's shoulder bag we'd brought her down to Malaga as a present. She'd taken the high-speed Ave to Madrid on Monday, her day off, to confront Vicente about the money she believed she was due. Anna was apprehensive about the meeting, but more anxious about not being paid. We'd schooled her in the gift that Roman jurisprudence had bequeathed to Iberia: *'pacta sunt servanda'*, contracts are meant to be honoured.

Vicente met her at Atocha station; he was double parked. 'How long is it since you've been to Madrid?' he asked.

'Five years,' said Anna. 'It's five years since I sold my apartment above the Hermès shop.'

'I'll show you some of the sights on the way,' he offered. And he took off in the car cutting across four lanes, and he was pulled over by the police. Anna was absolutely incredulous to hear Vicente give his domicile as Florida when they asked for his papers: seemingly, his car had Florida plates, and he'd never mentioned that connection to her before. After a curt conversation about Vicente's insurance, the police said they were going to impound his car. Vicente then reached under the dashboard and produced another set of papers. The police glanced at them, and in an unprecedented move for Spanish police that took Anna by surprise, they apologised to the both of them for causing them disturbance. 'Despite the freedoms following Franco's death, the old alliance in Spain between a few wealthy families, the Guardia Civil and the Church still seems to hold sway,' she concluded.

When they entered his office on the outskirts of Madrid, Vicente's mother was there. He was very affectionate with her, kissing her on both cheeks and holding both her hands, delighted to see her. Señora García greeted Anna warmly and let her know that Vicente had spoken well of her. She complemented Anna for not putting colour in her hair. And no, she wouldn't be joining them for lunch, but would be walking home in the bracing spring air, despite the offer of the chauffeur.

When Vicente was initially wooing Anna to come to work in Restaurante Alborán, he invited James and herself down for a meeting at the family's summer home, east of Malaga. As they arrived, he was standing out in the road waiting for them. Vicente is a handsome Spaniard in his early sixties, of commanding height, with curling black hair which straggles over the collar of his shirt. But Anna thought he looked like a little boy, dressed in threadbare clothes. The house was decorated in the seaside colours of blue and white, with impersonal furniture which Anna recognised as being in the style of the American designer Ralph Lauren: even the sun hats casually placed on the hangers in the lobby looked American. Vicente's wife, Alejandra, was introduced to them in the garden, where a large table had been laid for lunch. She was an attractive businesswoman in her fifties: 'I don't cook, you see, and I didn't know what to serve you. You know all about the glassware, Anna, and the way that a meal should be presented . . .' The maid served salmon, and Vicente opened a bottle of his favourite wine from the *bodega*, a very expensive red. It was at that point that Anna understood she wasn't in a subordinate position, but that Vicente was attempting to buy what couldn't be bought, despite his considerable riches. Anna had style, from the wavy locks of her greying hair, to the toes of her leather pumps. It was innate, a product of her background and education in Denmark, and her subsequent married life among the wealthy of Palm Beach.

'I want you to marry me,' Vicente had joked, as he filled her glass. It was a remark that she noted nevertheless, surrounded as it was with lightness and laugher.

Over a dinner in La Mairena, we'd discussed the psychology of what was happening to her. Vicente continuously talked in terms of millions, of the deal which was about to be signed with the banks whereby his cash flow problems would be solved. He spoke of his chateau outside Bordeaux which she was to visit, the hunting lodge and hotel in Doñana National Park which he owned with other investors, and which was available to her for a holiday. At various times he promised her a car, a free apartment in Elviria above the restaurant, and several other inducements. Over time, Anna came to realise there was a great deal about this high-powered businessman that he concealed from her, despite his apparent openness, which initially she found seductive. 'Always there's a repositioning manoeuvre, a further deal in the offing, but the upshot is that I'm not being paid properly for my work, which is what I want.'

'From what you're saying, Anna, it sounds as if he's gambling with your affections, grooming you, but always keeping you in a powerless position: the devoted woman, the good wife, the mother who never complains, essentially a family member who's not on the payroll. You're the long-suffering Madonna who's not to be paid like a whore.' Terry added, 'Maybe I'm being terribly unfair in this analysis of the situation, because I've only got one side of the story, what you've been telling me.'

'I like to give everything,' Anna admitted, 'and that has become a problem for me, on many levels: it's no longer working for me as it used to do.'

When Terry and I were invited to join Vicente and his wife for dinner in the restaurant, they proved to be an unusual and interesting couple, cultured and well-travelled, who'd met each other at the Woodstock Music Festival in 1969, when they were both enrolled at Harvard Business School. As well as raising several children, who are now working in Singapore and in London and New York, Alejandra runs the Ropa De Diseño chain of department stores all over Spain, selling clothes which she designs, and then has made up in China. She visits there four times a year, and her insights on the psychology of the Chinese were revealing. 'From the cradle, they're brought up to work: it seems to be their whole *raison d'être*, to the exclusion of everything else. In that, I can really feel sorry for them, and their unbalanced lives,' she said, and I wondered whether she was deliberately making reference to Anna: she had to be. 'In each factory there's an overseer, whose sole function is to make sure that the workers are not slacking.' And she held out her emptied glass of wine to her husband.

Vicente had been sent to boarding school in France by his industrialist father, who'd created the family fortune. He told me that one of his passions is books, particularly French literature, which I found to be surprising in a businessman. We discovered we both share a love of Albert Camus. I told him I did my Master's thesis on Camus at the Centre Européen Universitaire de Nancy, and he warmed to the subject. Vicente said, 'I have lectured my fellow businessmen on the absurd, which perplexed them, until I explained that dealing with the building bureaucracy here in Spain resembles Camus' take on the myth of Sisyphus. You roll the stone to the top of the mountain, and watch as it rolls back down, from whence you have to push it back again towards the summit. I went into the Town Hall, and personally confronted those who were holding up the planning permissions I needed. I'd discovered that person number four had lost the papers, so I handed the copies to him, watched him sign off on them, and physically brought them to person number five, and then on to person number six, seven and eight where I repeated the process. Ultimately, it was the only way to get the permissions cleared. More wine?'

I demurred, and so did Terry. 'Pity: it's very good,' and he filled his glass.

'Oh, I complained to the mayor, but he said the bureaucracy was immutable, everything apparently geared towards accomplishing nothing. I'm a realist,' he said, 'and you've got to do whatever it takes to survive. The only advantage in this business is that you get to push the stone up the hill.' And then he quoted Camus, and I joined in the quote: '"The struggle itself towards the heights is enough to fill a man's heart. One must imagine Sisyphus happy." That's my philosophy,' he offered.

'And mine. Which of those two sentences do you prefer?' I asked.

He ignored my question.

Anna, who'd sat down with us at the table, looked away, taking in the activity in the restaurant: 'Would you excuse me for a moment?'

Anna still felt unable to ask Vicente for money. 'How can I stop people ripping me off?' she questioned.

We were lounging on the sofas in La Mairena, about to watch a DVD. Terry looked over at me, and my heart hesitated. Anna is a good person, staunch and true. She'd never harm anyone, and I hated to think of people taking advantage of her good nature. 'Anna, Vicente somehow represents the past for you. It's my belief that if you were to revisit the divorce with your ex-husband, Carl, which is where all of these recent difficulties began, then the exploitation would stop.' Fifteen years ago, while divorcing her husband, Anna said she'd been told by his lawyers that his money was tied up in the family trust fund, so regrettably he wouldn't be able to make a proper settlement with her. Relations were so bad between them at the time that she was relieved to walk away with nothing, although the separation had left her devastated emotionally. For the longest time afterwards, she'd been unable to stop crying, and through a friend, she'd approached Terry, who was on holidays in Spain, to help her, which is how they met.

She raised her head: 'By revisiting the divorce, I'd be doing something about it . . .' she concluded, and her tone sounded hopeful.

I squeezed her arm.

'He told me that I came into the marriage with nothing – I was only seventeen – and that I was entitled to nothing. After twenty years of marriage to him!'

'So he bullied you!' declared Terry.

On the following morning, Anna was spooked to get a phone call out of the blue from Carl, who was crying on the phone. 'My house in Mijas has been robbed!' he sobbed.

'But that's terrible!'

'All of the furniture, the paintings that we had in storage in London, everything we bought together has been cleared out. Would you look into it for me?'

Anna was taken aback: she hadn't spoken to Carl since their divorce. 'Well, I don't know . . .' she said, playing for time to get her bearings.

'Anna, I'm tied up here in the United States, and you're the only one who can recognise this stuff: please, help me!'

'Very well, Carl, but I can't promise anything. I'd need to get into the house in Mijas, and I don't have a key.'

'Richard still has the key,' referring to the neighbour, who lived beside the house they once shared together. 'And I've offered a ten thousand euro reward for anyone who can help find our furniture!' Carl's manipulative use of the determiner *our* which he slipped into the conversation didn't go

unnoticed. Whether Carl was holding out the ten thousand as an induce-
ment, or whether the offer didn't apply to her because she'd once been
family, Anna knew that Carl would never share his wealth with her, if he
could help it. She noticed that his crying had stopped.

What Carl didn't know was that Anna's cleaner had asked her to get a
job for her son, Mario. Anna had recommended that the young man go
and talk to Carl, but to say nothing about her, otherwise Carl wouldn't
employ him. And Anna knew that Carl had been employing Mario for the
past few months as a caretaker: she hoped he hadn't had anything to do
with the robbery. When eventually Anna walked through the house she
hadn't set foot in since the day she'd packed up her car with her clothes on
hangers that she laid out on the back seat, although the place had no fur-
nishings, not many memories came flooding back. Carl had always wanted
to build an apartment over the swimming pool, and the new extension
onto what had been their home was what surprised her. Anna enquired of
the neighbours whether they'd seen anything suspicious. A woman told
her, 'There were four truckloads taking everything away, but the man said
that the furniture was being removed because of the woodworm . . .'

Anna confronted the cleaner about her son.

'We don't know where he is,' she admitted. 'We haven't been able to get
in touch with him.'

'Then I'm going to have to let you go.'

Anna questioned herself about why she was being faithful to Carl,
whom she considered had treated her so badly, and who'd ignored her
since they split up. Fidelity was a quality which has marked her life, not
always for the best. The obligations she feels towards people who need her
help, her committed loyalty to those whom she considers friends, the
necessities which flow from her practical sense of duty, these qualities
aren't always respected by those who benefit from her kindness. When she
was asked in the restaurant by a customer from Ireland, 'Are you the Anna
in Michael Murphy's book?' She bashfully conceded that she was. The

man then said to her, 'Such a pity he's gay.'

Anna was offended on my behalf by his remark, and her face flushed.

'My son is gay,' he justified, 'and I cannot accept his partner.'

'That doesn't sound very generous of you,' she replied honestly, refilling his wine glass, and the man had got up from the table and stalked out, leaving his friends to apologise for his boorish behaviour.

With James's help, Anna embarked on a tour of all the antique shops on the coast, from Malaga down to Estepona. They must have visited fifty, before looking in the window of a shop near Puerto Banus, Anna saw a sixteenth-century *bageño*, a type of small chest with many drawers in it, that she recognised. 'I posed as a spoiled bitch with money to burn, and talked to the woman, very cheap and her hair wasn't good, and told her the type of furniture I wanted for my new home. All the time I was looking at everything, and recognised piece after piece. But what I was really looking for was a walnut table, a solid piece of walnut in a light yellowish-brown colour, that was used as the marriage table for Philip and Isabella, but there was no sign of it. I asked her whether they had further shops, and she said yes, in Granada and Sevilla. So she came with us when we drove up to Granada in the pouring rain, hoping for a sale. We got on fine – she told us her husband was having an affair – and we found another shop which was full of Carl's paintings that I hadn't seen for years, because normally he kept them in London. We used to have to pay forty pounds a month for the storage: I still have the receipts.'

She saw my interest.

'I kept all the receipts for everything we bought together,' she explained.

'You really have to visit Roberto, the lawyer. He has told me he wants to see those divorce papers.'

'Anyway,' she deflected, 'I'd rung my friend, Antonio, in the Guardia Civil, and reported to him what had happened. He told me to be very careful because I could end up cut into little pieces. We didn't know who was behind the robbery: the Russian mafia, or the *gitanos*, or what criminal gang was involved. So he joined us up in Granada, and I said to the woman that he was my architect, and I identified many pieces that I pretended I wanted, but the walnut table wasn't there. I decided to ask for an antique table, very special, for a room that I had, and the woman told us she also had a house in Granada, and that there were many items there. So we ended up in the mansion of Luisa, the Duchess of something or other, a beautiful woman, who obviously knew nothing about any of this. There, in a back kitchen leaning up against a wall, was the top of the walnut table.' Anna's eyes were dancing with excitement. 'I was really worried that they were selling off the legs somewhere else. And there was a break-front cupboard there, English, from the early sixteenth century. I opened the door, and there were the hooks that I had put in. I asked the woman what she thought they were for, but she didn't know. So I suggested that maybe they were for cups.'

We looked at each other, astounded at her effrontery in having updated an antique!

'But I used it in the kitchen, Michael. Anyway, there was this garage, a big garage for about four cars, and I'm not exaggerating when I say that Carl's paintings nearly fell out the door on top of us when it was opened. I told the woman that I wanted some pieces, including the table top, and she asked me for forty thousand euro. I told her I didn't have that sort of money on me, but that I'd get her the money on the Tuesday, because Monday was a bank holiday. I borrowed three hundred from James, I didn't let the woman see, and I had two hundred in my bag, so I left a deposit with her of five hundred euro.'

'Your money, Anna.'

'Yes. And poor Antonio had to sit in his car outside the *palacio* of the duchess for the whole of the weekend in case they moved any of the furniture. And with his colleagues in Malaga, Granada and Sevilla, he organised for raids to take place on all of the woman's antique shops and on the mansion, to be done simultaneously on the Tuesday morning early.'

Anna's brown eyes were alive. 'You should have seen me!' she said. 'I was standing there in the rain on the Tuesday morning dressed in a yellow Guardia Civil overcoat, when the police vans pulled up at the mansion. I can tell you that all the *señoras* from the neighbourhood were out with their brooms sweeping the footpaths in the pouring rain!' Her laughter echoed around the apartment. 'The husband of the duchess was there, and he wanted to know what this was about. Antonio did the talking. The man said that he was into racehorses. A cousin of his ran the antique shops, and he promised us that he'd sort this out, and that Carl would get every piece of his furniture back. I was able to identify every piece, and the Guardia Civil photographed each one before loading it onto a lorry. Antonio knew all about the divorce from Carl, and he said I should take what I wanted, but all I took was a nineteenth-century Pontremoli rug which they didn't photograph. It's a beautiful piece, a part silk needlework rug, pale green, with birds and butterflies, signed JMP, London. And when I got it home and unrolled it, inside was my old Leica camera! It took the whole day up there. We'd spent about ten weeks altogether driving out every day!

'I rang Carl from the police station in Ojen to say that we'd found all of his furniture, and I suggested that he give two thousand euro from the reward money to the Guardia Civil because they'd been so conscientious in getting his furniture back, but he wouldn't hear of it, and he asked to speak with Antonio, so I passed him over the phone. Carl told him that I had been behind the robbery all along, and that he was going to sue me!'

I was shocked. 'Anna, that's not possible.'

'Yes!' she said, and her eyes were filling with tears. 'Antonio was furious. He knew the amount of work that had gone into getting the furniture back, and he swore at him and put down the receiver. But Carl has sued me! He contacted the police station in Malaga, and now I've a *denuncia* hanging over my head, and I don't know what to do about it.'

'What does that mean, Anna?' I asked her.

'It means there's a lien on everything: I can't get a loan in the bank, that's if you could get a loan in the bank in these days of austerity.'

We were talking about the Stefan Schmidt case to our solicitor, Roberto, in his office overlooking Church Square in Fuengirola, and he enquired after Anna. We told him about her heart complaint, which he was sorry to hear about, and we mentioned what Carl had accused her of.

'But that's a crime in Spain,' he said, 'to accuse someone in the wrong. Tell her to come in and see me. And get her to bring those divorce papers. I'll have a look at them, and see whether there are grounds for an appeal. Let's hit her former husband where it hurts!'

When eventually the electricity was turned on, and the empty fridges for the catering began to fill up once again, James didn't move back in, and Anna regained the girlish, gamine look that had been absent from her personality over the past few years, as though a shadow had been lifted. Her former boyfriend moved from Richard's house up to the apartment he'd bought with Linda in Alicante, and says he'll come down to collect the rest of his belongings by the end of the summer: at the moment he's occupied with visitors. Vicente drove down the road to the restaurant from his holiday home outside Malaga, and had a day-long business meeting with Anna, during which he again made no reference to what she says she's owed. Instead, he informed her about the enormous mortgage he has on Restaurante Alborán. While the restaurant is thriving, he showed her that they needed to increase business fourfold in order to cover the mortgage as well! 'Vicente complained about a bad smell in the restaurant, as if some food had gone off, really rank. It followed us everywhere, and I pretended not to notice.'

'Do you know that "rank" once meant its opposite?' I pointed out 'Ranc is Old French for straight or noble.'

'There's a bad odour around my dealings with Vicente,' Anna said emphatically.

Anna has received an appointment with a heart specialist in Madrid to see if they'll replace at least one of the valves in her heart. She doesn't know whether she'll continue to work in the restaurant. 'I might finish out the year. I realise that the mortgage on the restaurant isn't my problem. My health must come first.' She has yet to talk to Roberto, the lawyer, to revisit her divorce settlement with Carl. 'I don't have any time,' she told us over the phone. 'I had my hair cut at the restaurant with Bernard the other day,' she said, 'and I kept him waiting for over an hour. He sends his regards, by the way.'

A further year on, and Anna was still working at the restaurant, although she'd cut back on the mad hours she used to work. She's gained enormously in confidence and status from successfully running the business, and had made many important contacts. We attended the gala dinner as her special guests the night of her induction into the Marbella Lions, but still she insisted she wasn't being paid properly. 'I know Vicente doesn't have it.' was her excuse this time. Terry and I looked at each other, immediately hearing something else in her remark, but there was no point in labouring the point, because the hurt she was feeling was enormous. When Vicente texted a photograph of himself and two of his sons on a trip to Kiev to watch Spain play in the final of the World Cup, she was spittingly angry. 'That was my money he used. And some of the *proveedores* that provision the restaurant have to wait for several months to be paid, and they have families to support: they can't go to bloody Kiev!' Anna worried about them, and about how to keep the restaurant going on a shoestring.

When she rang Vicente in Madrid on his return, he told her that if the *proveedores* were causing trouble, to get rid of them. He said they were lucky to work with his family, which had very many enterprises, not just the restaurant, and if they didn't like the way he did business, then replacements could be found easily. 'No one is indispensible, Anna!' In the course of that conversation, he told her that he'd received money back from the revenue, and after she pleaded on behalf of the suppliers, he conceded to her that some of that money could go towards paying them, and settling the most outstanding bills. So Anna fully expected to get her own money when Vicente arrived down for another meeting with the accountant, Carlos, in the restaurant at Tuesday lunchtime, an appointment that he kept putting back from day to day, much to Anna's exasperation.

It was late Friday evening before Vicente strode into the restaurant with Alejandra, demanding a table out on the terrace, although all the tables had been fully booked. A table was organised. Towards the end of their meal, he called Anna over, and for the first time in their relationship he attacked her. 'I keep getting complaints in the office,' he said, 'that you're constantly demanding the use of a plumber or electrician.'

Alejandra was concentrating on her mint tea.

'Because you're not investing in a new fridge for the kitchen and it keeps breaking down. We need new fridges, Vicente.'

'All the money is going back into the restaurant,' he said evenly. 'Isn't everyone now being paid?'

'Except for me,' Anna stated. And looking down at him, she said, 'You owe me money!'

Alejandra appeared to be shocked, and she glanced around at the other diners in case they'd heard.

Vicente ignored what Anna had said. 'You're not managing the place properly; otherwise these constant breakdowns wouldn't be happening.'

Alejandra moved slightly in her chair, but it didn't appear she could leave the table out of loyalty to her husband.

Anna felt that Vicente was getting at her because of the difficulties being posed by her heart condition, of which he'd have been told, and she wondered whether he was now attempting to get rid of her. The anger boiled over suddenly. She raised her voice and became animated, even though the waiters could see and overhear the confrontation. 'You play the *grand seigneur* and treat people like commodities,' she said. 'I'm the one in the front line trying to do my best by the suppliers who are owed money. They bring their complaints to me, their loyalty is to me, but you're insulated up there in Madrid, and have no idea what's really going on. Or maybe you do, and that's where the underlying problem in this situation lies. Believe me, this is a thankless task, and it stresses me out. But I'm beginning to tell everyone here on the coast that you're not paying me what I'm owed.' And a flash of inspiration, she said, 'The staff think that the only reason I work here is because I like the adventure.' The word she used was '*aventura*' which can also mean 'an affair' in Spanish. Alejandra looked at her squarely for the first time.

Anna turned on her heel, walked up the steps into the restaurant and collected her bag from behind the bar. She was sobbing with the emotion of the encounter by the time she'd sat alone into her car, and locked the door on the cruelty of the outside world. She sat there unmoving for half an hour because her heart was beating so violently. 'I had a hole in my chest,' she later told Terry.

Anna was clear that what she'd done was wrong, because there was no truth in her intimation of an affair with Vicente, and in a fury, she'd deliberately fed a doubt about his loyalty.

'Alejandra came up to me in the restaurant the next day, and with the eyes of a deer ... yes?

'A doe?'

'Bambi! She said that she had no idea I was in dispute with Vicente, and in the same breath she told me that they share everything: they have no secrets from each other! Vicente just ignored me. And when I went up to him and said "I want my money," he waved me away with the back of his hand, and said "Later!"'

Over a breakfast in La Mairena, Anna shrugged, then ran her fingers through her damp hair, tousling and shaking out Bernard's new cut. 'He has no intention of paying me,' she stated gloomily, 'and Roberto, the lawyer, says it's my word against his.'

'In what way?' I asked.

'I just have an understanding, a verbal contract, if even that, because we never clearly discussed the terms of my employment. In a court of law, he has right on his side.' She poured some Greek yoghurt over her fresh fruit salad, then, gaining in spirit, she turned towards me again, and explained with a wicked grin, flashing a glimpse of the old Anna that we loved: 'Michael, in a man's world, sometimes a woman has to do wrong, in order to be right!'

Part Ten
Conor

Portraiture is a mysterious art that has always fascinated me, because in that recognition by a great artist I can hear some paintings speak. The calling voice is that of the sitter, so strong in communicating the person's truth, that time collapses and space loses its characteristics. Through tracing a line on canvas and drawing forth the image of a person's soul, I can intuit what a person is like from what the artist has brought out into the open. It's a divine talent which I don't possess, but in which I can share. The artist and I stand side by side listening to the voice of what the sitter wants to say, hearing at the same time what the sitter has tried to conceal, because the artist pulls back a veil so that emotional ambivalence is on display. My understanding of human nature is transformed, and it deepens at the sound.

In writing about a person, and using the pen to paint their portrait, courage is required. It's a disposition I have sought unceasingly, to follow through on what I've learned about them, and to reveal the truth while preserving discretion, a word which goes both ways: writing in such a way as to avoid the person social embarrassment or distress, while continuing to uphold my own freedom to make judgements, and to act as I see fit. As a Producer/Director in RTÉ, I developed the ability to look at the monitors in the television control room, and in a big close-up instantly see what a person is like, because a television camera paints with light. The image is like an X-ray: when the sound is turned down, I'm able to see the truth speak through the individual's eyes. It reverberates in harmony with the voice of my soul, supplying a commentary on what I see there, and directing with accuracy the calibration of the lens and the aim of my approach towards the protagonist, in the particular television programme I was making at the time. Despite any conscious intention on my part, the complexity of the truth when it emerged wasn't always agreeable.

Conor, the photographer, has steady blue eyes. He uses them to look through as he does the viewfinder of a camera. They swivel slowly in their sockets, sometimes aided by the tilt of his head, so that when he talks to you, he's sheltering behind them, coolly watching everyone on the other side, waiting in expectation. I can see him behave as a child would, scanning the room for a place of safety from the unpredictability of adults. And yet, he's looking for the unguarded moment when a sitter is open: *el momento de la verdad*, the moment of truth. When he was photographing Terry on the balcony of La Mairena, there was a moment when Terry forgot the intrusive camera setup. He'd turned to me to enquire happily, 'Well, Cook, how's the barbeque doing?' and then turned back to Conor.

Click, click, click: 'Yes!'

Conor tries to capture through his lenses this revelation of being, a point in time which affords him a glimpse through to eternity. His quest for that connection is importunate, like a demanding child, although his speech is soothing and gentle, hesitant almost, delivered in an emotionless monotone, as if the expression of personal emotion were too dangerous an act. In a rare burst of opinion making, he pronounced from the passenger seat of the car: 'We always bring our own prejudices to bear, be it middle-class, or liberal, or western.' Chuckling to himself, he admitted, 'I do have my own thoughts, like,' rolling heavenwards those clear blue eyes in mock horror. Ultimately Conor's demand is the simple one for love, which I could see that he paints with dancing, yellow sunlight into the photographs that he'd taken for me previously.

Conor had informed me of his plan for the new photographs in Dublin. 'I won't bring any lamps down,' shifting uncomfortably in his chair, then reflectively, 'just use the natural white light of Spain.' His simple apprehension was a lure, a decoy that deflected from his probing photographer's intelligence, for his artistic desire has many layers, and it's driven by hope. I was taken aback to find that his favourite time for photographing turned out to be late evening just before sunset, when the light levels are low. It's a soft, mellow time of magic and romance, when the stark contrasts generated by the blinding white light of Spain is obscured, and appears yellow. 'More like the filtered light in Ireland,' I muttered under my breath, apprehensive for our project of capturing in vibrant colour, the passionate arm gestures of the swirling, foot-stamping, extroverted soul of Spain. I'd in mind that Conor would emulate the treatment that the great cinematographer, Greg Toland, gave to the film *Citizen Kane* with Orson Welles: essentially, the harshly radical approach of the film noir. Conor chose to place me within a Spanish landscape at the end of the day, working in the briefest interval of time before the darkness takes over. Maybe he sensed that, as a writer, I was beginning a career too late, and this was his photographic commentary on autumn: he hoped to paint an elderly man with kinder light, perhaps?

Conor's method of working also knocked against my training as a producer/director, where once I'd called the shots, and the cameraman would challenge me for a direction: 'Well, Michael, what do you want?' I quickly realised that I was to have no input into what was happening about me in Spain, and through good manners, I felt compelled to acquiesce in this, and to trust him. When Conor was photographing Helen, I'd glance out through the window to find out how he was approaching her, alarmed to find that in one of the locations, he'd stood her up against a neutral wall, giving a photograph without a sense of place, although his scrutiny would concentrate on the sitter.

The band behind us in the stalls of La Maestranza struck up a carefree *paso-doble*, blasting out support across the sand for the twinkling *torero* performing a series of death defying passes with the bull in the arena. He shone with wavering light in the scalding afternoon heat, each successive move captured by Conor with an extended lens, click click click, before the bullfighter brought the sequence of *muleta* passes to an end with the classic *paso de pecho*. Standing still, the lonely figure waves the *muleta* as the enormous animal bears down on him yet again. Without flinching, his cloth arm and the widespread horns of the bull move across the torero's chest, click, click, click. At the last minute he sweeps the cape upwards and caresses with his cloth the whole length of the bucking bull as it passes under the *muleta*, click, click, click, and beyond. To an explosion of applause, the bullfighter continues the turn with his body, and walks away from the encounter with the puzzled bull, trailing his cape behind him across the yellow sand, raising a hand to greet the crowd, striding out of the simmering, swirling whiteness of the Spanish light, a hero who has overcome his brush with death at five in the afternoon.

I viewed a remarkable, fascinating Self-Portrait hanging in the Alte Pinakothek, the old picture gallery in Munich; arguably the greatest portrait in existence. It resembles the conventional representations that are normally reserved for Christ: the mid-shot full-frontal pose, the position of the right hand raised in blessing with the forefinger erect, even to the extent of the short lock of hair extending down from the centre of the forehead as in Byzantine images. It was painted on a wood panel in 1500, and was astonishing in its audaciousness, because this is a secular self-portrait by the greatest German renaissance artist, who has painted himself in the image of God. The Latin inscription to the left of his face reads, 'Thus, I Albrecht Dürer, painted myself in my true colours in my 28th year.' His fellow countrymen refer to him as 'The Prince of Artists'.

The painting is highly symmetrical, very close to the vertical axis, built up of pyramidal planes. Ringletted tresses spread out onto the tips of the shoulders and frame the mask-like face. A moustache and neat beard draw attention to the sensitive mouth. But the soul of the picture resides in the eyes. They're focussed ever so slightly to the left, which gives them an uncanny power. In the early 1900s, a woman found the connection they made with her so disturbing, that she scratched at them with her hat-pin, and the faint marks of her desecration remain. The eyes' uncompromising gaze proclaim that this artist is no mere artisan, who in Renaissance times might have painted himself as an anonymous face in the crowd, but a man who's so modern in his sensibility, steeped in the new intellectual currents of humanism, that he regards himself as being at the centre of the universe, and symbolically imbued with the authority of God's creative spirit. His portrait crashes forward into the twenty-first century like a prophecy.

This is the most important of Dürer's great trilogy of self portraits. The two preceding fashionable likenesses are painted in the technically more difficult three-quarter length pose, which was the convention at the time. The first, which now hangs in the Louvre, was painted in 1493 in Strasbourg, when the painter was twenty-one: it's entitled *Self-Portrait with Eryngium Flower*, and shows Dürer in his new role as a young husband. The second precursor, *Self-Portrait with Gloves*, is on display in Madrid's Prado. It was painted in 1498 after Dürer's travels in Italy, and shows him as a wealthy young gentleman of twenty-six. But the *Self-Portrait at Twenty-Eight Years Old, Wearing a Coat with Fur Collar* shatters the conventions and confronts the viewer directly, full on. The absence of any background shows the sitter outside of time and space, so that the primacy and universality of the artist's distinctive being is the only subject matter of this picture. The conflation of Anno Domini, the year of the Lord, with Albrecht Dürer in the 'A.D. 1500' inscription, written to the right of his face which seems to hang in the air, and by the positioning of the fingers of the right hand, which mimic those letters, re-emphasises the specificity of Albrecht Dürer's name. Through this advertising self-portrait, Dürer has succeeded in painting the impossible: the immanence of an eternal God, who has incarnated in the individual nature of this particular artist.

Conor's eyes caught mine briefly. 'I presume this second book will be brighter.'

His take on the book surprised me. I hadn't given any consideration to its temperament, to the mixing of qualities in proportion, because a book writes itself. The writing draws up the threads of life as it's lived now and spins it into a finished narrative, almost like the spoken accompaniment to a film. During the producer/director training course I underwent in RTÉ, I was shown how the visual content of a film is primary, carrying its explanation within itself, while the verbal accompaniment is incidental, and always in the service of clarifying the image. At the time, I'd never considered that this perspective could put a photographer and a writer onto a collision course. Yes, I was thinking, Conor is probably correct in his assumption: the new book will be a celebration of being above ground. As I continued to watch him, he switched his attention to the chilli con carne that Terry had prepared.

'This is very good, Terry.'

Bright means reflecting much light, or being pervaded by sunlight. I was aware that such an unqualified rejoicing would pose a difficulty for me. Grief, particularly from the cancer and its lingering aftermath of incontinence and erectile dysfunction, is like the purest soprano voice singing a plaintive melody, a Richard Straus lied for solo voice and piano, as a soundtrack to my life. I sometimes hear it defiantly piercing the solitary quality of the silence, in those inadvertent moments of absence when I feel no longer held in the gaze, and I begin to fade. Some psychotherapeutic clients get anxious when I bend to scribble a note on my pad: I notice they raise their voices unbeknownst, scrabbling for my undivided attention. The voice also sounds through those moments of relaxation that form the basis of living, which surface in Spain particularly, when the force of my concentration is loosened and time is forgotten, when the simple delights of the day seem to drive themselves, and the pagan pleasures of eating when hungry and sleeping when tired, punctuate the haze of the summer heat. They're wordless, playful moments of pure being that pass us by, then begin their circuit again, with the voice always humming softly in the background. My mother has been overtaken by that ease: she's lost her grasp on structure, whereas I can still accept the tightness of that discipline once again.

'It's going to be brighter, yes?'

'Yes!' I yielded to Conor's persistent ultimatum impatiently, trying to cover over my reluctance. The book will be cheerful, full of animation and promise; a comedy as opposed to the cancerous tragedy of *At Five in the Afternoon*. I was anxious, because the underlying emotional complexity, the negative as well as the positive, would have to be managed carefully, in order to give a surface impression of cheerful simplicity as a decoy.

The figurative meaning of a portrait is to picture in words, to describe or illustrate, literally to drag forth or bring to light the likeness of an individual through the use of prose. It refers especially to a verbal description of a person's character. The word portrait is a contraction of the Latin *provorsus*, straightforward, moving straight ahead, turned forward. 'Forward, forward with courage!' were the words that I offered to Helen when she'd completed her analysis. During those years when she faced down her shadow, Helen had divested herself of all the props that had sustained her in a previous life, choosing to act more and more in accordance with her true self. She'd become a pilgrim in Spain, facing into life as a *soltera*, a woman alone, in a language not her own, in an adopted country where she still feels a stranger. And 'Forward, forward with courage!' was the same phrase that I repeated to myself, a motto I adopted to help me to survive 'the with, through and the beyond' of my cancer. The practical method I chose of writing my memoir every day was a living out of that concept, leading to the assumption of my own history. The permanence of the written word was a portrait that held me above ground. Like the sudden shock of yellow from massed spring daffodils, the yearning of my spirit for the hope of another chance, for looking forward, for a future, incarnated in the words that I wrote at my computer. They burst into flowers of wishing and expectation, blooms that beckoned me forward from the half life of disease and into health, into joining once again with the legions of the living, nevertheless permanently marked by the scar of death on my body, and bearing in particular on the non-functioning organ of regeneration, which badgered my being with a fierce questioning about being a real man.

The fundamental fantasy of a psychoanalytic client has been to have my erect penis inside her. This erection, and she has specified it has to be mine, has acted as a guarantee of her world, a supplement of sanity, until such time as she can function on her own. Since the operation, she's berated me fiercely for my impotence, for literally letting her down. 'You're fucked!' she said. Once when I complained about the increasingly hurtful and deeply personal nature of her attacks, she questioned whether I was allowing her the right to say anything that occurred to her. Wasn't that what she was paying me for? She was right of course: I've a good-mannered sensitivity problem, which clothes the brutal horror of what cancer has done to me, and I apologised to her for letting that intrude into her analysis. The analysis requires me to have balls, to challenge her and to struggle with her in the transference, and to put my being on the line for her. Recently, she'd a dream that she was lying on the couch, and that I was seated behind her, which is the configuration in the consulting room. She said I leaned forward and put my forefinger into her back passage, and touched her G-spot. That was the dream. She found it very consoling, very sexual because she had an orgasm in the dream, and afterwards I noted that in subsequent sessions her complaints had diminished. She decided that I'd been doing 'anal-ysis' with her, and that my erect finger substitute had hit the spot. We were both relieved, and she continued to come.

I was speaking the dream to another, lying on a psychoanalytic couch, tip-toeing around the words, unpacking some, wary or forgetful of others, unravelling a particular thread of association, bemused by and unable to comprehend the warp of another. Such a method portrays the truth when it has just woken up, with a face full of creases. The folds and ridges in speech can hide the deepest emotion that gushes out to irrigate some long-neglected fields. The truth swells the bulbs that are hidden underground so that their stems can tunnel up and reach for the sun. 'I have . . .' it begins, the dialogue that seems to speak me, 'I have . . .' it continues, as I position myself in a world of words, translating the images into prose approximations and paint a picture for a silent listener, over my shoulder and out of sight, who has one ear attuned to what is not being said. The drama of the dream can be inconsequential, irrelevant, insulting, difficult to put into speech, but it's where I live and have my being. For the dream is my portrait, illustrating the combination of traits and qualities that's been put there by the engraver's tool. And the impossible piece occurs when eventually I can slip sideways and inhabit the poetry of the painting, and not feel confined within a frame: when the eyes can see off-centre and set my soul aflame.

At University College in Dublin, in the crowded, raked lecture-halls of Earlsfort Terrace, Professor Denis Donoghue had schooled me in the Cambridge school of literary criticism. 'My college was Magdalen,' he'd proclaim proudly, so that I believed my book should stand alone within that tradition being handed on, and be my ambassador. I'd made sure that all of the necessary information was given there in 'the words on the page'. I'd worked at and re-worked the text so that each word counted, and as far as I was concerned, within the covers was where the reward had to be sought. The first intimation I had that matters were arranging themselves otherwise, was a phone call I received from my publisher, Steve, down in Dingle. He requested that the photograph for the front cover be my portrait, open and smiling. The photograph that I'd suggested to him was a striking one of me with my back to camera in a bullfighter's pose, walking down a parched country lane within the evident, oppressive heat of late summer in Spain. After my account of the bleakest winter battling with prostate cancer, I felt that the image would lead the reader into the subject matter of the book, which was entitled At Five in the Afternoon, the time that the bullfighter's dance with death traditionally begins in the arena: *a las cinco de la tarde.*

By putting my face on the front cover, Steve seemed to be hoping that my fame would sell it. Always I'd known that I wasn't a celebrity. I'd never courted publicity in my career as a broadcaster, preferring to hide behind the inherent authority of the news bulletins, which don't have to be sold because the news sells itself; however, the publisher had set me on that politician's path of garnering votes to come top of the poll. After publication, FMcM Associates, Steve's publicity machine in London, had organised the book tour.

One Saturday afternoon in Cork, I stood dressed up in my finery in the middle of a shopping mall beside a table overflowing with copies of my book, in front of the small Eason's bookshop in Mahon Shopping Centre. Harassed shoppers walked up and down the wide mall passing me by, trailing kids and pushing trolleys and buggies, sometimes audibly asking, 'An' who's yer man?' I was unable to hawk my book by calling out in the street, and thrusting it into their faces: too effete for that. It was a humbling experience, and very awkward, because I felt that I was letting Steve down by not fulfilling my promise. The painful mortification I was feeling had tapped directly into my sense of inadequacy. I didn't believe the insight of the kindly Eason's manager, who joked that their put-down was delivered 'in typical Cork fashion!' in that they knew who I was really. I could see that I didn't matter to them, and neither did my book: they had more pressing concerns. Eventually I sold one copy to an elderly man from Wexford, out for the day with his son, who wanted a souvenir, any souvenir. He asked me who I was, flicking through the pages of my book like a gambler shuffling cards, and told me he'd never heard of me, never listens to the radio. Then, 'Is it a good read?'

'Yes,' I answered unhesitatingly, 'and it will surprise you.'

I'd seen a remarkable photographic exhibition entitled 'Untold', a piece of work about the women of the Troubles, hanging on the walls of a gallery in the former British military barracks in Glencree, outside of Dublin. The large, perceptive portraits were taken by a young photographer, Conor Ó Mearáin, for which he was awarded the Salisbury Bursary. I contacted him, and he agreed to come down to the south of Spain with Terry and me, to do a photo shoot for the first book. He'd taken the cover photograph that I'd suggested to Steve, one hot afternoon when we'd stopped the car on the road to Ronda. I was feeling very depressed, finding the recovery from prostate cancer too slow and intermittent. I was plagued by incontinence, which was as vile as the fishy pollution of Anna's jeep, a defilement disgusting to the senses and emotions. As I walked away from the camera crushing the dried golden grasses underfoot along a laneway lit by the slanting sun, yellow light which seemed to diffuse through different gradations of smoky blue mountains, hardly aware of Conor's instructions, 'A step to the right, forward, hold out your right arm, a little more...' my head hung low, and I was turned in on myself. I wanted to be gone, out from under the oppressive autocracy of the disease which had imprisoned me. I was blind to the harsh beauty of the tawny, Spanish countryside, until I looked at Conor's printed image. If you examine the photograph closely, you can see the outline of the heavy pad I was wearing at my behind; as I remember, it seethed and squelched with urine. Steve was of the opinion that the photograph would look well on the back cover of the book. Conor said we could do a version of the same photograph again for the second book, with me approaching the camera, walking uphill.

But the intervening three years had changed both of us. Conor wanted to take some photographs in a bullring, so in company with Anna we drove the thirty kilometres inland from the coast to the Real Maestranza de Caballeria de Ronda. The Ronda bullring is the first purpose-built space for fighting bulls in the world, and the birthplace of modern bull-fighting. It's a baroque structure, built in 1785, surrounded by an elegant two-storey sandstone arcade of Tuscan columns. We positioned ourselves on that upper tier, where Anna sat on the wooden bench holding a fan in the colours of the famous bullfighter, Manolete. As Conor checked and rechecked the light and found his focus, I heard Anna say, 'I could move my foot a little this way?'

Conor confidently replied from under his blanket, 'If I wanted you to move your foot, I'd ask you.'

My director's eye saw a shot that would be perfect for the new back cover. The highly carved baroque entrance to the bullring was lit by the evening sun. The light was reflecting off the polished stones of the ramp, which rose up in deep shadow towards the two wooden half doors that gave onto the bright yellow sand of the arena behind, blocked off on the far side by that wonderful pillared arcade with the shadowed arches. If I were to position myself in the sunlight before the entrance, having just left the arena and the brave performance of that dance with death behind me, then such a photograph would give the brighter message that I've survived my cancer, and that I'm emerging into the sunlight following that battle. For whatever reason, the sharp contrast between shadow and light, the difficulty of photographing in a public space with day-trippers around, and the expense of the photographic plate, Conor didn't give me the photograph that I wanted.

There was another evening when I stood in a field outside Ronda staring into the scalding sun as it sank lower in the sky, constantly repositioning, being shuffled into the lengthening shadow of a cork oak tree, as Conor got me to hold his lighting meter to my chin while he adjusted the lens, and tried the flash. 'Open your eyes while I check the focus.' And so it went on and on, for well over an hour, as the light levels continued to drop rapidly, and the glaring sun mercifully retreated behind a hill. As it grew dark, Conor eventually told me, 'I've been having trouble with my focus, and I can't figure out what's wrong.'

I was aghast. 'D'you mean to say you haven't taken any photographs at all?'

He was staring dismally at his camera. 'None, I'm afraid.'

My anger breached the code. 'Conor, it would have been easier if you said immediately what was wrong, instead of putting me through that pantomime.'

He looked around at me, and he held my gaze. The irony of my advice to him, expressing the truth which I hadn't put into practice, hung in the heated air between us.

'Oh, let's go down to Yanx and have a burger.'

During the meal, a gulf opened up for me, and I began to fall. 'I've had a hard life. I've had to work hard all my life. There was the sexual abuse as a child, I worked in the States during the summers to earn the fees to put myself through college. I'm working at two jobs to try and make ends meet: up at four o'clock in the morning: incredibly stressful on all sorts of levels, trying to sound cheerful. And then there was the cancer, abusive, horrible, and it's likely to come back in the future, and I don't know when ...' I'd said too much suddenly. I sounded unhinged, ugly, but it was fluent, boiling over and flowing. 'I hate it: I really hate it,' I said. It was as if somebody else were berating me with this: I was inhabiting my shadow personality, and while I was feeling desperately distressed, I didn't know the precise reference: what was it that I hated? The truth, was that it, or more properly, my seeming inability to express it? I felt like the over-tired child again, beyond it, inconsolable, unable to work out what was wrong, rebuked, sent to my room for bad behaviour, sitting alone in the *cúinne dána*, the bold corner, beaten and terrorised. Good manners reasserted themselves and prevailed, and while Terry, sitting opposite, caught my gaze, neither he nor Conor commented on my remarks. I finished my meal in silence. It was tasteless, but the repetitive movements with my knife and fork, the ice-cold beer, served to calm me. Afterwards, I bought Conor a big ice-cream for dessert, 'No, no, you have it,' and I paid for the meal. We'd begin again, tomorrow.

In January, the shadowy blue mountains in the south of Spain seem to float on wisps of greyish cloud. During the day, the sudden lash of rain showers brings down the tepid temperatures, until the sun shines out once more, raising the light levels and the warmth dramatically. On one such winter's day, Terry and I met Helen for lunch in the Ke Club at the Puerto Deportivo de Sotogrande, as the waiters continually swept the glittering raindrops housing the sunlight off the outside glass tables with plastic wipers, turning them into sheets of falling diamonds. We kissed her delightedly on both cheeks, embracing her slender warmth, and saw that she looked happy and healthy.

'You remember the last time we met in August, I was madly enthusiastic about raw food?' she said. 'Well, I went along to this Chinese doctor in Gibraltar, and he took my pulse and he asked me what was wrong.' Helen had suffered from cancer; she'd had a tumour removed from her brain. 'He said the raw food wasn't nourishing me, and that I was seriously depleted. He listed off several symptoms, and I had all of them: no energy, difficulties with my memory, no desire to take exercise or to meet people, no desire to do anything. I wasn't at my best through all of last year. It was a depression that I'd been struggling against for several months, and I hadn't realised why I was feeling so low. So I asked him "Will I be able to turn this around?" And he said, "If it's not too late!"'

'And, are you alright, Helen?'

'He's been giving me a course of herbs since September, alternative medicine, and I perked up almost immediately. I'm feeling really well today.' She looked glowing.

We'd brought down with us from Dublin as a Christmas present, the photographic portrait of Helen that Conor had taken in August last. I'd spied on the two of them hard at work in the heavy evening heat, amidst the lush gardens of the Punta Sur Hotel outside Tarifa, and kept out of their way, in order, as I told myself at the time, to permit the artist total freedom to interpret what he saw. With hindsight, this was an abdication of my responsibility to direct the shoot, a diminishing action which had the effect of distorting my relationships with Conor at the time, and also with Helen. It was a necessary fight I should have accepted in order to retain what cannot be given away, and I'd let myself down. I viewed the portrait when I saw it for the first time, as a representation of my failure. And I had reservations whether an intelligently perceptive soul like Helen would warm to it, so we'd left it in the boot of the car.

Towards the end of that enjoyable lunch in Sotogrande, when we'd relaxed and exchanged our news, and wrapped ourselves up once more in each other's lives, I went outside to retrieve her gift. At the table, Helen cautiously removed the black tissue-paper and looked at the picture, holding up the frame with both hands before her, like a mirror.

'Oh my goodness!' she exclaimed, surprised.

The photograph showed Helen dressed in white linen, in a medium-long-shot static pose, looking unsmilingly straight down the lens. Her pepper and salt shoulder-length hair was swept off her face, and her hands were held behind her back so that she was unprotected.

'What d'you think?'

She said immediately: 'Older women should be approached with a greater softness of touch: they need that kindness.' She was examining the woman that Conor had seen, and she crooked a finger under the kohl-outlined eyes, blotting out the lower part of the face. 'Look at the suffering in those eyes,' she said, incredulous, 'they're so sad.' And she shivered involuntarily. We'd prepared Helen by telling her that I didn't intend to use the portrait in my new book. Some of the other photographs that were taken paparazzi-style through the bustling streets of Tarifa earlier on that carefree August day were brimming with life and movement, and would suit the writing better.

'I see that you've folded your arms out of the way behind your back in that portrait!' I joked.

'Oh, my poor hands, gnarled from all the reflexology work: they're old beyond their years, and of course I hide them,' she protested. 'It's not a question of vanity. We've all been battered by life; you can see that in my face: it's a battered face,' she declared, and Helen turned the frame around so that it caught the light, which heightened the dappling effect on her skin from the trees in the Punta Sur Hotel garden. She went on, 'This photograph has taken away my privacy. I feel as if I'm standing there naked.'

'It's not how I see you, Helen,' I assured her truthfully, in an effort at mitigation, since for me Helen is a warm and beautiful woman with an exquisite face of unusual delicacy, graceful, stylish, constantly in motion.

'I'm relieved to hear that,' she said, laughing ironically, still closely examining the picture for what it revealed. I gave her a hug, feeling guilty about my part in its production.

Terry intervened from the other side of the table. 'Conor made his name by taking a series of photographs of the women of the troubles in the north of Ireland. They're studies of courageous women, who've been through a lot of suffering. Perhaps Conor has used the same technique on you? Maybe one day you'll be able to see your portrait as a work of art, hanging on the walls of a gallery as well. Conor is an extremely sensitive man.' And he added an amendment, 'He's more comfortable under the dark cloth, under the blanket, in the shadows.'

'I gathered that from the first time I met him,' Helen responded, sounding puzzled. After a thoughtful moment, she said, 'We all present a certain face to the world which covers over our inner privacy. And while we share that privacy with our friends and those we trust, we choose not to reveal our private nature in the public forum. We all behave in the knowledge that there's an incongruity between what is expected to be, and what actually is. It's a dissembling that we accept for the sake of good manners, a pact that smoothes the way for our interactions.'

'Impeccable manners is what I associate with you, and with Anna: it's an overriding characteristic. Conor has approached you forensically,' I suggested.

'Precisely! I've heard you say, Michael, that when you meet a client, you could reach in behind the wall they've constructed around themselves and pull out what they're concealing. But you don't do that violence, because they'd go into shock.'

'People go to the trouble of constructing that wall to help them to cope with life,' I contributed, 'so that it has to be dismantled brick by brick, even if the barrier is no longer working for them, and is keeping them imprisoned instead.'

Helen laid the picture down on the table, so that we all could see it. 'An older woman,' she explained, 'although presumably she's wiser from having lived longer, she doesn't have the resilience of youth to recover easily or quickly. She deserves a respect, where the beauty of youth can still be found, written within the aging process on her skin: all of that, both ends of the spectrum if you like, should be present without any exclusion. I appreciate that Conor is a young man, with all the ebullience of youth. Perhaps such an ethical approach is itself a measure of the aging process, and derives from the accumulation of life's wisdom. I think that Conor has achieved a remarkable portrait, of which he should be justly proud. He's a wonderful photographer to see what he saw . . . But where's the soft focus, for pity's sake?' she pleaded, suddenly striking a lighter note, and sending herself up to gales of laughter. I indicated to her with my fingers over the glass, the out-of-focus dappled foliage which surrounded the clarity of the figure in the photograph, and noticed for the first time that a splash of sunlight had highlighted the side of her neck.

Helen had arrived at a conclusion. 'Now that it's been done, you can use the photograph in the new book if you like,' she stated. 'I don't mind, Michael, because Conor has captured the truth.'

For the first time, I saw Conor's portrait in a new light. 'I agree with you, Helen: an older woman deserves respect. What a good, good word you've chosen, because as well as meaning to pay attention, respect derives from the Latin *specere*, to look. The *re* indicates a return to a previous condition, a looking back, so that the whole spectrum as you've described it, the whole range of a person's life can be observed written on the face. Conor has looked with his professional photographer's eye and revealed what he saw, maybe, as you've indicated, the depression you were experiencing at that time. I didn't pay sufficient attention to you on the day and preserve your discretion, which is my failure, and I apologise to you for that. I didn't fully realise the impact of my inadequacy until now: I should have protected you and overseen the shoot.' I placed my hand in the centre of the portrait so that it blotted out the figure. 'I suggest you take it home and place it on a table rather than on a wall so that you can get used to it,' I offered, 'and then hang it in your bedroom, or somewhere private. The photograph has been chosen by Conor as one of his best, and we must give due respect to that. And you've generously justified to me and Terry why it truly belongs to you, but to no one else. I'm happy that you're taking it home to Tarifa.'

Terry interrupted, 'Helen, would you trust yourself to that woman in the portrait; could you rely on her experience?'

'Of course!' was the unhesitating reply.

'Then I think you'll come to like it,' said Terry. 'It's a wonderful portrait of you, Helen, particularly since it has revealed something to you that you hadn't seen before.'

Terry understands the sacred nature of the soul's secrets, and the vulnerabilities of a brave woman who's living alone in a foreign country, which was mediated for him now through the commentary that Helen had provided.

'It's like Mum,' Helen said, folding the tissue paper around the frame, before slipping the picture down into the bag, 'when she wasn't well. And,' she added, 'wearing her cross face!' She glanced up at the two of us. 'Don't tell me I've said what I've just said about turning into my mother!' she rasped, and we roared with relieved laughter, the three of us bound together in our daily struggle to survive as best we can on our individual journeys, always courageously putting our best face forward. And Conor, as a brilliant artist who has fearlessly shown us that a portrait is like a palimpsest, increasing in interest as it matures, was lifted up into that lightness as well. Through his persistence, he had succeeded where I had failed.

Part Eleven

Helen

Helen lives alone in a little house near Bolonia beach in the south of Spain, a fishing outpost founded by the Romans two thousand years ago. It's surrounded by the outlines of ancient fields in the middle of the Spanish countryside, and very rural. Helen was emphatic. 'I feel more at home here than anywhere I've ever been in my life. They all know me in the local village, Fascinas, as the woman with the perfect hair!' and she made a square gesture with her hands, laughing. Helen's shoulder-length hair is a natural pepper and salt colour, because she has eschewed dyes since the surgeons in Dublin removed the cancerous tumour from her brain. 'I feel totally safe, even in the blackest of nights. Sometimes Moroccan migrants come ashore from across the strait, but they don't pose me any threat. I think that I've become hard,' she concluded, 'like the country people have had to do, because life can be unforgiving out in the *campo*. Although when the farmers separate off the calves from the cows, I can't bear to hear the looing sound of the mother's distress calls searching frantically for their young.' She shuddered.

Terry had warned Helen not to allow her loneliness turn her into a cat woman. 'If I hear you've been searching through the *basuras*, the rubbish bins, I'll take the first plane down,' he'd joked.

The week before the concert reading of *At Five in the Afternoon* in the National Concert Hall, Helen rang us in great distress to say that she wouldn't be able to attend, because her nearest neighbour, a tall, beautiful French woman, had that morning left her front door on the latch, and walked into the sea. The woman was a recluse, and she'd been minding over twenty cats. Helen felt obliged to house them out of respect for her dead friend; she felt unable to abandon them to their fate. Eventually, she paid for the bulk of the cats to be shipped to a cattery in Valencia. Helen had held onto four, the sleekest black ones with amber eyes. A friend who'd attended the concert, and who knows Helen, had queued up afterwards for me to sign a copy of the book. 'What did you make of the cats?' she asked, conspiratorially.

When next we met Helen, she told us that Chantal's suicide had affected her profoundly. The Frenchwoman was a single mother who'd been unable to find work in the south of Spain. She'd been estranged from her wealthy family in France, because they disapproved of her stoic decision to submit to destiny, and live out her life in the Spanish countryside. When her daughter had arrived to claim the body, she found that nothing worked in the house where her mother had lived: not the cooker, nor the shower, nothing. They concluded the landlord must have been trying to get rid of her, because she didn't have any money. Chantal's circumstances and death forced Helen to see clearly the straitened conditions in which she too was living, and the dangers that come from too much isolation. She had to confront within herself possibilities about how to cope with life's difficulties that she'd closed off, that she'd never normally entertain. While her training had equipped her to seek help and to talk over difficulties together, it was still further territory to be mapped and to be conquered by this brave explorer of the soul.

Eight years ago, Helen sold her house in Dublin, and had arrived in Andalusia for the first time. She said she felt like a pilgrim, a person undertaking a journey to a sacred place. She'd boarded a bus in Marbella, turning her back on the empty glitter of urban sophistication, and headed west into the windswept open spaces beyond Tarifa, where the wild olive trees bend double in the wind under the fierce force of the *levante*. She discovered a place where her soul could walk upright under the sun, with room to grow in harmony with the changing seasons: the meadows bursting with masses of colourful wildflowers in spring when the *señoras* wash down the walls of their houses with bleach, the incessant racket of the crickets when the roads clog with campervans during the heavy heat of summer, those cool autumns of soft winds when the countryside empties of the young surfing crowd and life is handed back to the locals, resuming the rhythms of its calm and steady pace, until the cold, driving rain of winter weeps into the houses, and blackens the walls again with mould. That seasonal cycle embraced Helen with its certainty, and she lived her life well. On those days when the *levante* isn't whipping up the sand into the air, Helen strides out with the rising sun past the ruined columns of a Roman basilica to an empty beach by the ocean, and goes for a cleansing swim in the waters of the Atlantic. The baptism renews her commitment to a life of tranquil simplicity in the south of Spain, which is a life of the mind, emptied of what is unimportant. Future terrors wash away with her regrets under the powerful stroke of the present, as she swims strongly in an ocean of pure being, and follows a pathway of sparkling light until she melds into the brilliance which is held openly within each day. 'People here treat you as you are,' she said. 'They don't know your baggage, which is immediately attractive. There's a freedom in being anonymous, in saying "*Me llamo Helen*," in naming yourself, and holding out your hand to another, devoid of expectations.'

That first night she'd booked a room in a hostel in the little town of Tarifa, the most southerly town on the Iberian Peninsula, and set out to explore the narrow, whitewashed streets and small squares, without noting the name of the hostel, or looking to see where it was situated. 'I thought, my God, what have I done? It was late November, cold and wet, and I felt bereft.'

We were climbing a narrow, winding street, and Helen popped her head around the *rejas*, the ornamental railings of a gateway, from where there was a strong smell of oil paint. 'Hello Henrie?'

A woman with clear hazel eyes, paint brush in hand, pulled them open. 'Come in Helen, come in. I want to thank you for your encouraging words yesterday. I'm really sorry, but I'd just collapsed under the daunting pressure of getting all these paintings ready for the exhibition in London. After you left I felt able to continue, and I worked all night at them. What do you think?'

The large paintings, which varied in size, were piled on tables and stacked behind each other on the tarpaulin-covered floor of the tiny room. As Henrie busied herself with rearranging them to make more space, a glut of abstracts bursting with washes of colour, pinks and turquoise and hazy white, flashed by before our eyes. They were obviously landscape inspired: the light and the Mediterranean and Atlantic air masses that converge in Tarifa over the turbulent gyre of sea were captured in the flood of feelings which the canvases called forth.

'They're beautiful portraits,' I told her. 'Your soul and the life you lead in Tarifa is on show here, Henrie: you're a good person.' She texted Helen later to thank her for inspiring her with much needed confidence, and that she appreciated the valuable support she received from those two visiting Irish friends.

Helen admitted she hadn't shown what I'd written about her in *At Five in the Afternoon* to her daughter.

'Why ever not?' asked Terry, surprised.

'Michael, with Tania's teaching job, and looking after Jeremy and the boys, and they've had five different sets of visitors, they lead such sociable lives, so different to mine,' she explained. 'My daughter is even more beautiful, but too thin. She rings me whenever she's driving alone in the car,' she continued, acknowledging with a glance her laconic use of language. 'And the grandchildren have their lives with their friends now in Sotogrande. They go on sleepovers, so I don't babysit as much as I used to.'

'You were a safe and imaginative counterbalance in their lives,' I recalled.

'Oh, the two boys are wonderful, tremendously competitive, total opposites. The older, Nicholas, is tall and rangy like their grandfather. Things come easy to him. He'll be a big hit with the ladies. All his shoes are lined up neatly in his wardrobe. While I can see that James, the younger one, equally bright, has to fight for his place in the sun. So I showed them their Chinese horoscopes. Nicholas is a rat, clever and successful, and I felt that James needed a little boost. So I showed him that he's a tiger, the most beautiful cat in the world, who's a naturally solitary creature, a superb survivor, but a bit messy where he lives. And he said, "Nan, Nan, that's me, that's me." And you could see him straighten up.' Helen sat upright, nodding in satisfaction: 'I call him "tiger" now!'

'If it wasn't for you,' Terry reminded her, 'they all wouldn't have come down to Spain. You're a trailblazer, Helen, always have been, and there are many people who owe you a debt of gratitude because of who you are.'

'I've pulled back, which I think is a good thing, because I was too available. There was a time I used to keep every weekend free in case I was needed, which is a problem of mine. Tania rang me last Friday morning to babysit that night, and I declined: I said I'd need more notice to arrange matters.'

She was referring to caring for her cats, and she sparkled. 'They always run to greet me when I come home from Gibraltar. They're so very affectionate,' she said. 'The big male, Beauty Boy I call him, hadn't come to say hello, and I went looking for him. He was under the bed with a trophy he didn't want to let go of: a big rat!'

We grimaced in disgust.

'Oh, that sort of thing doesn't faze me: it's country living,' she laughed. 'When first I married Simon, we packed up the Land Rover and travelled through Iraq and Pakistan. I was seventeen years old, yes that's right, married at sixteen! We arrived in Bangkok at the most important time in my life, when I was expecting my beloved Tania. From the back of the jeep, I saw a group of men around a campfire throw something into the flames. The little creature would run away; they'd catch it again and throw it back in. When they all fell asleep, I rescued what turned out to be the most beautiful cat, with big ears. It was badly singed, but I nursed it back to health. I really loved that cat: he was my companion when Simon was away working for the BBC. And after I had Tania in the hospital, I couldn't wait to bring her home to introduce her to my cat. When I arrived at the house with Tania cradled in my arms, Simon somehow released the guard dog, and it killed the cat before my eyes. It was a horrendous thing to happen.' Tears pricked her eyes at the memory, and she shuddered. 'I sank into the most frightful depression.'

On one day a week, Helen drives into Gibraltar, where she works in a holistic centre as a reflexologist. 'I give each client about one and a half hours of my time, because they all want to talk.'

'It's about time that you worked directly as a psychotherapist,' I told her.

Helen was shocked. 'Wouldn't you have to have pieces of paper to hang on your wall?' she protested.

'The work comes from the heart, Helen, and not from the head. You're doing it anyway, just as you've described. That's what your own personal analysis has equipped you for,' I told her. 'How long had you spent? Nine years was it? At the end of analysis you're constituted an analyst according to Jacques Lacan: it's a self-appointing vocation which your own analysis prepares you for. And,' I pointed out, 'nobody licensed Freud!'

She still appeared hesitant. Her sense of integrity appeared to be an obstacle in the way of grasping at this opportunity to make some extra money. Or maybe she found the psychotherapist label too stark, too onerous a responsibility, too draining of resources, despite her proven fearlessness.

'All students are required to work with clients. Terry and I would supervise you from Dublin over Skype, so give it some thought.'

Helen has to make do with very little, because the downturn in the economy has wiped out whatever investments she had. She has no health insurance, because she can no longer afford to pay the premiums. The only luxury she permits herself is her cleaner, who comes to her for two hours on a Tuesday morning. Pepa is one of an army of Spanish cleaners who vigorously chase the dust out of every miserly corner, upturning in the process any pieces of furniture that block their path. The drawback is that Pepa has the Spanish love affair with *lejia*, bleach. There are shelves filled with this dangerous chemical on open display in every Spanish supermarket. Pepa throws *lejia* about everywhere. 'Look,' said Helen, showing off her beige linen slacks, 'those white spots are bleach marks, and this was hanging up on a rail in the bedroom!'

During the eight years that Helen has spent in the south of Spain, she has gradually moved to inhabit the shadow side of that freedom from being judged, from being placed and labelled, that she once experienced as being attractive when first she landed. 'This countryside around Tarifa is very like Africa,' she said, and there was real affection in her voice. 'Some of my friends have had to leave everything behind in Rhodesia, or Kenya, everything they owned, farms that had been in their families for generations: we have that colonial background in common. We also share the divestiture of context; we can recognise that in each other,' she admitted. Helen, Terry and I were seated in thirties-style cream leather armchairs by the open French doors of the Punta Sur hotel near Helen's home on the Costa de la Luz, and the soft, warm westerly wind, the *poniente*, was blowing in off the raised blue ocean, carrying with it the scent of the honeysuckle twining about the balustrade. There was a very large map of Africa hanging on the wall behind the billiard table, and some blown-up photographs of life in the African bush, hunting scenes, were splashed with hot sunlight, which crossed the brown tiles in the evening shade of the lounge. A large dog, an elegant creature with a ridge of hair down its back, was boisterously playing with its young owner at the far end of the room, plashing up and down.

'It's a Rhodesian ridgeback,' said Helen. 'They're very powerful dogs, bred for taking down lion.' Helen grew up in Kenya, where her father was Chief Medical Officer. 'People wash up on the shores of southern Spain for an infinite variety of reasons. They're a motley crew made up of many nationalities,' she explained. 'Most people here, including the local country people among whom I live, can't tell who I am. They can't read my accent,' she said, sounding sadly pensive. Helen has impeccable manners, and she speaks beautifully in an Anglo-Irish accent. 'They see that I live in a tiny house out in the *campo*, and that defines me for them, whereas I'm much more than that.' We'd been speaking earlier about family holidays travelling around Europe in the fifties. Each summer, Helen's family used to take a ferry from Mombasa to Trieste through the Suez Canal, with their large Citroën Pallas, which her father bought in Paris. 'When I lock up for the night, and gather in my tiny family around me, you come to realise how very little you are in the universe,' she said.

The deadly truth she entrusted me with demanded no response, and we fell silent. The dog approached us sniffing the air, then turned back to its owner.

'I brought with me in my suitcase a box overflowing with photographs: there's one of me with my father at the Rift Valley, another of all of us with Mum and Dad standing rigidly to attention outside our home in Mombasa; Michael was wearing in Indian feathered headdress. I think I shall have them blown up at the local photo shop in Tarifa.'

The pilgrimage that Helen has undertaken is a spiritual one to do with her being. In travelling to the most southerly point of Europe, where she could see the North African coastline thirteen kilometres away across the Straits of Gibraltar, Helen has journeyed back to her roots. She has travelled deep within to rediscover a time when she played unconcernedly with the native children in heat of the African bush. It was a time of pure being in the moment, when the lofty adult concepts of the past and of the future spoke a different language, and were incapable of stooping down to join in the games and the laughter, brimming with life. Those moments of play, which she recaptures during her morning swim in the ocean, are derived from the body, and in particular, its continuity after the deadly interruption of the cancer which had caused her to hold her breath. Now that she's been given another chance, the daily miracle of her continuous participation in southern Spain's sunrise fills her with joy and with gratitude. In addition, the play of pure being has become for her a function of the aging process. 'All of my life I always had a man on the go,' she confessed, 'but now I have developed deep friendships with women. At my sixtieth birthday lunch hosted by my daughter Tania, there were ten women around the table, all of them interesting women with wonderful stories to tell, and hugely supportive. Life here is so on the edge that women are more open, and speak the heartfelt truth to each other. In summer, Tarifa is heaving with a young crowd who are concentrated on surfing during the day. Their enthusiasm is infectious and hugely admirable, and they party at night, but not so hard as to interrupt their sport. Women of my age are confined to the margins.' Helen looked at me, and her kohled eyes twinkled with humour. 'We inhabit the blank space surrounding the text of a page, Michael! So what we tell each other has added importance, like scribbled notations. It holds us in a collective of wisdom, binding us together, like a patchwork quilt. My German friend, Christa, married to an English alcoholic, had an affair four years ago with an evangelical minister from Denmark, who told her that he was going to end his marriage and come here to live with her. And after four years, she still hopes that he will. When I attempted to nudge her in the direction of reality, pointing out that it appeared the minister was more concerned with protecting his position, she told me that she needed to believe, in order just to continue. Her belief was a fantasy that sustained her, and I can understand that. Such pain and honesty is a gift. It's a usual exchange among the women here. I am truly blessed,' she said.

'Don't you get anxious, Helen, living on the edge like that?'

She reached out and patted my hand, quoting the Benedictine nun, Julian of Norwich, telling both of us: 'All shall be well, Michael, and all shall be well. And all manner of things shall be well!' I wanted to reassure her in return, but my words would have sounded glib after her reach for such poetic mysticism.

Helen chided, 'What could you possibly write about me? I lead such a little life.'

My rejoinder led to a lively discussion of Lorca's 'aesthetic of the diminutive', the sensual perception that all of life is contained in a small piece, held together as it is in the important detail of a dream, which is more often neglected, hidden on the periphery in the shadows, but which nevertheless confirms us in our humanity. Helen has the understanding that always there will be difficulties in life. Her belief in the resilience of human beings to face and overcome their challenges has led her to invite in strays, who've warmed themselves at her hearth for a time, before she's opened the door again on an uncertain world, and encouraged on their way those pilgrims who are passing through. They leave that little dwelling in the south of Spain enriched by Helen's bounty, more certain of their value, having grown bigger under the watchful quietness of her love.

Part Twelve
You Could Make an Olive
Dance

'You could make an olive dance!' Terry has great faith in my writing. The significance of the impossible image he painted is underlined by his suffering from polio, where even standing upright to walk a few steps poses a painful challenge. Terry lives daily with a malicious representation of the human body. In his particular case, the everyday reality for most people was altered subjectively in the mind of his creator, so that Terry has been forced to respond to life resourcefully and without complaint. He has an unshakable belief in the limitless, transforming power of the imagination, and an equally strong conviction borne of fate's arbitrary cruelty.

The image of a green olive dancing with all the emotional intensity and grace of a flamenco artist as it ripens towards black under the harsh Spanish sun, expresses the confrontational drama of living life on the edge by the Mediterranean Sea in the south of Spain. Yielding to those subtle, sprung rhythms within the day keeps attention directed effortlessly onto the here and now. One day succeeds another in tranquillity, freed from the strict disciplines of time and the anxieties of achievement. The human spirit flourishes in such an environment, meditating deeply with a part of the mind that otherwise never would be given voice.

This *llanto*, the deep song of Andalusian folk music, is like the warm wind that blows in late summer. It scours the land, whistling through the pines and the cork oaks by the Mediterranean basin, dancing especially around the beautiful broad and pendulous white-leaved *hojiblanca* olive trees, bowed down to the ground with their bumper crop. The song gathers up the perfumes of the parched grasses, the nuttiness of sweet almonds, and the fresh taste of exotic fruit. It tells of the various civilisations it has experienced, those of the Phoenicians, Romans, the Moors, and of the Christian and Jewish peoples who made this land their home. Enriched with such a broad heritage, it confronts the intense white light of day that hurts the eyes, with the starkness and the ambiguity of truth.

'You could make an olive dance.'

I can see through the window where I write at my desk, the light go on in the sky behind the blackened, gnarled branches of a cork oak, an imperceptible brightening at the eastern horizon. Soon it will be time to water the plants on the terrace. It is cool this morning, just 23 degrees, and there are clouds in the sky. A sheet of mist from the sea extends over the valley beneath the blue peaks of the mountains, creating nature's first mystery of the day. Later, a gentle interruption over my shoulder, 'Good morning! How did you sleep?'

The intimate abundance of those August days, the repetition of waking up to more of the same under the oppressive heat of southern Spain, soothes the spirit like some soft, intensely aromatic olive oil spreading over broken breakfast bread hot from the oven, glistening like the greenest liquid gold. *Aceite*, the Spanish word for oil, is a survival in everyday speech of the Arabic *al zait*, meaning juice from the olive. At the core of its sound (despite the brutal overthrow of successive administrations in Spain) the word retains the continuity of handing down from generation to generation the civilising custom of tending to the olive tree, and harvesting the fruit to extract its juice. *Aceite* represents the transformation that occurs when olives were ground between two large stone wheels turned by mules. This paste was then loaded onto circular mats stacked high on a press, which was squeezed by turning a large wooden screw, until the liquid dripped down on the outside of the stack and into a container. After a day, the oil floated to the surface because it was lighter than the vegetable water. It was then skimmed off and stored in cool, earthenware jars.

'You could make an olive dance.'

The sun was sinking down behind the sierras, painting the clouds pink against the blue of the sky. The Alhambra lay protected by sentries of the darkest green cypresses, stretched out along the side of the hill over fields of pumpkins and aubergines and vines, in silent repose now after throngs of people had clambered through its royal halls and patios during the fierce heat of the day. The jewel of Granada was surrounded by a pale yellow aura, yet the walls of the palace glowed red in the mellow sunlight, the silhouette of the turrets slowly fading to black as the sun disappeared and the stars came out in the soft velvet sky, to the clacking applause of the crickets and the hissing of the water sprinklers. A little to the north, in the open air auditorium which is surrounded by the gardens of the Generalife, the country estate of the Nasrid kings, the air was fragrant with the scent of the box hedges and the clumps of chive and lavender, as the brick walls released their heat, wafting the perfumes into the night air.

The dancers, a dozen of them dressed in black, turned and twisted as one, stamping out the flamenco rhythm with their high-heeled shoes. They bowed forward in an over-arm gesticulation, then arched their backs to a cascading windmill of arms, and held the arrogant pose on the slow rotation, clicking their fingers overhead with a most delicate movement of the wrist, tapping out the beat with their toes. A sharp turn of the head to the right, to the left, as they travelled sideways across the stage, drumming their heels and swirling around again to the intricate guitar music. Through the spasmodic frenzy of their gestures, raising and shaking their skirts in a furore, the men wielding a cape around their bodies like a matador, the dancers embodied the pent-up emotion, the desire in the raucous voice of the singer, that insinuating thread on which they were carried. As this fusion poured out relentlessly, continuously, filling up the thick night air so that we were drowning, the dancers ascended slowly towards the heavens trailing gasps of wonderment and awe, and at the sudden, unexpected surcease, frozen in death together, there was relief that the threat had passed us by, at least for now.

The dead spirit of the bullfighter dressed in black, and the poet who had loved him, clothed in an impeccable white suit, danced a *pasodoble*. The shock of seeing two men openly dance their love one for the other, and lament their loss through a tender embrace in front of Granada's conservative audience, was intensely moving. This city has been traditionally Catholic since the re-conquest, and the final overthrow of the Moorish civilisation. As the two men steadfastly continued to dance side by side alone on the huge stage, tears of admiration coursed down Terry's cheeks, and he squeezed my arm until it hurt. For the first time, the performance provoked isolated cries of '*bravo!*' from around the amphitheatre. The emotion it evoked was grief, deep sorrow for humanity's burden of vindictive hatred which was laid upon the shoulders of Federico Lorca, a son of Granada, and Spain's greatest modernist poet of the twentieth century. With three other intellectuals, he was lined up against an olive tree, still standing in Viznar outside of the city, and shot dead by the Escuadra Negra, the death squad of the Fascists, early in the Civil war. He was thirty-eight years old when his life was cut short. The four bodies were dumped together into an unmarked grave which has never been identified. At the termination of the ballet, some members of the audience had risen to their feet, and they gave to the liberal challenge of the choreography a sustained, standing ovation; others remained firmly seated, fanning themselves with their programmes. The lament over Spain's recent political history, and the implied criticism of the reactionary powers that be, had been heard.

Lorca's greatest poem, '*LLanto por Ignacio Sánchez Mejías*', an expression of sorrow on the death of his friend, Ignacio, was danced in a *metáfora flamenca* by the Ballet Flamenco de Andalusia. In the beginning, a voice had quoted the opening line '*A las cinco de la tarde . . .*' which I'd employed as the title of my first book, concerning my battle against prostate cancer, and the blackness which had threatened to engulf me. That struggle with death in the arena begins in Spain at five in the afternoon. As the *pas de deux* progressed, and the beautiful sequences continued to dance deep in my heart long after the performance has ceased, I was strengthened in the awareness that this socially engaged writer who was a committed defender of the dispossessed, a homosexual who was assassinated by the uncaring evil of a philistine's bullet, with two further bullets fired 'into his arse for being a queer' (as quoted by his biographer, Ian Gibson), had composed a poem which speaks to the world of how human beings should live and behave towards each other.

Afterwards, I pushed Terry in his wheelchair down towards the car park. We didn't talk, bobbing amidst the sea of Spanish voices. The fact that he was reliant on my holding him bound us together in a physical expression of our intimacy. I laid my hand on his shoulder, and he raised his hand and placed it quietly on top of mine. What we'd seen, and the experience we'd been through, was deeply personal to us as gay men, and it had made us proud.

'You could make an olive dance.'

Through the years, I've heard myself carried in Terry's voice as an animating presence. The reflection he upholds for me has some of the alienating qualities of a mirror, inverting what's seen. Nevertheless, his portrait is a loving one, often tinged with wry humour, which Terry has made into his life's work. He has created a well-defended area of freedom within which the two of us can flourish. His unshakable faith in my writing pushes me forward centre-stage, but the original expression 'You could make an olive dance' comes from him. I give him voice, which dances with all the colour and tone, the inflection and modulation that's required for the message to be received properly. The manifest emotion propelling 'You could make an olive dance' is love. The implicit meaning in Terry's impossible phrase is 'I love you!' By employing it, Terry crowns me with the highest honour of an olive wreath.

The archetypal evergreen tree of the Mediterranean region, the olive, with its fragrant white flowers in spring, and its autumnal fruits that are black when ripe, marks in its longevity the everyday transitions that occur in the cycle of life, when the ending reached is timely. Those recurring periods which naturally succeed each other so that events can grow towards a completion, is the fruit of continuous caring and of love, of tenderness over time, as in the golden gestures of husbandry. These repeated acts are ordinary, indeed diminutive, but they impart to life its vigorous juice. The harvest leaves all parties, and every living thing, transformed without limits.

'You could make an olive dance!'

Part Thirteen
Aengus

On the third floor of the new St Vincent's Private Hospital, I walked up to the nurses' station. 'Is it alright to visit Aengus?'

A wide, cherubic smile. 'Yes: he's expecting you, Michael . . .' and he glanced at his watch '. . . at three o'clock.'

It showed seven minutes to three on the clock high up on the wall behind the nurse, so I went back out into the foyer to wait by the lift. What I knew was that Aengus was the editor of the highest-circulating Sunday newspaper in Ireland, the *Sunday Independent*, and deadlines obviously had to be important to him. I took the opportunity to bathe my hands in the disinfectant gel which was available at the double doors outside the ward. He was suffering from lung cancer, and according to his wife, Anne, a traumatic incident had thrown him into a sudden and ferocious depression, which had caused his morale to plummet. Although Aengus hadn't read my book, he would have been aware through the interviews I gave on television and radio of my experience in coping with prostate cancer, and the loss of my brother to cancer. Those were the obvious reasons I was called to visit him. Anne's hope was that Aengus might open up to me, but I didn't know what to expect.

When I walked into the bleakly functional hospital room on the dot of three o'clock, I met a tall, well-built man with shoulder-length grey hair who was standing by his bed in a dressing gown. The blinds were down, blocking out the winter sunlight, but in the gloom I could see that Aengus was handsome, not particularly fierce-looking for a successful chief executive, about my own age, and he invited me to pull up another chair. 'How are you?' I asked.

'Arrah, just ok,' he said, weakly. 'I'm a bit down today. And how are you?'

'When I was going through the cancer I was down as well. Are you taking anything for it, Aengus?'

'Zispin, but it's a very low dose.'

'You can take up to forty-five milligrams, which is what I took, was glad to take. It's like a bandage: it keeps the two sides of the wound together while the healing is going on. So be sure that you take it, Aengus.'

Thus began a series of bi-weekly visits to a man that I came to admire for the even-tempered nature of his endurance, and the bravery with which I saw he underwent the vicissitudes of his illness. More than that, I found he had an emotionally intelligent, sensitive nature, which was beautiful to behold and very attractive to experience. I was comfortable in his courteous presence. He pressed the bell, and when a nurse appeared, he surprised me by asking, 'Please, would you bring a cup of tea for my guest?'

Early on during our getting-to-know-you discussion on that first day, Aengus laid down the ground-rules. 'People ask too many questions,' he said, smiling at me, 'don't you find that?' The smile lit up his face, and extended up into his eyes, which twinkled with devilment. I came to love that smile, which was ready, despite his suffering. He had a slight Kerry accent, which showed itself in the Gaelic underpinning of the way that he spoke English: 'nach dtuigeann tú é, or perhaps in the native Corca Dhuibhne dialect 'cad déarfá?' don't you find that?'

I was maybe too eager, a restless intrusion into the measured pace of his recovery. I soon understood not to ask him anything about himself unless he volunteered the information. I was also reticent about contributing anything into the conversation which would divert him in any way from what he wanted to say. I reined myself in to accept the inevitable silences without showing any impatience or anxiety, because my psychoanalytic training would have impelled me to interrupt the reverie of one of my clients, inviting them to clothe what was going on for them in words. These visits with Aengus had a different tenor: they were being framed differently for a start. Aengus was to be my guide on a journey whose destination was withheld from me: the travelling was all. I was also entering as a guest into his domain, and accepting the good manners of that designation. Aengus gathered his resources before releasing what he decided to say, which took effort because of the pressure on his breathing. He had the security of an oxygen mask at his nose. At times, I felt that he was teaching me.

'What broadcaster do you most admire?' he asked me once.

'Gay Byrne,' I said.

'I was watching the Queen's visit. Wasn't it wonderful? At one stage in Dublin Castle, President Mary MacAleese becomes over excited, and I saw Gay Byrne intervene and talk to the Queen, and deftly steer her around out of the way. It was extraordinary to watch. He has that skill he used on air: it's a simplicity which conceals art.' He looked across at me from the bed, 'People think anyone can read the news, and they can't.'

'It requires grace under pressure, which is Hemingway's phrase,' I added.

He repeated the phrase, 'Grace under pressure: I like that,' he said, chuckling to himself. At the time, I hadn't realised the devastating truth with which Aengus was grappling.

Oftentimes we sat in silence, and he would close his eyes briefly, until he wanted to say something again. Those silences were powerful. They had the effect of blocking out the hospital bustle so that the two of us existed inside a companionable bubble, each of us concentrated on the other so that the words when they arrived could splash over us and have their full, drenching import. I'd focus on his mouth, and remain still until he spoke, which he did with increasing frequency as he began to trust me, and as I began to trust myself. Those encounters were intense. The intimate setting of Aengus's bedroom allowed for a divesting of the worldly masks in which we clothe our real selves. When he became agitated, and began to ask where his sons had gone to, I knew that he was tiring, and that it was time to make a move to go. 'I could come back and visit on Thursday next if you'd like, Aengus?'

'I would like that.'

'I'll see you on Thursday, so.' And I'd grasp his hand, swollen with drugs, outstretched from above the bedclothes, and walk gently from the room.

He was keen to take exercise, to get air into his lungs: 'Crown says it's a good thing.' I guessed that this must be part of Dr John Crown's narrative of hope, allowing Aengus to get through his days while keeping up his morale. So we'd walk slowly and with great effort on his part from the hospital room up to the Family Room, where he'd reach for a chair to sit down gratefully, and hold out his shaking hands for a plastic beaker of water. Often there'd be visitors inside, talking or watching television. We'd sit there in that attuned silence we'd brought with us while he recovered his strength, and the rapid gulping of his heavy breathing became quieter, and eased. When he signalled he was ready, we'd walk back deliberately, he leaning on the walking aid, pushing it ahead of him and trying to steer it impatiently around the nurse's trolleys in the corridor. Those walks were conducted in semi-silence, because Aengus didn't have the breath to talk and to walk at the same time. Occasionally I'd encourage him with a 'Well done, Aengus: you're doing really well,' because the undertaking he'd chosen was enormous, at the outermost limit of his reserves. He quoted back to me Santiago in Hemingway's *The Old Man and the Sea*: 'I went out too far.' But he'd insist on completing five rounds, ten walks. 'I'll try again,' he'd say, counting off each of them until he'd achieved his target. It was while we were resting in the safety of his hospital room during the turnaround that Aengus would venture some personal comments, which were pithy, going directly to the heart of the matter. Oftentimes he bounced his remarks off my experience of surviving cancer.

'I get very anxious: feel I can't breathe,' he said, looking up at me searchingly.

'Like a panic attack,' I offered.

'Yes, that's it. I get into a panic. Do you have that?'

'I did, Aengus, when I was undergoing the illness.'

'It's like drowning,' he said. 'I felt something in my chest was broken,' and his eyes were wild with the fright of remembrance.

'It's a terrible feeling when it's there, but it does pass, Aengus.' And from his face I'd read whether I should continue on and venture a possible solution for dealing with his terror, or whether validating his experience was enough, which made us brothers in arms, caught up in a gallant fight to the death against that unscrupulous foe, cancer. More often, the acknowledgement that what he was feeling was appropriate, seemed to be sufficient to help him cope with what was so alien to the previous life he'd led as a healthy man, up to just six months ago. His experience since then was so profoundly shocking, and driven on with such celerity, that he didn't have time to catch up with the assault from the disease, nor have the personal space to recoil from the savage wilderness of the medics where immediately it had taken him.

It was the October Bank Holiday Monday, and the ward was relatively quiet. Aengus had been admitted for side effects from the 'wonder drug' he was on. A scan had been done, of which he hadn't yet had results. October had been a happy month, the only really happy month since Aengus was diagnosed in April. He'd managed to go to work, to have meals out, and to play his tin whistle. He told Anne, 'I want to die at my post!' Aengus and Anne were happy on that afternoon sitting in the Family Room, waiting for a doctor to give some steer about the symptoms he was suffering. An oncologist, not on Aengus's immediate team, arrived with the oncology nurse in charge that day. And without ado, pronounced, 'I've seen your scans, and the disease is progressing!' Their world fell apart as the doctor moved on, leaving behind that primed bomb. From being a free man, overnight Aengus was held captive, with his life delivered into the hands of another, who treated him as the object of their specialty, an additional cruelty of which he was made painfully aware. The change was bewildering. Cancer had unmanned him. Aengus held himself with great dignity, but he was in deep shock. Anne responded by asking if she could stay the night with him, and the staff was wonderful about that. She slept beside Aengus in the hospital almost every night from then on, until he came home for Christmas.

'It's a catastrophe!' As a journalist at the top of his profession, Aengus chose his words advisedly. His short utterance in my presence was making known that the incomprehensible misfortune of being diagnosed with lung cancer, a disease which was progressing, was a tragedy whose dénouement ended in disaster. 'Crown is hoping to shrink the tumour with the chemo,' he explained, but his tone sounded unconvinced. 'I think I'd be better off out of it altogether, if I don't improve. This is no life. I sleep alright with the drugs, but it's not a restful sleep. I can't read anymore. I just sit here, waiting.' He'd been staring straight ahead, his head on the pillow. 'It's like an out-of-body experience,' he said, incredulously. 'I'm looking on, and I don't know what day is which. Did you find that?'

'Yes, Aengus.'

'Sure, what's the point in that?'

I was listening intently to what he had to say, and there was consent in my silence. On another occasion, I named it emotionally for him: 'You have great suffering, Aengus,' which seemed to take him by surprise. He said nothing in response, perhaps unwilling as a man not to downplay it, but he pondered what I was saying. Some days later, I overheard him admit to Lucy, who was busy affixing tabs to his chest in order to take a cardiograph, 'I'm very sick, you know.' I questioned whether I was one of the only people around Aengus who gave him the freedom to think about giving up the fight, since everyone's effort was aimed at getting him better. All the members of his team had managed, without lying, to keep up his morale. I felt his subversive thoughts to be more in tune with the rebellious demands of his spirit, a truth he was silently concealing out of respect for the resolute efforts of the medical team, and of his loved ones. I saw the evident love and protection with which all three of his adult sons, Dion, Evan and Stephen, surrounded their father. At various times, I witnessed each of them solidly by his side, publicly holding his hand. How could their father willingly break those links, and abandon them?

What I didn't know at the time, what Aengus didn't tell me immediately, was that his joy in life had been robbed from him, and his hope, so important for recovery from cancer, had been stolen by that callous, throwaway remark '. . . the disease is progressing', which hadn't sought to match where the patient was at. Aengus had never suffered from denial. As a newspaperman he could accept the horror of reality, and at times he chose to escape from it as well. But now, there was to be no escape from so profound a loss of hope, which attacked at the roots his soaring, human spirit.

'I'm trying to live with what I've got,' was what Aengus had said. I came to value his remarks for their wisdom, and his open acceptance of the human nature which they displayed. He quoted Kant: "The crooked timber of humanity can never be made straight." I think Marx and the Church both got it wrong on the perfectibility of the human being: it can't be done,' was another of his conclusions. Aengus was processing a lifetime of experience, the good and the bad, which he embraced even-handedly. I realised that I was in a very privileged position to have such access to him. The narrative we constructed over several visits had the feel of one long, extended metaphor. Aengus described it to me as 'a meditation'. Our conversation was picked up where it had left off, coloured only by the mood of the particular afternoon. It was a type of poem, where the chosen words resonated widely through many layers of experience, so that the truth in all of its fullness was built up stroke by delicate stroke, a portrait presented with warmth and great gentleness. Veritas stood framed in the window, looking out shyly from behind a lace curtain of words, which she was in the process of pulling aside, and she was wonderfully beautiful.

Aengus ranged widely over the present and his past, shining a beam with exquisite felicity on what he chose to show me. When he talked about his meetings with the British actor Oliver Reed, he described him as being 'an aristocrat, who constructed his bad boy persona purely for the media. He was a most sensitive man.' On another occasion, Aengus said 'I don't believe those various accounts you hear in Dublin about drinking sessions in Paris with Samuel Beckett. He was dedicated to his writing. Beckett was an intensely private man, a recluse.' Tenderly over time, Aengus was taking me into his confidence, and telling me about himself through the anecdotes and the stories that he told about other people. 'What is your next book about, Michael?'

'I've written about those who appeared in my first book, and brought their stories up to date.'

'I have many stories, but they're peripheral to the main events. I was never able to write a book myself, although I tried.' He thought for a moment, and then stated, 'You can write about this, if you like,' and he smiled at me, affectionately. At the time, I didn't know what he was asking me, and I didn't want to probe. We'd been discussing Joyce earlier, 'A very selfish, unsympathetic man, although his short story, 'The Dead', is a masterpiece,' and it crossed my mind that Aengus had in mind for me a secretarial role along the lines that Beckett had played for Joyce, and that he was giving me permission to write his biography. It was a formulation of the truth, that our important work was always ancillary to the resolute, loving endurance with which Anne carried him every day. Hers was the conversation which would continue on. Aengus told me that his wife was exceptionally in London, for the first overnight she'd spent away from his side. The visit was for a theatre opening: her daughter Nancy had a new play on in the Bush. 'Do you know Anne?' he asked.

'We've spoken on the phone,' I admitted.

'She's a wonderful woman!'

Aengus had met many well-known figures in the course of his long, twenty-eight-year career at the helm. 'Being editor must have been a very pressurising job?'

'It was at times, particularly in the early days, from governments, and from individuals. Hector Legge was editor for thirty-one years. He sent me a note when I was appointed that I wouldn't beat his record.' Aengus became thoughtful for a moment. He looked over at me from the bed and sought my eyes. 'I'm going to say something now that I've never said before, to anyone, least of all to myself. I don't think that I'll ever be editor again.'

I was seated in the armchair by his bed, with my two hands resting down over the armrests. I didn't move, fully concentrated on being calm in order to hear what he had to say.

He continued, 'It's very peaceful, don't you think?' For a cancer ward in a busy hospital, suddenly there was no noise at all. We savoured the peace, as the reverberating impact of the conclusion Aengus had reached affected both of us profoundly, and changed the solemn atmosphere in the room so that it became noticeably lighter. At that moment, the evening sun came out from behind the barrier of the clouds and streamed into the room. Aengus was letting go, and accepting the possibility of his retirement. 'D'you know 'London Snow' by Robert Bridges? He also had lung disease.' And he began to recite:

> When men were all asleep the snow came flying,
> In large white flakes falling on the city brown . . .
> Deadening, muffling, stifling its murmurs falling;
> Lazily and incessantly floating down and down . . .

He paused. 'Isn't that a wonderful adjective "brown" that Bridges employs, not black or grey, but brown.' He was silent again. 'I think we understand each other, Michael.' And he smiled at me, crinkling up his eyes, secure that like the gallant knights of old, we'd forged a faithfulness to the truth in the sacred stillness of Aengus's room, which would see us through to better days. 'This lunchtime, I had a golden sleep,' he said, 'it was recuperative.'

The following morning at the psychoanalytic practice during a break between clients, Terry called me urgently, flinging open the door of his consulting room, and he approached me holding up his iPhone on loud-speaker mode. 'Listen!' he commanded. It was Anne's voice from London airport. 'Aengus died an hour ago. He had his shower early, and he was sitting out on his chair when he suddenly leaned forward. They got him back onto the bed, and when Dr Crown asked him, "Are you alright, Aengus?" He said he was, and he just died.'

I wept, overwhelmed that Aengus was no longer alive, that he was now at one with the sudden silence. He'd been so at peace yesterday afternoon that we'd talked for over an hour and twenty minutes: it was completely absorbing. And I was to see him again on Thursday. I'd left the whole afternoon free for him, I'd even put it into my diary. Now it was over.

'I'm sorry, Michael,' said Terry.

'I found it very difficult,' I sobbed. 'On the way into the hospital, I'd play Bach in the car to calm myself down, and put my mind in order. I'd sit listening to the music in the car in the underground car park until it was time to take the lift to the third floor, and the oncology ward. I never knew what to expect when I'd knock on the door, how he'd be, who'd be there, whether he'd remembered. On one afternoon recently, Aengus was asleep, and when he was woken up by his youngest son, Stephen, to "Michael is here," I overheard him say from outside the door "I was expecting him on Thursday?" "But today is Thursday," was the reply. And I walked in, and he apologised to me several times for sleeping. Dreadful, dreadful. I felt I was imposing. Did he feel he had to see me? The indignity of bloody can-cer! His son, Dion, said to me yesterday in the corridor that it's so unfair, and all I could do was repeat what he said, so unfair. It was like visiting my brother Kie in hospital, when he was dying: it brought it all back. I found the emotional demands very troubling. What must it have been like for Aengus? He was such a courageous man, he never complained: he even died like a gentleman . . . I said "I'll see you again on Thursday," and he said, "I don't know whether I'll be here, or at home." And I gave him my word, "Don't you worry, I'll find you Aengus, wherever you are." I am so, so sorry that he's dead, really sorry, about all of it.'

And Aengus said:

> For now the doors are open, and war is waged with snow;
> And trains of sombre men, past tale of number,
> Tread long brown paths, as toward their toil they go;
> But even for them awhile no cares encumber
> Their minds diverted; the daily word is unspoken,
> The daily thoughts of labour and sorrow slumber
> At the sight of beauty that greets them . . .

Part Fourteen

A Poem for Terry

'Not a wedding!' corrected Terry.

I offered as a riposte: 'You are cordially invited to "not a wedding."'

'I'd thought I'd go along to a hatch, and sign,' he said, referring to our civil partnership looming up in June: yet another solution to an Irish problem, this time how not to call a gay union a wedding. We'd queued on the path in the spring downpour outside Teddy's in Dun Laoghaire for an ice-cream, and when Terry arrived at the window, he asked the girl, 'Could I have a Civil Partnership, please?' As she looked nonplussed, to smothered laughter we settled for two 99s.

Wedding is an old word, over a thousand years old. It means to pledge or to covenant: it's an engagement to do something, which has within its utterance the idea of a solemn agreement, a promise or a guarantee. Perhaps it does fit the vows criteria of a civil partnership ceremony after all. We'd made an appointment with the registrar to give notification of our intention three months in advance. She was a warm woman, who gently took us through the form filling with a minimum of fuss. One of the impediments to a civil partnership turned out to be heterosexuality, an unexpected and contradictory outcome which we found delightfully ironic, and we chuckled over it. The registrar informed us that we were the 217th couple to apply for a civil partnership in Ireland, and we left her office hoping that she'd be the one to perform the ceremony on the most suitable of the two available days which were offered to us, Tuesday, 14 June 2011. The choice was dictated by the holiday plans of our witnesses, our friends Barbara and Tiernan, who had planned their holidays for later that month.

In the kitchen, around their generous dinner table, we'd been listening to them with an increasing sense of disjunction, as they fondly recalled their wedding day in Slane Castle, at a time when Dundalk girls held their receptions in the Ballymascanlon Hotel. It sounded to have been a very elaborate affair attended by many business associates of Barbara's father. We weren't able to relate to it, possibly because we don't go to weddings. They got married in 1986, the year after Terry and I had met at the Rutland Centre, where I was making a television documentary about an addiction treatment centre for RTÉ. Properly, Barbara pointed out: 'At your stage in life—'

'Old!' I interrupted drily.

'—you don't have to do it that way. I think the weddings we've most enjoyed over the years have been those where the couple were obviously mad about each other, and the people who were there really wished them well.' She was slicing up a banoffee pie that she'd taken out of the fridge. 'Warm,' she concluded briskly, 'that's what it was, we went away with the warmth that we'd received that day.' Honey, the Labrador lying stretched out on the tiles under the table, farted viciously. 'Out!' yelled Tiernan, scraping back the chair and thrusting open the patio door, 'Out: bold dog!'

Our headlamps swept over Barbara and Tiernan waving at the gate, I beeped the horn and saluted, heading for home, subdued within the silent swishing of the car. Terry and I have lived together for twenty-six years. We know every step of the road, every elaboration of the saga that we've constructed in each other's company. Our assessment comes from the perspective of that experience. 'I want a quiet affair,' I murmured, glancing over at Terry.

He squeezed my arm. 'You need to be more robust,' he said. 'He was annoyed that you wanted the spare iPhone, which to be fair I'd promised to him.' Then, 'Will you ever use that phone?'

I didn't reply.

'We're not getting married,' Terry stated, 'and we don't have to use the heterosexual model of a reception. And anyway, I'm a socialist.'

I looked across at him.

'Keep your eyes on the road!'

'So you won't be wearing a dickey-bow, then?'

Terry carries off a bow tie very well.

A client of mine said she'd a ticket to go and hear the Dalai Lama. 'D'you mind me asking,' she said, 'what d'you believe in?'

'I believe in the goodness of human beings.' The answer surprised me, but since it was given within the open dynamic of a psychoanalytic session, I valued the statement as the truth. We'd been watching a BBC *Panorama* programme about Iran on television last night, a theocracy where gang rape is used as an instrument of torture by the security forces. A young homosexual man who's now living in Turkey spoke about the all-encompassing helplessness and despair he was plunged into from such repeated, inhuman treatment. He was incarcerated in an Iranian jail by the security forces because of his sexuality. A young woman now living in Norway told of the number of operations she'd undergone for the unspeakable pain, following the physical and emotional damage that her Iranian captors did to her. I reflected that terror bubbled just below the fragile surface of our civilisation, like magma waiting to explode.

I wondered at the revolutionary social changes that had taken place in Ireland over the past twenty years, an apparent liberalisation of outlook that had replaced the catholic theocracy of a failed and abusive Ireland, and questioned how far those changes had penetrated beneath the surface skin of our culture, and whether they were trustworthy and would hold. Our Taoiseach, the Prime Minister Enda Kenny, who had eruditely launched my book in the Castlebar library in a relaxed performance before his home crowd, stood up in the Dáil, the Irish Parliament, and declaimed, 'For the first time in Ireland, a report into child sexual abuse exposes an attempt by the Holy See to frustrate an inquiry in a sovereign, democratic republic as little as three years ago – not three decades ago … The rape and torture of children was downplayed or "managed" to uphold instead the primacy of the institution, its power, standing and reputation.'

We got the merest hint of the terror in the unanticipated robbery of our suitcases from the hire car at Fiumicino Airport in Rome, an assault which floored us with shock. But I can imagine that when evil rises from out of the depths to incarnate in the blind beliefs of our fellow human beings, the non-negotiable drunkenness of being filled with such power, with the psychotic certainty of righteousness, can ultimately drive some people to kill those with an opposing point of view. No feeling of empathy quickens in their veins, even though the eternal and reverberating effect of murder nullifies our shared humanity. I too experienced the effects of a symbolic murder in relation to my uncle and aunt: first being murdered, and then, murdering in my turn. The evil that lurks within my soul is but a step away, as is the reaction of guilt.

After the diagnosis of prostate cancer and the subsequent prostatectomy, I often feel that I live my life on borrowed time, and that a day of reckoning is a sudden early-morning knock on the door away when my bail will be revoked. Kafka captured the horror of this reality in the prescient, opening lines of *The Trial*: 'Someone must have been telling lies about Joseph K., for without having done anything wrong he was arrested one fine morning.' The theft of our belongings in Rome proves that the protective middle-class certainties I surround myself with and live within are a vulnerable illusion.

Since the horror of cancer, I never feel safe anymore. The television news about the Arab Spring, those brave young people who are defying the authorities in the Middle East, teaches me how simply an entire people can be held captive by the autocratic few. Jung's in-depth analysis of the problem was accurate: 'It is merely incumbent on us to choose the master we wish to serve, so that his service shall be our safeguard against being mastered by the "other" whom we have not chosen.' Yet, I believe in the goodness of my fellow human beings, because daily I experience a reaching out in kindness and fellow-feeling from Terry, with whom I feel totally secure. However, I'm also cognizant from my work with clients that from time to time I feel I've to explain to them about the hole that exists in our personalities. We've a large cushion which we place over the opening that leads to the abyss. It smothers the unbearable harshness of the real, and prevents us from falling through. I know from experience that sometimes, as in the depression that both Aengus and I had suffered from, the cushion is pulled out from under us, and then we simply drop through the hole and fall forever. After the devastating shock from cancer, which threatened to unravel completely the widening rent in the webbing of my existence, I had to take anti-depressives for a period to balance my equilibrium, until such time as my natural composure returned. Like the staples in my belly after the prostatectomy, the medication held that split together, and kept the insanity at bay, while I was healing.

I seem to come from a disagreeable family. My uncle and aunt come over to us for Sunday lunch about once a fortnight. Terry is careful to cook food for them that's nourishing and tasty, and easy for them to manage. Just before dessert, when Terry had left the room, I told them that he and I were going to have our Civil Partnership ceremony on Tuesday week next, and that they were more than welcome to come. I could see them freeze slowly in their chairs as my words landed. It was as if the blood in their veins had suddenly thickened, and they became immobile. There was no movement. My joyful news was received by them in stony silence: both of them appeared stricken as if I'd broken wind, and caused a noxious smell. I've learned over time not to try and fill silences, so I let it continue on. Eventually, my aunt was moved to ask stiffly, 'And where is this going to take place?'

Sensing the danger, I chose to speak about the reception. 'In the Herbert Park Hotel in Ballsbridge.'

More silence. Aunt Mary is an aunt by marriage, and we'd been talking earlier about the recent civil wedding of her niece. My aunt had described the outfit she'd worn, so she did have something new to wear. I began to collect the dinner plates, and left the room to total silence. In the kitchen I was furious, and angrily whispered to an astonished Terry to bring in the plate with the fruit-topped flan that he'd made for dessert. 'Just take it in, take it in!' I ordered desperately, flailing about, filling the dishwasher with their dirty plates, demented with the ugliness of the situation. I was shocked because I hadn't expected such a discourteous response. Even though they were schooled in a different era, I never imagined that they wouldn't be supportive of us. When I followed on with the sweet plates, the conversation was continuing without any reference to my invitation, even when they repaired to the couch afterwards for a hurried cup of tea. The pair left our apartment without delay for the journey home, and made no reference to what had occurred. To my shame, neither did I, wanting to forget the whole episode as an incidental digression. When I waved them away, I was left with the crushing impression that my aberrant behaviour had spoiled the Sunday luncheon of good humour, and I felt out of place and in disgrace. The letter inviting my uncle and aunt remained unopened, propped up against a decanter on the side-board. And the envelope is there still: I haven't been able to touch it. Their names which were written across it in such joyful anticipation, reproach the living like an inscription on a gravestone, acknowledging a relationship which once was.

We noticed that the usual phone call on the Monday night to thank us for the Sunday lunch didn't come. Finally on Thursday night, when we arrived in late from work, there was a message on the answering machine. 'Auntie Mary here. Please ring me urgently.' And unusually, 'If you've forgotten the number, it's 295 635.'

I should have been warned by the edgy, sarcastic tone of that addendum, but for a second time I didn't perceive that anything was amiss. 'They've probably thought better of it, and want to come,' I remarked to Terry. But the seating plans had already been settled and delivered to the hotel. After their horrified reaction to our invitation, we'd presumed that they weren't going to be there, so what to do?

'Tell them we don't want them there – and I don't want them there – but make it light and fluffy. Say that it's going to be a young crowd that they wouldn't know: they'd probably be delighted anyway to be let off the hook,' said Terry, turning on the television, and pulling over the armchair.

I rang my aunt. 'Hello, Michael here . . .' Uncle Robbie answered the phone. He asked how we were, and then said, 'Your Aunt wants to speak to you.'

My aunt came on the phone. 'I'm in a state of shock,' she said. 'We've just had a call from my sister in Limerick an hour ago.'

Oh my god, I thought, I wonder who's dead?

'She told me she read in the paper that you and Terry are going to be married.' She laid emphasis on the word *married*. It was spat out.

Some of the newspapers had run with the story following on our recent radio interview on the *John Murray Show*, and sensationalised the head-line, 'Radio Star to Wed'.

'We knew nothing about this,' she berated. My aunt was the youngest in a family of several children, and a persistent cry over the years has been, 'Nobody tells me anything.'

'Don't you remember I invited the both of you to our Civil Partnership ceremony last Sunday at lunchtime.'

'I don't remember that.'

'You asked me where it was happening, and I said the reception was being held in the Herbert Park hotel,' I reminded her. I decided to tell the truth about what I was feeling. 'As a matter of fact you were both very rude, and said absolutely nothing about the invitation.' As I spoke, I wondered whether I'd been too forward in naming what had happened around our table that Sunday lunchtime.

'We were in a state of shock about it,' my aunt responded vehemently, almost shouting: so she did remember. Her voice sounded frenziedly angry, and shot up an octave. 'You know that one man can't marry another man!' she screamed at me down the phone.

I felt assailed by what she was saying and by what she was about to say, and I put down the receiver into its cradle to bring the conversation to an end. I stood there looking at the answering machine, horrified and shaking, as her poison continued to emanate into the room. Her attack was deeply personal, which went to the heart of who Terry and I are as a couple. I didn't want our home to be polluted by her vituperation, but it was too late: the damage had been done, and could never again be undone. When Terry several days later named the attack as homophobic, being seized by her hatred which had fastened itself to the doorjambs like a bucket of splashed paint, I recognised the truth at once. 'Your Aunt wants to speak to you,' my uncle had said, preparing the ground for the launching of her missile, and pointing it in our direction. The two of them had an hour to plan the ambush. I know that I'm fortunate, because this is the first occasion in my lifetime that I've been the butt of such malice.

I don't know whether my aunt's rage was about having ruled themselves out of the running for attending our partnership ceremony by refusing our invitation, or whether she was furious that other people like her sister now know about our homosexuality: my conjecture is futile. I remember the fracture in her voice, her scornful tone, and the vigour of her attack. The altercation was deranged: it was a crank call, but it was rancorous and rancid, and it was better to have called a halt to it, because from my psychoanalytic experience, there's no treating with the intractability of madness. If you enter into the *querencia* of the bull, his favoured territory in the arena, you're liable to lose your domination.

I warily took the phone off the hook, and dropped it rapidly onto the desk, still shocked. I kept looking at the receiver, listening to the beep beep

beep, deriving comfort from the repetition, as the bullfighter inviting the bull to charge out from his safe place into the *torero's* territory makes a succession of *verónicas*, passes with the cape, and starts to impose his will over the unpredictable animal. Later on, I made the decision to leave the phone permanently off the hook until the joyous celebration of our partnership was well and truly over. I decided not to afford my elderly relatives a chance to undermine our happiness with religious diatribes, if that was the likely motivation for their attack, or even excuses and platitudes papering over their bigotry to retain our friendly and supportive services: the indignity of accepting those impossible apologies for the sake of good manners had to be obviated.

Terry was exasperated that I put down the phone. 'Be a man about it, and take her on, even if she's nearly eighty.'

I did protest their rudeness, and that was an advance for me. I go into shock too quickly for my own good. It renders me incapable like a child, and leaves me unprotected. The encounter with such overpowering anxiety lacks the mediation of words so that it has a traumatic quality outside of language, impossible and inassimilable. My physical reaction, that striking back or acting again, anew, is the instinctive, early one of cutting off contact with what causes me harm. I remember being beaten by my father when I was very young. Then I stayed in my Granny's house next door for days on end at the times when I knew that he'd be around, at lunch or after tea, to register my disapproval of his behaviour, and to punish him by withdrawing my sunny presence. Eventually, after yet another beating, I moved house permanently.

Terry grimly pointed out, 'And Uncle Robbie was probably listening in on the other phone!'

Of course he was. He always does, although he says nothing. My brother used to refer to them as 'the stereophonic phone calls'.

That night I had a nightmare. There was a raging wolf with bared teeth snarling into my face. At chest level, I was bringing down the lid on a stainless steel cage trying to contain him as he threshed about, and attempting to fasten it shut with a simple clasp which had no strength in it. Outwardly I appeared calm, but inside I was fainting with fright because this berserk, wild animal was so close in front of me; in my arms really. I awoke with a start, and lay there panicked on the bed, breathing heavily in the darkness. It was several minutes before I could bring myself to get up and go to the toilet, wondering what the dream was about, and what it could mean, and where it applied in my life.

Too close for comfort! Some days later, I decided that the dream was a memory. The wolf is a pack animal: it operates within the intimacy of a nuclear family. And while the attack from my father when I was little set the template, the assault from my aunt had revived that. The cage represented my inadequate attempt to corral the problem, but the situation was beyond my skills. The wolf is a dangerous predator, a wild animal not amenable to immediate domestication, so I was right to keep clear of it. In both Greek and Roman mythology, the wolf is associated with the prophetic and oracular god, Apollo, the god of the sun, light and truth, of music and poetry. As an archetypal disposition, he favours thinking over feeling, and distance over closeness. So paradoxically, I can use his energy to protect myself through the creative medium of writing as author or composer, because the wolf represents an instinctive potentiality deep within myself. The image of the snarling wolf also displays the strength of my anger, where good manners are foolishly irrelevant. We had a cat once called Myrtle, who sat in front of the Aga. My mother would say to her politely, but vainly, 'Excuse me, excuse me,' when she wanted to get at the lower oven to heat the dinner plates.

The People of the Book

The People of the Book
Condemn me for being

A person who loves
Those of my own sex

The Christians the Muslims
And even the Jews
(Who attest to the lack of redemption)
Believe that God says
For me to be loving
I'd have be living in sin

The Nazis decided I'm '*unter-mensch*'
A sub-human person
To be burned in the ovens at Buchenwald
The German Pope
Following on in that tradition
Decreed that as a human being
I'm 'intrinsically-disordered...
With a tendency towards evil'
A ranking so far beneath
That of the heterosexual elect
I'm destined to be burned in the fires of hell
For all eternity

The People of the Book
See nothing wrong with that prejudice
They consider themselves nice people
'If it were up to them. . .' But it's not
God is the despot here

The People of the Book believe
I have a dialect of sexuality

Which must be suppressed
For the sake of the family
Or because the 'grotesquery' of gay marriage
Poses 'the biggest threat to our civilisation'
Bigger even than global warming
(I recall from those harrowing documentaries on television
The same threat was laid at the door of the Jews)
Do the People of the Book hope that the millions of us
Will be obliterated off the face of the earth?
Or should we voluntarily submit ourselves to castration by dogma
For differing sexually from the majority?

The People of the Book
Ignore the advances in human psychology
Which say that my dialect of sex
Is a normal outcome of the Oedipus complex
They say they take their instruction
From Moses and Jesus and Muhammad
Whom they preach with all the fanatical certainty
Of the ignorant and insecure

The People of the Book suggest
That I should press my sexuality
Between the leaves of the good book
So that it can wither away like a desiccated flower
For according to them my 'out' sexuality
Is not orthodox not sanctioned
By people who monopolize the deity

The tragedy for me
Is that the People of the Book

Would exclude me from a sense of the sacred
Which I find in the wonder of love
And in the various expressions of human nature

I can hear God speak through the human voice
That tells me I'm alright despite my differences
That encourages me to continue on when times get tough
Helping me to hope for better
That is humble enough to walk beside me on the road
On every journey of my life
That makes a commitment to a fellow human being
Reaching out to lift the heavy burden off my shoulders
That trusts me unconditionally with the courage
To live out my truth in spite of doubt
Responsible only to the best that I can be
Flowering in my own way and at my own pace
Without feeling the need to berate me as the scapegoat
The outsider the stranger
The prodigal son the neighbour

That can always say to me the Jew
Me the Christian me the Muslim
Me the son of God
'I believe in you
Because I love you'

And also (a dialect the People of the Book conveniently forget)
'Because you are mine' says the Lord

During the twenty-six years that Terry and I have lived together, love between two men was a topic we shied away from in public as if it were something unseemly, because for most of that time, our existence as gay men was judged to be illegal. That was our training, as we lived life occasionally looking over our shoulder in case of an attack. My uncle and aunt haven't had the benefit of the schooling that living with these realities has bestowed. Shortly after the legislation was updated to take account of present realities, there was a court case where a solicitor queried the probity of someone because they were gay, and the justice, Mr Cyril Kelly, interrupted to remind him that homosexuality was now a legal way of being in this country. His simple statement, and the way that he had phrased it, had a profound effect on us. We felt vindicated when we read about it in the *Irish Times*, and his words seemed to free us, cleansing us from a lifetime of dishonourable secrecy.

An Ode to Those Labelled 'Intrinsically Disordered'

We remember the terror of the men and of the women
Who are still denounced
Once they were burned at the stake
Their lives extinguished at Buchenwald
Who are still in prison

To have a legal way of being
                                        powerless
Because they happen to be homosexual

I owe them so much honour

After our television and radio appearances, I received an email from Germany: 'I left Ireland in 1986 not just because of the economic situation but also because of the homophobic and hateful environment against gays at that time . . . One morning after a weekend of clubbing I went to work, and my boss said to me "Can I give you any aids or assistances with that? Do you need any help or AIDS?" The sentence was repeated at every possible opportunity in front of as many people as possible. Seeing as it is not perfect English it was clear to me what the real message was.' And the writer concludes, 'What would a confrontation with one of the owners of the business have got me in Ireland of the '80s?'

Although the edges of my consciousness have been deformed from having worn the straitjacket designed by Church and State for far too long, I had forgotten how profoundly crippling those times were, and how many people's lives are still being damaged by ignorance.

When Terry and I talked it through, we decided that the day of our commitment was of such great consequence for us, that we wanted to be surrounded by goodwill as we celebrated our love, one for the other. We wanted people to be present at our civil partnership ceremony who've wished us well in our lives, and in particular, all of those friends who've supported the two of us around the time of my cancer, and also around the publication of my book, and its subsequent reading in performance at the National Concert Hall. 'If anybody asks what I thought of your book, I'll tell them I haven't read it, and that will be the truth,' was the hostile response from my uncle to the story of my life, which astounded me. When I told him that I'd found a publisher for my book, my exciting news was deleted from the conversation through ignoring what I'd said, as if it hadn't been heard. This wearying aggression, overt and passive, wasn't something I wanted to have to deal with on the day of our civil partnership ceremony. On a solo run, eliciting a sharp intake of breath from me at the sudden flooding with foreboding feelings when I learned of it, Terry had reached out to my uncle in a text message earlier this year. He got back the rebuff, 'We have maintained a dignified silence around Michael's book.' The vehement telephone attack I'd suffered from my aunt had buttressed their response. But I'd no idea why my life story, which previously had been lived in the silence of shadows, warranted such a depth of disapproval, dignified or otherwise, when it was lived out loud and in the open.

Terry had argued from my uncle and aunt's point of view. 'You've torn away their privacy and revealed the truth in your book. Your uncle and aunt grew up in small towns in Ireland, and you've revealed the truth to their doctor friends, businesspeople, solicitors, what they felt was unnecessary to reveal about their background, about your father, and you expect them to be delighted about that?'

'But you'd have imagined they'd all have been horrified by what I described,' I said. 'It merits an apology from somebody, anybody; one of them, whoever "them" could be . . .' trailing off, feeling dejected. 'Well, that just confirms that they can't be present, seated in the middle of the room like some baleful, simmering presence, and while all around them people are celebrating us: it'd be dreadful, for all of our sakes.'

I looked at Terry seated in his armchair, tired from a day's work, the strain from battling the pain of his polio holding his face in a mask. He made an appeal to me. 'I'm finding it very difficult to deal with you these past few days. I wish it was different with your family, but it's not. They're very undeveloped,' he suggested.

'You don't want them to be there.'

Terry shook his head. 'It's your decision, and it has to be your decision, but for my part I'd be relieved if they weren't there.' So my partner had made up his mind that he didn't want my uncle and aunt there on his special day, and his welfare is my priority, as mine is his. I too didn't want to be worried about anybody's responses on the day: I didn't want to have to limit myself through minding the susceptibilities of others when I've already revealed the truth in my book. When I'd publically say to Terry, 'I give you this ring as a token of my love,' I didn't want to feel that there were people looking on who were cringing inside with embarrassment at the openness of our affection for each other, whose heads hung lower as they shrank back into their seats, or who were in two minds about any aspect of our lives together, or worse, were so crippled with shame about us, that they felt they had to maintain 'a dignified silence' which excluded me.

'Imagine!' was my mother's injunction. Imagine for a moment that these hostile and disagreeable people weren't related to me. Would I want to have them present on the occasion of our civil partnership? Would I even regard them as friends in the first place? The answer to both questions comes winging through the air to present loud and clear before me like the apparition of a ten-foot archangel rolling open a scroll of parchment. Inscribed there in large golden lettering is the phrase 'under no circumstances!' And yet, I catch myself ambling about at the edges of my thinking, seeking a way in for them unbeknownst to myself, in order to wangle for them yet another invitation to come and participate joyfully. The archangel with the scroll metamorphoses into an elegant matador holding his cape, who shifts position slightly on the sand, moving his weight from one leg to the other. But he holds steadfast, and raises the open cape so that it directly crosses my line of my sight: 'under no circumstances!' is writ there large, waving in the wind, portending the eruption of danger.

'I'm finding it very hard,' I said. 'There's the strongest pull deep in my guts to overlook all of the mess and to just invite them once again!'

'Well, you love your family,' proffered Terry, clear-eyed, matter-of-factly. It was a concept that I hadn't considered, until it was named. 'You always said that if you won the lottery, you'd share your millions with them!'

That was the truth: I love the members of my family, and I always have. 'Love and aggressivity both: they seem to be interdependent. And the conflict is tearing me in two.'

'If you plump for one side over the other, the conflict will disappear,' he said airily. 'But what I don't understand is why you constantly reference them, why they matter so much to you?'

'I love them,' I said, 'and love matters!'

I still feel guilty over the sadness of an incident that occurred, when for some reason I'd spent one night in the family home. My brother and I were seated around the dining table at breakfast eating our porridge, when my grandmother came around the back way, carrying a small jug with the top of the milk for me. I was happily triumphant in telling her that I'd almost finished my porridge, so I didn't need the cream. Instinctively I knew that by rejecting her kindness, I was demonstrating that there was no differentiation between me and my brother, and that I was where I wanted to belong. Granny turned away without saying anything further and went back home carrying her jug. As I swallowed the final spoonfuls, I felt desolate in the knowledge that I was displaced, yet unable to comprehend a truth which my parents had in their possession, perhaps locked away even from them. Today, I still feel like an only child longing for playmates, perplexed by the intricacies of negotiating friendships. I want my two remaining relatives in Ireland to be there to witness and lend familial importance to a major event in my life, and to be happy for me. Declan Dunne, the Chief Sub Editor on the radio desk in the RTÉ newsroom, sent me an email entitled 'joyous day' accepting his invitation. He wrote, 'I would be delighted to attend and celebrate a great day with you, your other friends, and family,' so he takes for granted that my family will be there. But any appeal to my family for validation has always been marked by insecurity, because it never has had the desired outcome. I should look for the guarantor elsewhere.

I'm hoping that by signing the register, the defining relationship will shift from that with my family to the relationship I've forged with my partner. To validate means to have the force of law, and to be legally binding, which will be one of the effects of entering into a civil partnership. After the ceremony, a new phenomenon in Ireland, we were invited to come onto the *Saturday Night with Miriam* show on RTÉ television, and she asked me how Terry and I met. I explained that I was producing and directing a programme for RTÉ on an outside-broadcast unit at the Rutland Centre, Ireland's premier addiction treatment centre, where Terry was working as a psychotherapist at the time. Since we couldn't film the clients, staff-members role-played those in treatment, and Terry played himself running a group therapy session. I told her I'd the opportunity to see him in action over the three long, twelve-hour days that the taping took. I explained that a producer/director is trained to make an instant judgement about everything and everyone that appears in shot. I could see Terry's integrity, and the truth that guided his explorer's soul: Terry was somebody I could entrust my life to. Over those three days, my conviction about him grew. When we held a celebratory dinner at the end of the recording, I made sure that I was sitting beside him.

There was a phone call to the Sandyford consulting rooms from a producer on the *John Murray Show*. The fiftieth anniversary of the death of the great Swiss analyst, Carl Jung, was coming up on the following Tuesday, and she wondered whether I'd be in a position to come on the show and talk about his life, his achievements, and what effect his legacy has had on people.

'I'd be honoured to talk about one of my psychoanalytic heroes!'

Terry drove me in to the radio studio, and he sat in the control room while I talked about Jung's achievements with John Murray, after the nine o'clock morning news. At the end of what was a long interview in radio terms – twenty minutes – John asked, 'What's this I hear about a big event in your life coming up soon?'

'This day week I'll be undergoing a civil partnership ceremony with Terry, my partner of twenty-six years.'

'We'll talk some more about this after the break,' said John. 'And maybe Terry, who's out there in the darkness, will come in and join us on air.'

During the break, a shocked Terry joined us reluctantly in the studio, and he talked about the ceremony. 'Being gay is a legal way of being. For me that's what it means . . . The state requires a solemn moment when you have to make a vow in the company of a registrar and two witnesses.' And he went on, 'I'm remembering about my father who fought in the War of

Independence. He fought for an egalitarian republic. He was a fine man, troubled: Ireland hurt him, and we were hurt as well. One thing I can say about him – I can never speak for him, but my experience of him – he would be standing proud beside me today, proud of this era in our history. He taught me to have allegiance to a republic . . .'

'. . . that all of us are to be cherished equally,' I added, quoting the 1916 proclamation.

There's no word for it: there's as yet no designation for two men who've signed the register at a registry office. A card from my cousin Mary in Chiswick was printed on the front 'MR & MR' which was the first of its type that I'd seen. It formed a satisfying graphic. Taragh sent an email in which she referred to 'You and your partner, now husband Terry are an inspiration . . .' which sounded an incongruous further step, with ambivalently disparaging echoes about who's the wife which weren't intended, even though *husband* means master of the house, male spouse, married man, developed from *hus*, house, and *bondi*, householder. My lawyer in Spain wrote, 'I think the positive coverage will be a cause of great hope and pride for many who may have had apprehensions about taking the CP step,' his legal training confining him within the civil partnership context, but which remained abbreviated, as if awaiting formal ratification, a secret yet to be spoken about. It showed hesitancy appropriate to the newness of the situation. Ultimately, from my experience of living in a relationship with Terry, I feel most comfortable with the word partner, one that shares or has a part with another, a companion or ally, even though the word never before passed into my speech, and certainly never was acknowledged publicly by us up to now. The word partner encompasses both the state of affairs prior to signing the register, and one who's become part of a contractual relationship, which a civil partnership is. Partner can also mean being a member of a married couple, without straining the understanding of the word. Nevertheless, a specific word for same-sex couples who've signed the register is absent from the vocabulary.

Our progression towards a public civil partnership ceremony has been part of a deeper process that has burgeoned since the publication of my first book, and I have cancer to thank for it. Over a quarter of a century, Terry and I have lived a private life together within the safe and constant parameters of friends who've supported us, and of family, who had seemed to regard our living arrangements with forbearance. But when my memoir appeared in print, those boundaries disappeared. Strangers would stop me in the street to say how much they enjoyed reading my book. On the Publishing Ireland stand at the Craft Fair in Dublin's RDS, I was signing my book for a middle-aged woman, when she turned aside towards Terry, who was seated behind and to my left. 'Is this your partner?' she asked. 'Hello – my name is Mary,' and she held out her hand to him.

He looked astonished.

'I've seen your photograph in the book,' she explained.

I reflected that so much has changed in Ireland, where a person in a greeting can indicate recognition of a same-sex partner. In the hospital before the prostatectomy operation, I was asked, 'Who is your next of kin?'

'Terry O'Sullivan, I suppose.'

'And what is her mobile number?'

'Terry is a he. His mobile number is . . .' A programme of education has since been rolled out in the major teaching hospitals to bring their personnel up to speed on the legal changes that have been put in place. The simple question, 'Who is your next of kin?' is not a legal question that I'm used to answering. It's all bewilderingly new.

We were driving back to Dublin from Castlebar, having undergone, yet again, the grief-filled trial of visiting my mother in the nursing home. She'd been sleepy, and had mostly kept her eyes closed, and said nothing during the visit, hadn't really acknowledged our presence. It was spitting with rain, and there was a double rainbow arcing across the threatening skies. Terry was doing the driving. I turned down the music on the radio.

'When I was little,' I said to him, 'I earnestly believed there was a pot of gold in the field at the end of the rainbow.'

He looked over at me. 'There is, Michael,' he said simply, and he took hold of my hand. His loving gesture bound us together.

The magic of poetry returns to the world when fear disappears. As the former president, Mary Robinson, said in her preface to the first book, 'I wanted to shine a light in the darkness, a darkness of ignorance, of prejudice, violence, fear and hopelessness, all of whose spreading cancers assault us as human beings, and which attack at the roots the free flowering of the human spirit.' It takes special people who are graced with the gift of love to remind us of that: they merit being held dear in a loose embrace. And my partner, Terry, is one of those special people.

Anna came up from Spain to attend the not-a-wedding. The night before the ceremony, Terry and I sat with her on the floor of the bedroom surrounded by several different ties and bow ties, and she helped us choose the ones which looked the best: a light blue bow tie with white spots to go with Terry's white shirt and dark navy suit, and a pink tie with white spots for my blue shirt, and the dark navy suit. In the subsequent laughter-filled photographs, they worked well together.

Tuesday, the fourteenth of June, dawned clear and calm. The sun shone out of a cloudless blue sky. It warmed our backs as we stood outside the gates of our apartment in Stillorgan, waiting for Tiernan and Barbara to arrive in the Land Rover, and the beginning of our progress towards the Registry Office on Grand Canal Street, and the start of an exuberant, emotional day that was to carry us shoulder high on the palpable goodwill and well-wishing from everyone that we were to meet.

The Registrar began by asking Terry and me to reaffirm that there was still no impediment to a civil partnership, and then she led each of us in turn into the declaration of the three vows. It was an intense, emotionally charged experience. For over a quarter of a century we've had to wait for this moment, with no expectation that it would come to pass in our lifetime. We realised that we were undergoing a definitive ritual in formally committing ourselves to each other, and blocking off the possibility that we could simply walk away from the relationship when it no longer suited, a possibility that we'd never seriously entertained. Our future path was to be together until death parted us. Because of the newness of the legislation in Ireland, we knew that we were also making a little bit of history.

'I declare my intention to love and support you, and I declare that I accept you as a civil partner in accordance with the law.'

The legal basis which grounded our relationship was not only welcome, it was a relief. We always operated a joint bank account without reckoning who was earning the most money at any particular time, and the joint assessment of income tax would make sense of the notional reality by which we operated in any case. We were of the opinion that this public declaration in front of my family of friends put beyond reach any potential challenge to the wills that we'd drawn up, a real fear of interference after my death that Terry had expressed to me on more than one occasion.

'I pledge to share my life with you. I promise to love, honour and support you. I will respect you and be true to you, through good times and bad. To these promises, I give my word.'

These promises were easy for me to make where Terry was concerned. I have respect for who he is. He carries an ideal which makes it easy for me to love, honour and support him. Over the years we've forged an alliance which has been tested through the good times and bad. We've grown closer in our likes and dislikes in music and in art, and we understand how we like to spend our time, and enjoy our holidays.

'I give you this ring as a token of my love, a symbol of all that we have promised, and all that we now share.'

When I suggested to Terry that we buy rings for the ceremony, he pointed out that he loves the Cartier ring he wears, as it happens, a lanières wedding band in yellow gold that I'd bought for him previously. He likes the fact that it's chunky, and has bevelled sides. 'What d'you take me for?'

he asked, incredulous. 'I'd never wear a second ring at the same time!' For my fiftieth birthday that we'd celebrated in Spain, Terry had bought me a Cartier trinity ring in pink, yellow and white gold. The day beforehand he'd made sangria with oranges, red wine and loads of sugar. The almost instantaneous migraine was so incapacitating that he had to call the doctor, who merely injected me for the death-inducing pain, when what I craved was a beheading. The following day I can remember swaying in a fugue outside Cohen's jeweller's shop in Gibraltar, when Terry went inside to buy the ring, trying to grip the cobbles with the toes in my shoes in order to continue to stand upright, and not to collapse in the street. I love the simple slimness of the trinity ring, because it embodies the Lacanian psychoanalytic concept called the borromean knot: the three orders of the imaginary, the symbolic and the real are interdependent like the three rings, which are linked in such a way that if one of them is severed, all three of them separate. In psychoanalytic terms, this unravelling results in psychosis, but the three working in tandem signify sanity. When I wear the ring, or touch it, rolling it around on my finger, I'm invoking this healthy, psychological position. Since we both appreciate the beauty of the Cartier rings we already possessed, we decided to consecrate them during the civil partnership ceremony, and set them apart as sacred symbols of our love for each other. That expression of love passed into language is still so new for me, that I hesitate after writing the sentence down.

My gift to Terry on the day of entering our formal partnership was a special poem I wrote for him, which I'd perfected over the previous weeks. I'd recited it over and over in my mind like a mantra, rearranging and refining the words so that eventually on the day, it was those words which were speaking me. The rhythm of the poetry became the heartbeat of the whole world, which characterised the extraordinariness of the day as a day of *duende*. The poem was both a prayer and an invocation, and it grew into a sacred text that we included in the civil partnership ceremony as an epithalamion, a song or a poem traditionally composed to celebrate a wedding. Perhaps it was the first epithalamion ever to be given on the occasion of a Civil Partnership Ceremony. Henceforth, it will be known simply as 'A Poem for Terry':

When I grow old and have no voice
No children there to care or to remember me
I shall always know
That there was once a midsummer's day in Dublin
When I was loved

Then I shall smile in the dream-time
Hearing once more
The dawn chorus announced with trumpet blasts
And see the vivid roses burst into bloom
And twine around the morning of that glorious day in June
When I was finally allowed
To be loved

I shall laugh inside through Stephen's Green
And leave my dancing footprints in the dew
So you can follow me
And take your place
By my side
On a day which was prepared
Since the beginning of the world
For you are my world
And I have always loved you

Whenever I would look into your questioning eyes of blue
To find myself reflected in your goodness
I could never feel afraid of other's judgement

Or their shame at these extolling words
As true as you have proved to be
For an everyday eternity
Of table fellowship and fun

The sun swept to attention and saluted us at noon
We did not stand in one another's shadow
When we vowed either to each
Three times before our family of like-minded friends
Who have supported us for better or for worse

The words were tolling in the golden air
They bathed us in light so that we shone
I shall honour you with my esteem because of your integrity
I promise to support and bear the weight
Of your open unprotected soul
I promised too to love you, as if ever I had stopped
And needed to commence what is continuous
And round as the ring you gave to me
Blessed with your affection

On that laughing summer's day
The wind was cheering and the leaves on the trees were waving
As we processed towards our future through O'Connell Street
Side by side we laid our bouquet of roses out at the GPO
Acknowledged those who gave their lives so we could be
    cherished equally
Proclaimed ourselves free
                                    and free to become
Better together than either of us could choose to achieve on our own

And we withdrew relevance from those who disapproved
Of our new and mutual republic of love

There is nothing I regret more than my compliance
That I was not in my life more undignified and reckless and awkward
Like you a fearless fighter joyfully at home in foreign lands
An encourager of dreams an explorer of the soul's secrets
And warm and tender as the pleasure of our private trysts

Whenever we shall be no more and nobody remembers us
These words of mine shall inherit the earth
They will echo in the heart of every season
That that there was once a midsummer's day in Dublin
When I was loved
                  and they will sing out loud

   my song
Repeat publically the poem I have told about you
And the treasure you endowed me with
The inestimable adventure of a meaningful life

This simple shining truth shall belong to you immortally
That once upon a time
                  on a Dublin midsummer's

   day at noon
I always loved you

On the day, I ended the poem at that point, and embraced my partner in public for the very first time. I've since composed a postscript, which revolves around the final adverb *too*, so that the mutual embrace will continue to radiate outwards for as long as words can express the truth:

Then you will be present in the wind and in the trees
And especially when the roses are in bloom
You will gladden with a smile or with a glance
When people feel your presence in the wonder of beautiful words
Lingering in a room like your fragrance
The blown petals falling to earth like prayers
Whispering over and over that I have always loved you
That I have loved you, too

When I signed the register, I made a mistake. The registrar leaned forward, and said, 'No, not there!' and indicated where I should sign. There was a ripple of amusement from the audience behind me, so I turned around and talked to them, saying, 'The French playwright, Jean Anouilh, said that nothing in this life has any business being perfect!' The transgression was a good omen for our future life together. Terry then signed the register, followed by Barbara and Tiernan, who used the special Italian Delta pens for the first time that we'd given to each of our witnesses as a gift. Then Terry and I stood up and faced each other. We were filled with delight at what we'd accomplished. The twenty-six years that we'd spent in each other's company, the effort expended in trying to work things out, to make things suit, the many triumphs, the losses, the horror of the family deaths, the assault from cancer, we'd survived them all. On this day we'd confirmed each other in our love, which had proved steadfast and had brought us through. As we embraced each other, our little family rose to its feet and gave us an ovation.

Geraldine Boyle was in Portugal at the time of our not-a-wedding, so she sent her regrets. After her holiday, she brought Terry and me out to dinner to celebrate with members of her family, and we had an uproariously warm and enjoyable evening. Geraldine told us that at a meeting of her Active Retirement Group, she'd overheard a woman regale a group of people about a civil partnership ceremony that she'd attended, albeit reluctantly. The woman explained, 'As a practising Catholic, I was worried about attending, so I asked the priest about it in Confession. And he advised me that it would be better not to attend lest I give scandal by appearing to approve. But I knew Terry from way back, so his invitation to the Civil Partnership ceremony posed a real dilemma for my conscience . . .'

'Are you talking about Terry O'Sullivan and Michael Murphy?' inquired Geraldine, joining in the conversation. 'They're very good friends of mine. I was at the launch of Michael's book.'

'But I didn't see you at their Civil Partnership ceremony: you didn't attend,' accused the woman, betraying her anxiety.

'Oh no!' said Geraldine, and before she turned away, 'I thought it'd be too sinful!'

Another of the cumulative effects on me of the journey I've undertaken following the prostatectomy and the publication of my book concerns perception. The Old French for journey, *journée*, means a day's work or travel. For the Celts, that journey began at sunset, during the dreamtime. At this stage, I've thoroughly grasped what it means to be an author. I've taken possession of that textual territory, planted seeds there, and caused them to grow. I've inhabited the sobriquet of writer, and woken up as somebody else, who is more truly me. All the unconscious events of the night and the conscious ones of that day have founded me in my new vocation. Towards the end of my passage through life, I've taken hold of evanescent words and combined them into a holding fiction, which has prevented slippage and a cascade of re-shapings, in order to make a reality out of the pleasure and play of pure being. Such a performance is to provide completely, to furnish or equip, to fill out a shape and to accomplish. It's a continual coming out into words, a resurrection into the visible development of this book.

I heard the accent tugging at me from somewhere behind us as Terry and I waited to board the Malaga plane. It curled forward like Christmas turf-smoke full of warmth, redolent with the richness of the flora and fauna in the Mayo countryside that has been layered over centuries, the whins, the sedges, the bog oak, deep and resonant and welcoming. From my seat in the third row, I saw the man enter and turn to move forward down the aisle, still talking in a loud, comforting voice to the companion he was leading, who was disabled. I leaned across, touched him on the arm so that he looked at me. 'Is that a Mayo accent?'

'It is,' he replied proudly. 'On the Mayo border. Clonbur. D'you know it?

'I know it well,' I said.

'Are you Murphy?' he asked.

'I am.'

'The broadcaster!' he exclaimed. 'I read your book!'

'Thank you very much,' I said, surprised.

'It was very human.' His comment was sincerely meant. And then he was gone, moving with his friend on down the plane.

Such truthful, fleeting encounters are like a baptism. They immerse me in the waters of my heritage, so that I'm born anew, filled with hope and strengthened in certainty. My grandmother was the Mayo woman, a Hoban from out the Newport road in Castlebar. I recognise the embrace of her intonation in the country accent I'm attuned to. Terry says he too likes the soft sounds of Mayo, the mist and the breeze that he can detect in the way that I use some words. 'You deliberately put in an "ee" sound in words like *today* and *pay*, correcting that sudden Mayo stop at the end of those words, which probably comes from the Irish,' he concluded.

'There isn't that English "y" sound at the end of Irish vowels. It's the same with Spanish: we say "no" in exactly the same way!' Terry is aware of the effort I make to iron out the local pronunciations when I'm broadcasting to a national audience. I felt joy that he overheard the original expression of the way that once I'd used the language, an intimate expression of my Mayo roots which I still wear like a fragrance, perceptible to a connoisseur's palate. Whether speaking or listening, the welcoming clasp is the same, and I'm indebted to those who've loved me for the continuous nature of their linguistic holding. It has enabled me to walk the road with a confident fluidity of movement, articulating the sounds as easily as I've come to inhabit my body at long last.

There's an agave plant in Spain beneath our balcony in La Mairena which flowers once in every ten years. This summer, in a final, desperate effort at survival, the succulent sword-shaped leaves suddenly grew a tapering stem six metres tall, with open-wide arms that held masses of tiny golden flowers to the delight of the bees who harvested its nectar in the early morning, scattering its seeds as the plant died, exhausted from the effort of giving so much. I see that I too have written such a love story, which was not my intention, although maybe it was ordained after having survived the assault from cancer. I've created a fiction which has revealed the truth: an invention of the mind, a feigning or fabrication, which has been shaped, formed, and devised to uphold my being above ground after the terror of being marked by death. In my own way, I've continued on what my mother has had to say, the dialogue my mother had begun, sustaining her desire to the point where it vanishes, that smallest measure of space and time to which she now has attained without the need for my help. I see her swaying unsteadily on the edge of the abyss, flashing a smile, a look, still playing the piano for me. She's celebrating a moment of pure being, which I deplete with my cancerous experience of the past and my foreknowledge of what awaits, an awareness with which my mother is no longer oppressed. She dwells forever in a house of pure being. Her now is the deepest meditation.

'I have something to say, Michael.'

My mother's dramatic statement pierces into the silence of the universe, and disrupts it. In the course of writing this book, I've come to see that there's no need of a response, not even an assent, much less an inquiry from her eldest son. My mother has said what she's said, and that's sufficient for an eternity. Mum always loved her hot summers in the south of

Spain, and she'd have delighted in the wonder of a plant that can soar so high into the blue of the sky, in a tangible illustration of the Assumption, being received bodily into the heavens.

'I don't know what comes next.'

It's clear by now that I'd never let a lie get in the way of a good story, but that's my way: that's the individual way that I would do it. And I have spoken the truth, notwithstanding. As they say in my native tongue, *má tá bréag ann, bíodh: ní mise a chum* . . . If there's a lie in it, let it be: I didn't compose it.

Imagine, just imagine . . .

www.michaelmurphyauthor.com

If you've enjoyed this book, then please tell others about it, and recommend *The House of Pure Being* to your friends.

And if you'd like to let me how this book has affected you, you can email me: info@michaelmurphyauthor.com. I'd welcome receiving your comments and insights.

For your added enjoyment, the website gives background information on *The House of Pure Being*. It features further photographs of some of the people who've appeared in this book. It also gives information about the various book signings and talks around the country, where I look forward to having an opportunity to meet you. You'll find the latest news there about how *The House of Pure Being* has been received by the professional critics. There's also a section on this website dealing with my first book, *At Five in the Afternoon – my battle with male cancer*, where some of the characters were introduced.

Finally, I want to thank you for taking the time to read what I've written. I hope you felt it was a rewarding experience.

Go dté tu slán!

Acknowledgements

This book is a fashioning of the truth by my imagination. What I've written is subjective, and meaningful only in the context of language. As a literary work, it has no end or purpose beyond its own existence: truly, it's a house of pure being.

I'm indebted to those who've allowed the events and situations in which they appear to be re-made, and serve the overall plot of the book. In order to maintain their anonymity in some instances, I have changed the names of individuals and places, and some identifying characteristics and details. I feel it important to state clearly that the analytic sessions described don't refer to particular clients. Anne Harris asked me to write the chapter about her husband. Aengus had already suggested that I write about our meetings, and I'd felt an obligation to honour his request, and find him as I promised. I want to thank his sons, Dion, Evan and Stephen, for granting me their permission to include it.

I wish to acknowledge the honour that Máire Geoghegan-Quinn, European Commissioner for Research, Innovation and Science, has accorded this book by writing the foreword. I feel privileged that her response was so personal and warm. I'm thankful for her insights and kindness.

I remember with gratitude Seán O'Keeffe and all those in Liberties

Press who helped bring *The House of Pure Being* to publication, in particular my painstaking editor, Daniel Bolger, and Alice Dawson and Amy Herron who cheerfully handled the publicity. My literary agent, Emma Walsh, and photographer, Conor Ó Mearáin, gave me their time and encouragement. Legal Counsel, Muireann Noonan, in conjunction with Jeanne Boyle, our solicitor, studied the book in such detail that they were able to quote individual words and page numbers by heart! Through their belief, protection, and unremitting desire for perfection, the manuscript has finally been turned into a literary work the whole production team can be proud of.

It's noteworthy that three women, Muireann Noonan, Anne Harris and Máire Geoghegan-Quinn, who have such pressured jobs, sent me back what was asked of them within the same working day. They gave me a lesson in how to be successful, but also in how to write.

The people I love and respect have told me they regard it as an honour to be immortalized by a writer and to appear in a book. I've been enriched by the open gift of their supportive friendship. *The House of Pure Being* is proof of that, and despite the inventions, it's also my way of saying thank you!

Rath Dé oraibh uilig.